MEWAT

Folklore •Memory•History

Geographical and culturally diverse country like India, regional studies have yet not got the attention they deserve. *Mewat: Folklore Memory History* is an attempt to study the hitherto understudied research. Being near to the two capitals Delhi and Agra, the region comprises parts of Haryana, Rajasthan and Uttar Pradesh. The people are known as 'Mewatis' who are scattered allover the country. Many of them are also settled outside India, in Pakistan particular.

The present work is a collection of different research articles mostly published in the journals of International recognition and attempt to illuminate some aspects of the life and conditions of the people of Mewat. The region though has played a signficant role in Indian History since the time of Mahabharta, the people have continued to suffer in the hands of the Hindu as well as Muslim rulers. They struggled for their survival throughout the centuries till the Khanzadas took over the reins of Mewat.

The Khanzadas played a very important role in the then politics of Delhi court during the fourteenth and fifteenth centuries and had become the king-makers at Delhi. They also fought against Babur, sided with Rana Sanga in the battle of Khanua under the leadership of Hasan Khan Mewati. Numerous buildings in the region stand mute witness to their cultural heritage. The Mewati played a significant role in the revolt of 1857 and were punished severely by the British. The author has provided a very well written survey of the region and raised certain questions to be re-considered in the context of contemporary debates.

G.D. Gulati (b. 1946) obtained his Masters and Ph.D. degrees in Medieval Indian History from the University of Delhi. Joined as a lecturer in History in Satyawati College (University of Delhi) and retired as an Associate Professor. The author is renowned scholar of medieval history. He has two monographs to his credit—*India's Northwest Frontier in Pre-Mughal Times* (1985) and *Central Asia Under the Mongols* (2010). Both the books were well-received by the academic community. Besides he has contributed a number of research papers at various seminars and conferences.

MEWAT

Folklore • Memory • History

G. D. Gulati

Dev Publishers & Distributors
New Delhi

Published by:

DEV PUBLISHERS & DISTRIBUTORS

2nd Floor, Prakash Deep,
22, Delhi Medical Association Road,
Darya Ganj,
New Delhi-110002
Phone : 011-4357 2647, 98102 36140
e-mail: devbooks@hotmail.com
website: www.devbooks.co.in

ISBN 978–93–81406–26–7
First published 2013

Printed in India

To
My Mewati Friends
and
Anil Joshi

Contents

List of Maps

Preface

I have happy memories of my childhood and schooling years spent at Firozepur Jhirka in the Mewat region. Hence this small venture is dedicated to my Mewati brethren.

The present volume is a collection of some research papers mostly presented at various National and International seminars, conferences and symposiums. For preparing this book I consulted the relevant literature available at different centres of learning and from the learned and knowledgeable persons of the area. In this endeavour many friends who had interest in the history and from culture of the region, happily extended their hospitality, shared the relevant information and gave valuable suggestions.

Muhammad Sualeh Khan, advocate of village Biwan in district Mewat, was very helpful in my tour to various parts of the region. He also provided me with some valuable texts in Urdu. Late Choudhary Rahim Khan, Member of Parliament, also encouraged me and took me to Indore to introduce me to the Meo friends who had migrated and settled down there. Presently, they are living in Indore City, at a location known as 'Mewati mohalla'. Their leader an advocate Mohd. Iqbal Khan Meo and his friends were of immense help to me in conducting field work. Comrade Choudhary Abdul Hai was happily surprised seeing a non-Meo, doing research on Mewat. He offered me to visit his office to go through his collection on the region. Unfortunately, due to his sudden demise I was deprived off his treasure of knowledge.

Safeda Mirasi of village Kolgaon near Doha in Mewat district, was one of those who entertained me with some folksongs concerning 1857 revolt and socio-cultural life in Mewat. Comrade Muhammad Ahmad of village Gumat Bihari in Nagina, a sub-division of Mewat district, was the first who told me about Yasin Khan, his carreer and *Yasin Ki Baat.*

During my tour in the region I happened to be in the Alwar court where I met Mr. Anil Joshi who had already earned his name by translating number of works available in English and Urdu into Hindi and was busy in writing more on the Mewati folklore (see bibliography). At this juncture I also met Dr. Jugmandir Tayal, Dr. Mumtaz Khan of Raj Rishi College, Alwar who encouraged me for this mission. Later on, I came to know about Shail Maya Ram, the wife of the then collector of Alwar Mr. Arvind Maya Ram, working on the oral traditions of the Meos. I discussed with her certain aspects of the Folklore of Mewat and later found her book *Resisting Regimes: Myth, Memory and the Shaping of a Muslim Identity* (Oxord, 1997) very useful in finalizing some conclusions in this book.

There is a long list of friends who have helped me in the writing and researching of this project. I would like to thank all of them who are especially mentioned in the introduction of some chapters and other at relevant places. Prof. G.S.L. Devra, Former Professor in History and Vice-Chancellor of Kota Open University; Professor B.L. Bhadani and Prof. I.H. Siddiqui of Centre of Advanced Study, Department of History, Aligarh Muslim University; Prof. Jigar Muhammad of Jammu University, Jammu; Prof. Azizuddin Ahmad, Dr. R.P. Bahuguna, Prof. Inayat Ali Zaidi, Prof. Sunita Zaidi, Department of History, Jamia Millia Islamia, New Delhi; Dr. M.M. Juneja, Jat College, Hissar (Haryana); Dr. Suraj Bhan, Moti Lal Nehru College, University of Delhi; Dr. P.K. Shukla, former Member Secretary, Indian Council of Historical Research, New Delhi; Dr. S.Y. Qureshi, Election Commissioner, Govt. of India whom I met when he was

Administrator at Haryana Bhawan, New Delhi in the course of my research work and Prof. Dilbagh Singh of Jawahar Lal Nehru University who helped me in preparing the project for financial grant from University Grant Commission, New Delhi. All these individuals deserve my sincere thanks for their suggestions, guidance and help in more than one ways.

I fondly remember the hospitality of Lord Sannu Khan Mewati and Maulana Mufti Jamaluddin whose knowledge about the Meos and Mewat was of an immense help to me for this study. Late Choudhary Tayyab Hussain, the Minister in Haryana and Rajasthan Governments also deserve my thanks for his guidance to carry on the project and providing me with some details about his father (Late) Chowdhary Yasin Khan. Dr. Munshi Khan too deserve my thanks who gave me an opportunity to interact with other scholars, working on the different aspects of the life and conditions of the people of Mewat. Among the non-Meo Mewatis, I wish to thank Shri Tara Chand Premi, a renowned poet of the region and Khem Chand Khurana, brain behind the 'Mewat Mitra Mandal', an organization of the Mewatis settled in Delhi who helped and guided me in pursuing the project. Shri Harmohinder Singh Sarna of Shri Guru Nanak Dev Khalsa College, University of Delhi deserves my special thanks for accompanying me many a times during my tours into Mewat, sharing my thoughts on various occasions and suggesting certain research tips. My special thanks to Dr. Shamsul Islam, my collegue in the Political Science department for acquiring some useful information and material through his e-mail service.

It is my duty to wish to thank the staff of the Oriental Institute of Rajasthan at Alwar and Bharatpur; Public Library at Alwar; National Archives of India, New Delhi; Delhi University Library System; Library of the Department of History, Centre for Advanced Studies, Aligarh Muslim University, Aligarh; National Library, Kolkatta; Nat Nagar Shodh Samsthan, Sitamau, Madhya Pradesh; University

Library, Maharishi Daya Nand University, Rohtak; Library of Panjab University, Chandigarh; State Archives of Haryana, Chandigarh; State Archives of Punjab, Patiala and the Library of the Indian Institute of Advanced Studies, Shimla.

I am highly grateful to my friends Jugmandir Tayal and Jeevan Singh Manavi of Alwar who spared their valuable time to go through the manuscript of this book and made valuable suggestions for making this work a presentable one.

Special thanks to Professor Bhagwan Josh of Centre for Historical Studies, Jawahar Lal Nehru University, New Delhi for giving me many valuable suggestions.

It is my duty to acknowledge Dr. S.P. Maheshwari, Delhi, Headmaster Dina Nath Khanna, village Mandikhera (Mewat); Master Inder Bhan Chutani, village Raoli (Mewat), Patwari Taneja Sahib, village Baroda Meo (Alwar); Isa Khan, village Shahpur Khera (Mewat); Kunwar Hazari Singh, Faridabad; Abdur Razzak, village Mohali (Mewat); Ibrahim Sahib, village Sarpanch, Bhagola (Mewat); Jaga Bhagwan Dass, village Ghat Khunteta (Alwar) and Shri Bharat Dogra, a free lancer journalist, New Delhi and other friends without whose keen interest in my work and ecouragement I would have not done justice to my job.

Finally, Pankaj D. Jain deserves my appriciations for showing his keen interest and taking up the task of the publication of this book.

G. D. GULATI

New Delhi
Dated 11-6-2012.

Introduction

Needless to say that the region of Mewat is without coherent history. There are reasons for it: the paucity of historical source material and little interest among the scholars to make a study of the region which is spread over on the borders of three states Haryana, Rajasthan and Uttar Pradesh. Another reason could be that the region had never been an independent state like Alwar, Bharatpur and Jaipur; therefore, no patronage to the scholars, hence no history.

In the beginning, I had a plan to bring out a series of research papers on the historical aspects of Mewat. Being a student of medieval Indian history, the first paper was presented at the Punjab Historical Conference held at Patiala under the title 'Mewat during the thirteenth century'. The paper was based on the contemporary Persian literature and the empirial records. But it was not possible to continue with my initial plan in the absence of enough source material in contemporary literature.

It was Professor Nurul Hasan who advised me that being a 'Mewati', I should work on a full time project on 'Mewat' which may include different aspects of the region i.e. social, cultural and historical. Therefore, I decided to work on this project and prepared the synopsis : 'The Folklore of Mewat'. Later on, discussed it with Professor Irfan Habib, the then Chairman of the Indian Council of Historical Research, New Delhi, for some financial assistance from the council. He advised me that the project should have some historical bias.

Therefore, the project was re-worked as "Folklore and History - Writing: A case study of Mewat". And now finally the title of the book *Mewat: Folklore Memory History* is before the reader.

The project required to visit different institutions and libraries and an extensive tour of the region. While making survey and conducting the field - work in Mewat, I met personally the learned and senior persons to know more about their socio-cultural life. It took me three years to give it a final shape and the detailed report was submitted to the Indian Council of Historical Research.

There was a symposium on the regional history sponsored by the University Grant Commission, held at Kurukshetra University, Kurukshetra. My friend Dr. K.L. Tuteja introduced me at this forum as a student of regional history. I had to justify my position as a student of regional history working on the region of Mewat. It proved a big challenge for me. I presented a long paper including some aspects of the folklore of Mewat and how it helps the scholars in bringing together the historical aspects of the region in the absence of written literature. It was a half-day session chaired by Professor Dwijender Tripathi. There were numerous querries and observations from the scholars present in the seminar. I received encouragement from the scholars and friends presented at there.

The folklore is an important aspect of the Mewati culture.

Culture which has been defined in different ways since the inception of the word 'Folklore' in 1846 AD. In brief the common idea present in all folklore is that of traditions, something handed down from generation to generation and preserved either by memory or practice, including the written records. The historians have begun writing on the social and economic formation and evolution of different cultures, shifting away from merely chronological or political history. They have recognized the oral literature as source of history which includes folklore, though with some hesitation. Not only this, many institutions have established 'Oral History Cells' or 'Centre for Contemporary History' which underlines the importance of the non - recorded history.

The main object of the first chapter is to study the region called 'Mewat' and how the rich folk traditions of the people make us understand their history. Folksongs sung by their *mirasis* or bards highlight the bravery and warlike qualities of its people, evoking a sense of pride in their history. Though some historical facts on the basis of the Persian chronicles have been taken into consideration, most of the chapter contains a survey of the folk traditions of the region. It includes certain folktales reflecting the position of the village bania without whose presence the agrarian production cycles could come to a halt. The same way the monopoly of the *qazis* has been highlighted and how it was challenged by their folk hero - Dada Heja on the occasion of *nikah* performing ceremonies. Many more miraclous actions of their folk hero have also been described showing him as a superman of his people.

The region of Mewat had been the seat of sufis and saints viz. Lal Das, Charan Das, Sahjo Bai, Allah Baksh, Shah Chokha and others. Among them, Lal Das, born in a Meo family could attract thousands of his followers to his sect *Laldasi* whose shrine is at Sherpur in Alwar district of Rajasthan.

The Mewatis played a significant role in the revolt of 1857. The folk traditions as well as official records throw sufficient light on their bravery and sacrifices. The twentieth century too saw the rise of the Meos as a political power under the leadership of Yasin Khan who happens to be a first graduate and an advocate in the Meo community. He played an important role in the then politics which resulted the exile of Maharaja Jai Singh of Alwar state. In his praise the *mirasis* of the community always sing a full length folksong at certain social gatherings.

In colonial texts, the Meos have been depicted as lazy and spent - thrift and have always been in debt. The Eurpoean scholars have highlighted this aspect in their literary works, specially M. Darling in his *Punjab Peasant in Prosperty and Debt.* He has compared them with Jats, Ahirs and Meenas who live in better conditions in the neighbouring areas of Mewat.

Women in Mewat are well-known as hardworking not only at the domestic front but also in the field work. The male folk just kill their time in smoking their *huqqa.* They work only in ploughing in the fields. There are many folksongs on the position of women and their relations with their spouses. Recently the drinking habit of male folks has become a curse in the region, which has been reflected in one of the folk songs sung by the *mirasis.* Thus the whole chapter is full of anecdotes, folksongs and folktales throwing light on the Meo society in the past and present.

In the chapter entitled 'Mewat during the 13th century' attempt has been made to identify the region and the origin of the Meos who gave the region its name 'Mewat' on the basis of the empirical records specially the gazzetteers of different districts of Haryana, Rajasthan and Uttar Pradesh. The importance of the physical features has also been taken into account which allowed the people to adopt guerilla tactics to harass the caravans of the traders and extend the depredations to the far off places of Haryana, Siwalik and Bhiana. Ulugh Khan, the *wizir* of Sultan Nasiruddin Mahmud (AD 1246–65) showed much zeal in ravaging the region of Mewat. The leader of the Meos, Malka had been compared with a gigantic demon and a serpent hued under whom the Meos had paralysed the movement of the royal forces. Later the brutality of the royal soldiers was intensified by the reward of one silver tanka for each head and double the amount for a living Meo. Such expeditions into the region proved only a temporary relief to the Sultans of Delhi. After ascending the throne of Delhi Ulugh Khan took the title of Ghiasuddin Balban. He gave top priority to the task of crushing the Meos of Mewat. He used to take hunting expeditions into the neighbourhood of the capital Delhi. A fortress at Gopalgir was raised for guarding the capital's south - western approach against the Meos or Mewatis garrisoned with the Afghans troops. Balban lost almost one lakh of his special soldiers in this act. This act was fruitful as we do not find Meos' turbulence for about a century.

In the course of the project, an international seminar on the folklore under the auspices of the Department of Slavic Studies was held at University of Delhi in its South Campus. This was my first experience to present a paper on the folklore in a gathering of non - historians. I read a paper on the image of a 'Village *Baniya* as reflected in the Folklore of Mewat'. The paper was well received by the scholars present. Some of them criticed the paper that these anecdotes were merely the local titbits. Professor Lokesh Chandra former Chairman of the Indian Council of Historical Research was presiding over the proceedings, supported my case and convinced the scholars that the paper was well within the theme. Later, the same paper with some modification, was presented at the Punjab History Conference held at Patiala and was published in its proceedings. The paper is based on the folktales, describing the village *bania* as a cunning fellow who with his sweet and clever tongue lures and exploits the villagers. Since the village herdsmen cannot survive without the services of the village baniya, therefore they had to believe what the *baniya* speaks. The economy of the village centres around him and he remains a significant player in the agrarian system of any village society.

A few seminars and symposiums were held at various institutions either on Mewat or folklore. A two day seminar on 'Saint Tradition' was organized at Jaipur. This, once again, provided me with an opportunity to highlight the importance of folklore as well as religious traditions of Mewat. Later, a detailed chapter was prepared on Lal Das of Mewat and his teachings, titled 'Tradition of Bhakti in Mewat and the controversy of Sant Lal Das and his shrine'.

During medieval period of Indian history the impact of the socio - religious movement was felt throughout the country. Sufi *silsilahs* and the teachings of the *Bhaktas* like Nanak and Kabir preached love and humanity. Mewat too produced number of sufis and saints who taught the lesson of equality and sacrifice to the people of this region. Among them Sant

Lal Das is most revered among the Meos and non - Meos. His teachings are available in a *gutka* called *Lal Das ki bani.* Among his teachings the most important are the condemning of begging, respect for the right to property of the others. In the above chapter many miracles of Lal Das have been referred to just like other saints of that age. The followers of Lal Das called *Laldasis* live a very simple life and believe in hard labour. They are Meos, *Banias, Kalals* and *Khatis.*

There arose a dispute over the proprietorship of the shrine of Lal Das when some Meos erected some structure inside the shrine and began performing *namaz,* thus challenging the very right of the *Laldasis* who were residing in the complex for more than three hundred years. Ultimately the dispute was settled by the court which went in the favour of the *Laldasis.* The paper is based on the oral traditions as well as written records. (Copy of the decision of the court is enclosed)

In January 2001, Dr. Vir Singh, Secretary, Suraj Mal Institute, Now Delhi approached me to prepar a research paper for a National Seminar on the *Jats in Indian History* organized by the Centre for Research and Publication of Suraj Mal Memorial Education Society. On his insistencce a paper entitle 'Jat-Meo Alliance Against Jaipur State: Evidence of *Murraqa-i-Mewat*' was prepared and presented. On my request the paper was not included in the publication of the proceedings of the seminar, as it needed little revision. Now it is one of the chapters of the book. The main object of the paper is to hightight *Murraqa-i-Mewat* for the study on Jats and how the Meos of Mewat played important role against the Jaipur State, allying Jawahar Singh of Bharatpur. Moreover this text in Urdu has not been used by the scholars working on the Jats or Meos. However, the Hindi translation by Anil Joshi is available which has been used for this article.

At Kurukshetra University, a National Seminar was held on the *Peasant Movements.* Its convenor Professor K.L. Tuteja once again provided me an opportunity to present a paper on 'Peasants' unrest in Mewat as reflected in a folksong of Mewat.'

In it was shown the rise of Yasin Khan as a leader of the Meo peasantry against the Maharaja of Alwar State who had imposed certain taxes on the Meo cultivators. They rebelled against the Maharaja and Yasin Khan led the movement in Mewat. The paper with some modifications was presented at the *Punjab History Conference* which was published in its proceedings in a summary form on my request. It has further been revised before its inclusion in this book entitled *Yasin Khan Ki Baat.*

Being the first graduate and an advocate among the Meos, Yasin Khan led various movements in the region, especially in the 'Meo uprising' in Alwar state against Maharaja Jai Singh in connection with the increasing taxes. He succeeded in his mission and ultimately became an instrument for Jai Singh's exile. The folksingers or the *mirasis* sing this event in admiration of their leader. The folksong has been used by scholars for their research purposes. I have also used the same with a different interpretation.

Zahiruddin Muhammad Babur, the founder of the Mughal empire in India was not only a good warrior and scholar but also a good traveller. He made his observations on various places of this region visited during his campaigns in India in his autobiography *Tuzuk-i-Baburi.* 'Babur is observations of Mewat' was prepared for Rajasthan History conference to be hald at Bikaner in February 2011 but due to a National Seminar at Jaipur during the same dates it could not be possible to present. The paper is based on the autobiography of Babur named *Tuzuk-i-Baburi,* originally written in Turki and translated into English by A.S. Beveridge with annotations. Babur is well-known for his descriptions of the contemporary political, socio-economic and cultural conditions of Central Asia and India. As a traveller also he visited various places of interest. Mewat also attracted his attention due to its natural beauty. In his autobiography, he makes mention of Mewat and its rulers, the Khanzadas, especially Hasan Khan Mewati who fought against him in the battle of Khanua, supporting the cause of Rana Sanga. In his account of Mewat, Babur makes mention of the mountain ranges of the Aravalli. It is through his autobiography, we come to know the Mewati nobles in the court of Ibrahim Lodi. Babur had ordered to destroy and plunder the region of Mewat.

In the year 2007, the country celebrated the 150th year of 1857 revolt. Seminars and symposiums were organized in different universities and institutions throughout the country and abroad. The Department of Historical Studies, Punjabi University Patiala organized a two day seminar on 1857 and Punjab. I was invited to present a paper on the theme covering the Mewat region. A paper was prepared on the '1857 in Mewat' presented at the said seminar which is now published in its proceedings. The same has been made a part of this work under the title '1857 : Mewat and its neighbouring region'. The paper is based on the published literature available at different libraries and research institutions in India. In the beginning a brief historical survey of the region has been made. It has been shown how after the Khanzada rule, Mughal established their rule over the region and after them the Jats, Narukas, Marathas and finally the British occupied the area of Mewat. The Mewatis had been in the imperial service of the Mughals as well as under British and were serving as soldiers in different regiments. The paper highlights that it was the result of a ruthless policy of exploitation of the British which made the people to raise their heads against them, hence 1857.

As soon as the news of the 1857 revolt spread, the Mewatis got an opportunity to ventilate their anger against the imperial authorities. The Mewatis were joined by other communities viz. Jats, Ahirs, Rajputs and other lower caste artisans and Harijans. Number of Nawabs too supported their cause and joined them against the British. Many houses of the loyal Eurpeans were plundered and destroyed including the District headquarters at Gurgaon. Mirza Ghalib who was present in Delhi, was surprised on the depredations of the Meos in the neighbourhood of the capital. He compares them with the devils.

The Mewatis were fighting not only in district Gurgaon but

also in Aligarh, Hathras, Agra, Etawah, Pilibhit, Mandsor, Indore, Allahabad and at many more areas. In the border districts of Hissar, Rewari and Gurgaon the Punjabis and Sikhs too joined hands with the rebels. Many European officers were killed with their supporters. Charles Ball, Altaf Husain, K. M. Ashraf, Dalrymple, Mirza Ghalib, Majumdar, Mallson, S. N. Sen, M. P. Srivastava and many other scholars have provided a detailed account of the Mutiny and made mention of the Meos or Mewatis who were fighting the British even after the revolt was suppressed. Hundreds of them were hanged and the process of the rigourous punishment continued till December, 1858.

Mewat mein Jang-i-Azadi, on the occasion of the celebrations of 1857 in Mewat an NGO, Mewat Development Front invited me to deliver a lecture on the subject in Hindi. It was addressed in a large gathering of the Meos and other communities on 11th May, 2007 at a village Doha in the district of Mewat on the occasion of the celebration of the 150th year of the 1857 revolt. Basically it is based on the above chapter.

In August, 2008, there was a three day seminar on *Mewat: Past and Present* sponsored by the Mewat Development Board, Rajsthan at Alwar. I was given an understanding by its organizer Dr. Munshi Khan to prepare a paper on the historiography of Mewat and present the same in Hindi, as the people present there would like to listen it in their own mother tongue. I could not resist myself and went through all the volumes published by Aligarh Muslim University related to the Persian sources, translated into Hindi by Professor Sayyid Athar Abbas Rizvi as well as *History of India as told by its own historians* by Elliot and Dowson and prepared a paper entitled *Samkalin Granthon mein Mewat: Tehravin se Solahavani Shati.* It is based on the account provided in the Persian chroniclers as well as Babur's autobiography pertaining to the period of early medieval Indian history with special reference to Mewat from the thirteenth century to the beginning of the sixteenth century.

As mentioned the paper includes the works of the contemporary and the near contemporary Persian chroniclers and Babur's autobiography in connection with the region of Mewat and its people. Each chronicle is important in itself due to the period covered by its author. The chapter is little lengthy highlighting the activities of the Meos and the role of the Khanzadas in the court politics of the Sultans of Delhi. As the region had been strategically important not only to the Meos or Mewatis but for the royal princes of Delhi who used to seek shelter under the Aravalli hills. Timur too could not ignore Bahadur Nahir, the Khanzada ruler of Mewat, who presented two white parrots to the invader. Babur himself made a survey of the region during his campaigns towards Agra and Alwar. He stayed few days in Mewat and gives a good description of various places of interest in Mewat, as mentioned before. The survey of the chroniclers of this period made in this paper may be useful for the scholars who are interested to work on the history of Mewat.

An article was prepared to be presented at a seminar on *Historical Monuments of Madhya Pradesh and Adjoining States* at Sitamau (M.P.) organized by the Natnagar Shodh Samsthan in December, 2009. But due the Gujar agitation at that time the reservations in the trains had to be cancelled. This paper is included in this collection as a chapter antitled 'Khanzadas and their buildings in Mewat. Thanks to Dr. Manohar Singh Ranawat on whose insistence it was prepared for the seminar. Obviously in the introduction of the chapter, a brief sketch of the region and its location has been made. Secondly, a brief debate on the origin of the Khanzada kinship among the Meos too was required. Therefore an account of the Khanzadas and their rule over Mewat makes a point in this chapter. Their role in the court politics of the Delhi Sultans has also been discussed briefly.

There are number of places known for their historical importance, either being the seat of government or due to their strategic location. Hence each place attracted the Khanzada rulers to leave some imprints, to be remembered for the coming generations. The chapter deals with these historical places and their buildings which are either surviving or extinct or otherwise in ruined condition. Alexander Cunningham in his reports gave a beautiful account of such places and the chapter is based on his reports as well as my own personal tour into the region and other literature available to us. The first amongst these is Tijara. It had been the seat of the government for the Khanzadas, surrounded by many buildings. Sarhatta too had been the capital of the Khanzadas and has some remnants of old buildings. Bahadurpur near Alwar was founded by Bahadur Nahar. Cunningham referred some Jain inscriptions in the city temple which are important for the study of the past. The city is famous for a *mithikui* which has been mentioned in the chapter on Lal Das.

Firozepur Jhirka named after a *jhir* or spring in the Aravalli hills, had been a shelter place for the royal troops of the Khanzadas. There are number of tombs and mosques on all sides of this city. The author himself belongs to the city, hence the details given in the paper are more or less the eyewitness besides Alexander Cunningham's report and other records. Babur's description of Mewat is interesting who visited the *jhir* and got built a *hauz* to mark his visit. Kotila had been the capital of Khanzada Bahadur Nahar which was protected from all sides. Lake of Kotila finds mention in *Tuzuk-i-Baburi* which invited the attention of Babur who described it at length. The fort and a fine stone mosque are famous for their historical significance and attraction for the tourists and travellers.

Six miles on the north of Kotila lies the old fort of Indor which was one of the strongholds of the Khanzadas. Presently only a village can be noticed. It is famous for the tomb of Jalal Khan which is 95 feet by 34 feet with three rooms. The place has well been described by Cunningham and Major Powlett. Sohna, famous for its hot springs and its mosque has been an important place in historical times. Near Sohna, Bhondsi on the way to Delhi is another important *qasba* or town, famous for its mosque.

Alwar has its own history and famous for its forts, palaces

and other buildings. It has been the seat of the Khanzadas and later the Naruka Rajputs. The buildings include a number of memorable tombs, *chhatris* and lakes. These days the city is on the world tourist map and attracts the people from within the country and outside. Babur during his campaigns made an attack on the city and placed the treasures of the town under the charge of his eldest son Humayun. Cunningham and Powlett both made a survey of Alwar and give their account on their own way.

Iran Culture House, New Delhi organized a three-day seminar on *Azhadari* (*Muharram*) in which I was invited to participate and write a paper. Hence I prepared a paper entitled 'Observation of *Muharram* in Mewat' and presented the same at this seminar. Though the Meos belong to the sunni sect of Islam, observe *Muharram* as if it was a kind of festival. Since my childhood I have witnessed the observation and used to get blessings during the *tajia* procession. In the Haryana part of Mewat the Meos have stopped to observe it, the Rajasthan part still continues it in different parts of the region. The proceedings of the seminar have been published in Urdu translation, therefore, the paper has been included in the book as an appendix.

In March, 2011, the Department of History, Centre of Advanced Study at Aligarh Muslim University organized a seminar on the 'Sources of Medieval Indian History'. My friend Professor B.L. Bhadani insisted me to be present in the seminar with a paper. I was already busy in preparing the material for this book. But how could I annoy my friend. In the fittest of the occasion I prepared a paper on *Arjang-i-Tijara* as a source of regional history so that it could be added as one more chapters of this book. It deals with the contents of the book *Arjang-i-Tijara* written by Shaikh Muhammad Makhdum. Basically the book is the history of Mewat from Mahabharata age till the year 1872 AD. It is a brief but a coherent history of the region which is based on some mythological traditions, Persian chroniclers and other written records. It is useful for the history of the Khanzadas of Mewat. The book also contains beautiful account of different cities and places of interest in the region including the monuments existed at the time of the author of the book.

To know more about the region one can go through the *Alwar Ank of Vinay* Magazine published by the Raj Rishi College, Alwar in 1969. After going through this *Ank.* I realized that a brief survey of the book be made and published as a separate chapter, being the part of this book. The contents are rich and thought provoking and may serve as a guide for those who wish to work on the history, socio-cultural and political life of the people of the regoin.

As mentioned above, the reader will find that there are two chapters in the book which are in Hindi while one is in Urdu. Many friends have suggested that I should translate or re-write these three articles in English but after reading them over and over again I realized that these chapters should be appended to the text as their 'linguistic flavour' carried considerable importance.

In the end, I must admit that there is a large scope to explore different aspect of the history, polity and society of the region of Mewat. There are numerous and neglected monuments which need the attention of the scholars. These monuments comprise a good number of historical buildings as well as the sufi shrines visited by the people of the region. My work is only an introductory one to apprise the scholars with the region and its people.

Since the region and its people are the main centre of the book, therefore, it was unavoidable to repeat few passages especially defining the region almost in each paper which otherwise is complete in all aspects.

1

Folkore Memory History*

I

In recent years there has been increasing interest among the scholars to study the social, economic and cultural aspects of different societies in India. And, the folklore is an important aspect of their culture which needs to be defined briefly. Since the introduction of the word folklore in 1846 by William Thoms, there arose a controversy about its definition. Twenty one definitions given by different scholars as quoted in the *Standard Dictionary of Folklore* prove the gravity of this disagreement.[1] However, one may agree that "folklore consists of the beliefs, customs, myths, legends, songs, tales and ritualistic ceremonies of the common people of any society. It has been established that the science of folklore is that branch of human knowledge that collects, classifies and studies in a scientific manner the materials of folklore in order to interpret the life and culture of the peoples across the ages and contributes in a great measure to the history of mankind. Folklore or popular knowledge, is the accumulated

*The Paper was presented under the title 'Folklore and History Writing: A case study of Mewat' at Nehru Memorial Museum and Library, New Delhi on the invitation of Professor Ravinder Kumar, the then Director in 1989. Later the same under the present title at a symposium, sponsored byUniversity Grant Commission at Kurukshetra University in 1991.

store of what mankind has experienced, learnt and practiced throughout life as popular and traditional knowledge which is distinguished from so-called scientific knowledge".[2]

Folklore is essentially a product of a community, handed down from generation to generation undoubtedly without a reliable ascription to an inventor or author.[3] In brief the common idea present in all folklore is that of traditions, something handed down from one person to another and preserved either by memory or practice rather than written records.

It is believed that every art including folklore is derived from the reality and reflects the same. It needs no evidence or proof. Difficulties arise when we attempt to interpret the historical process and decide how history has been reflected in it. And, history as we know is based on certain sources of information which are based on written material or records, epigraphy and numismatic and other methods to study it. But there are certain areas where no such material is found for historical writing. It gives relaxation or little free hand to the scholars to justify their thought and prove their thesis. Pre-historic art-efacts and archaeological tools came into use, followed by literature. Now, the historians have started writing on the social and economic formation and evolution of cultures, shifting from the merely chronological or political history. They have also recognized the oral literature or oral history as source of history which include folklore. No doubt there is always a hesitation to use folklore but if the lores do not create contradiction or conflict with the valid historical data, there should be no objection to their use. As a matter of fact, the choice of oral information becomes obvious in areas, where the documentary evidences are either inadequate or negligible. In the case of the social history of any minority group, the limitations of written documents are such that the use of oral evidences introduce an entirely new dimensions to the study.[4]

It is a moot point in history-writing that the deriving force of history is the people itself and the individual persons are a derivative of history, not its impetus. From this point of view, everything that happens to a people, belongs to history in one way or the other. In a broad conception of history the historical basis includes the whole of people's life throughout its existence.[5] Historical legends treat events and persons of the past as if they were real. By preserving the memory of the past events and narrating about the heroic behaviour of some persons, the historical legends live in the people's memory as oral and unwritten history.[6] Every tale or song is characterized by a specific relation to reality and by a method for its artistic representation. These are formed in various period and times have various fortunes, pursue various aims and reflect various aspects of the political, social, economic and everyday history of a people. Thus question why study folklore? One can suggest that to understand a people, it is necessary to understand their folklore. What is true of a nation is true of a smaller group or region as well.

Trained to use books, newspapers, diaries, letters, official reports—the written remains of the highly literate portion of society—historians too often ignore the orally transmitted folk materials and do not feel the need to preserve them.[7] As suggested by modern scholars, oral history loses power as time depth increases, it cannot account for the earliest eras. Written history loses power as social breadth increases, it cannot account for most people. The same problem is with the art factual record. We have more early works from men than women, more from upper class and middle classes than the lower classes. Thus it is upto the historians how they are benefited by the folk traditions of any class, society or region where one finds fuller treatment to their studies.[8]

On the other hand, we are familiar with what folklore can do to history, how it changes data, places and names to suit the pattern of the moment - the moment the folksinger is most concerned with the carrier of oral folk traditions-continually alters the tale, song or saying he has heard.

Therefore a meaningful approach to the folk traditions of any region, society or community must be made against its historical background and need to be verified through the indexes and reference works which form the scientific tools of the historians. We know that history and folklore develop side by side and the local pride, prejudice and passions play their part in the folkorization of history. Writing on 'Primitive materials for history' Allan Navin says that Folklore and ballads are among the most beautiful and alluring of the sources of history. They have the dewy freshness of the morning of the human race upon them, for they have sprung in the main from times and communities, innocent of written literature. The ballad in particular, which often throws a bright prismatic light upon manners, customs, beliefs and primitive emotions is the composition rather of a folk than of an individual. It rose from the heart and lips of a whole people. These compositions usually contain little explicit and authentic fact, but they are nonetheless valuable. It can not be denied that even today there are large number of tribes and communities who do not possess any written record of their history. We know them through their folklore or bards.[9]

In fact oral history has taken its roots in the Indian Universities and other institutions. The Punjabi University, Patiala is the first to have established in 1973 an 'Oral History Cell' as a wing of the Department of Punjab Historical Studies with four-fold objectives: (i) to collect oral traditions from knowledgeable persons in different walks of life (ii) to collect accounts of freedom fighters (iii) to collect account of historical monuments, site, forts and shrines which are fast decaying (iv) to collect the account of the villages especially of various tribes, castes and communities, land settlements, etc., and to survey and collect the manuscripts, documents, letters of historical significance. In this connection the Department of Punjab Historical Studies had organized a seminar on "Concept and Value of Oral history in the Historiography of Modern India" and brought out its proceedings in the volume of *Panjab Past and Present* in October, 1985, edited by Professor Ganda Singh. Prior to this a report of discussion from the Indo-American Seminar on Indian Folklore held at Mysore in 1980 was published by the Central Institute of Indian Languages, Mysore in 1981. In summarizing the discussion it was felt that folklore serves to express life-values and to offer metaphors for the shared understanding of life. It also preserves the past in areas where there are no historical records, linking the past to the present; and even where there are such records, it provides an alternative history, a democratized history that tells quite a different story from the facts selected by the journalists and historicans. We must learn to "understand India from the bottom as well as from the top."[10]

Recently a centre for contemporary history has also been established at Nehru Memorial Museum and Library, New Delhi. It has interviewed hundreds of freedom fighters, retired civil servants and other old and learned persons who either have witnessed the national movement or participated in the political, administrative or any other events of importance for national heritage. In Calcutta (now Kolkata), Subaltern Group of the scholars has also got recognition among the academics. It has brought out so far eight volumes. The first emancipatory act, as pointed out in a discussion on *Subaltern As Perspective*, that Subaltern studies project performs in our understanding of tribes, castes or other such groups, is to restore them their historical being.[11]

II

With this brief sketch of folklore and its scope as a source of history, now we come to the region of Mewat. Just few miles from Delhi there is a community called Meo after which the region is named 'Mewat'. In this chapter I have discussed some aspects of this land and its people as reflected in their folklore not only as a student of history, but as a native of the region. This is an outcome of the field work undertaken by me over the past three years while working on a project entitled "*Folklore and History writing: A case study of Mewat* for which the Indian Council of Historical Research, New Delhi was liberal to give me a financial support. To carry on the project, I had to travel extensively the region, meet and interview the learned and elderly people. During this period I had the opportunity to enjoy the folksongs sung by their bards (*Mirasis*). I have also had the opportunity to witness the cultural programmes in some schools through the good offices of some of my old friends and classmates who are teaching in the villages. These functions reflect on the Meo culture and heritage.

Mewat, the land of the Meos, included most of the parts of Gurgaon district in Haryana, Alwar and Bharatpur in Rajasthan and some parts of Agra and Mathura in Uttar Pradesh at that time. Though the information is furnished in the district gazetteers or other imperial records, but the following couplet describing the region is still current and equally relevant:

> इत दिल्ली उत आगरो, मथुरा और बैराट,
> कालौ पहाड़ सुहावनो, बसे जहाँ मेवात।

Couplet sufficies, 'where the Mewat is'? From Delhi to Agra, from Mathura to Bairat (the old Virat of Mahabharat's times which is about 30 miles from Alwar on the way to Jaipur) where the black charming hills of Aravali stand, 'here lies Mewat.'*

III

According to the traditions, the Meos claim their origin from the Rajputs and they still carry some Hindu traditions.

* Now a separate district of Mewat has been created in 2004 by the Haryana Government, Nuh being its headquarter comprising the whole Mewat region of Haryana.

For example they erect *Bhairon ji ka chabutra* (a local deity) before they start any important work. They still bear Hindu names, for example I met two brothers Bashir Ahmad and Kundan. There are prevalent other Hindu names like Hira, Suraj, Chand etc which are very common.

The scholars have different opinions about the origin of the Meos. Some agree that they are from the Aryan stock whereas the other relate them to the Meds who were present in Sind when Alexander invaded India. However, the explanations noticed in the district gazetteers seem to be the more accepted definition that the Meos are of the Rajput origin who descend from *Suryavanshi* and *Chandravanshi* being the generations of Lord Rama and Krishna.

There is a controversy about their leanings with the Minas. The Meos are divided into certain *gotras* and *pals* which are prevelant in the Minas. Without any prejudice one may suggest that they belong to the Hindu family as they still carry certain Hindu customs and rituals. They celebrate Dussehra, Holi, Diwali with equal fervour alongwith *Id* and *Shab-i-Raat.*[12] Though belonging to the sunni sect of Islam, they observe *muharram* and take out *tajiya* procession.

The physical features of the region played a vital role in the life of the people of Mewat. Due to deserts, hilly tracts or lack of arable land, there grew nothing but thorny bushes in the early period. Agriculture became the profession of the Meo especially under the Mughals, they hardly gave up their old habits of plundering the traders and their caravans. The region served as the shelter place for the fleeing princes of Delhi. Now the land is in much use under cultivation but the region is listed as the *backward areas* of the state of Haryana and Rajasthan.

The first reference about the Meos in the history is made by the Persian chroniclers of the thirteenth century. They mention that the Meos combined together with the disgruntled nobles of the Rajputs posed problems to the Turkish rulers of Delhi. They had developed a special guerilla technique to fight their enemies due to advantagous positions in the hills of Aravali. Like the Khokhars* in the northwest frontier regions of the Sultanate, the Meos also maintained their independence. The boundary of the Delhi Sultanate remained fluctuating to the south of Delhi because of the tribal depredations. Ghiasuddin Balban suppressed them and took puntitive measures by raising the fort of Gopalgir and garrisoned it with the Afghan troops as described by Ziauddin Barani in his *Tarikh-i-Firuzeshahi.* Minhaj the author of *Tabakat-i-Nasiri,* compares Malka the leader of the Meos with a gigantic demons and a serpent-hued. Owing to the fear of their activities the South-Western gates of the city were closed at the time of afternoon prayer and no one could dare to go out of the city after that time.[13]

We find the Meo chiefs embracing Islam as their creed in the time of Firozshah Tughlaq who bestowed upon them the title of 'Khanzada.' Bahadur Nahir Khanzada played an important role in the court politics of Delhi. On the eve of Timur's invasion he had been described a very powerful ruler of Mewat. Timur in his autobiography refers about two white parrots presented by Bahadur Nahir to him. After defeating Ibrahim Lodi in the battle of Panipat in 1526 AD. Babur established himself as an emperor. He found Hasan Khan a descendant of Bahadur Nahir as the king of Mewat. Hasan Khan supported the cause of Maharana Sanga and fought against the Mughals and lost his life in the battle of Khanuah. He has been described as the patriot of the country who fought for the independence of the country. The folksong is still common:

यह मेवाती वह मेवाड़ी, मिल गये दोनों सैंनाणी,
हिन्दू मुस्लिम भाव छोड़, मिल बैठे दो हिन्दुस्ताणी।

After Hasan Khan Mewati we hardly find references about

* See G. D. Gulati. India's Northwest Froniter in Pre-Mughal Times, (Delhi, 1985), Chapter III.

any leader of the high rank. Mewat remained under the control of the Mughal governors till the end of the their power. But Meos remained Meos and gave trouble to Aurangzeb who sent a powerful army under the command of Raja Jai Singh who conquered the fort of Alwar, the centre of the Meo power at that time. After the downfall of the Mughal empire, Meos fought mostly as an unorganized force resulting the Jat and the Maratha domination on some of the areas of Mewat. Later under the British the region came under their direct control with the creation of the District Gurgaon. Shamsuddin was raised as the Nawab of Mewat. He was instrumental in the murder of William Frazer, the commissioner of Delhi.*

During the 1857 revolt we find the Meos in a very strong position. They fought for the cause of the Mughal emperor Bahadur Shah. After the revolt the region was brought under the direct control of the British and partly under the states of Alwar and Bharatpur. Later in the freedom movement the region produced a number of leaders who played significant role in the then politics. The names of Yasin Khan, Kunwar Muhammad Ashraf (noted historian) and Comrade Abdul Hai are in point.

IV

As mentioned earlier, the region owing to the scarcity of arable land did not produce except thorny bushes. The Mughals realized this factor and to encourage cultivation in the region, began granting some incentives and concessions to the peasantry including exemption of land tax in certain villages. As we know Akbar was the first among the Mughals who gave serious attention to the agriculture and classified the land into four categories. The following anecdote relates to a village Ghata Shamsabad in Firozepur Jhirka sub-division

*See chapter on 'William Fraiser's Murder' in Perceival Spear's book *Twilight of the Mughals* (O.U.P. 1951) pp. 82–91.

of district Gurgaon at that time. It reflects on the policy of Akbar not extracting land tax from *banjar* category of land. But the Meos bards or *mirasis* describe this incident as if the Meo chivalry compelled the Mughal emperor to do so. The anecdote on the basis of a folksong was told by the *sarpanch* of village Biwan in Firozepur Jhirka sub - division, Mr. Sualeh Khan advocate. Interestingly, he is also a student of history and did his post-graduation from Aligarh Muslim University in the sixties.

The anecdote goes as under:

> The Meos of Ghata Shamsabad (a village in Firozepur Jhirka sub - division) were most fearless and never paid their land tax to the state officials. When Akbar ascended the throne he directed his revenue officials to collect the revenue. As usual the Meos did not pay any attention to them. Akbar sent some soldiers to Ghata Shamsabad to realize the tax as well as to teach a lesson to the villagers. The Meos fought bravely and killed the *Nazim* (revenue official) in the midst of the village *chaupal.* The Mughal forces were compelled to retreat. The Mughal army later made a success and succeeded to make the sarpanch captive. Akbar directed his officials to bring two bags of soil. The sarpanch and the soil bags reached the court. Akbar seeing the soil gave his decision of exempting the land tax as the soil was of such a poor quality which could not produce any thing. The sarpanch was also released.

The same incident when sung, gives different picture. Mirasis go to this extent that even in the court Meo sarpanch abused the emperor and compelled him not to send his officials to his village in future and Akbar seeing his anger gave the above decision. This is how the folklore exeggerate the facts of the events. But we can not ignore the way they appreciate their feelings, that at least the *mirasis* indirectly tell about Akbar's land revenue policy in context with the *banjaror* non-cultirable land category. If the illiterate peasantry cannot learn about this land system under the Mughals however they are made aware of this through their folk-singers in this way. This is how the Meo folk perceive the historical facts.

V

Mewat had been a seat of a number of saints in the medieval period, which do not find place in the literature of the contemperary chroniclers. However, there are number of shrines which are the evidence of their saintly life who lived in Mewat. Their sayings or teachings are possessed by their followers orally. The most famous was Saint Lal Das born in a Meo family in village Dhaulidub (near Alwar) in 1540 AD. His father was Chand Mal and mother Samda. He lived a very simple life and earned his livelihood by selling wood sticks. He died at ripe age of 108 years in 1648 AD. His shrine is at Sherpur a village in district Alwar on the border of Haryana. In the memory of the saint people from all religions and sects pay visits to Dhauli Dub, Sherpur, Nangla and Bandoli villages where quarterly fairs are held. Major P.W. Powlett in his District Gazetteer of Alwar gave an account of the life of Las Das and his teachings in little details.

The followers of Lal Das are called Laldasis. The Laldasi sect is close to Kabir sect. The followers are both married and unmarried. Every Laldasi hates begging and believes in hard work. Singing Ram's name rhyms accompanied with music form an important part in their worship. His saying are called *bani* or *gutka* in which some of the *Kabir's sakhis* are mixed with the *bhajans.* Lal Das was a great social reformer and always spoke for the unity of man and God.[14] The *gutka* opens with a strong condemnation of begging:

Let not the devotee beg, as the begging is shameful, wandering from house to house is wrong even if they be those of kings or queens.

Lal Das is held as a great Meo and Pir by the Meos. The day before each full moon and every Sunday are kept as fast. The Laldasis are chiefly Meos, Baniyas and *Kalals* who are more numerous in Alwar, Bharatpur, Mathura and Agra. On a true sadhu Lal Das said:

The sadhu should be one who earns the food he eats. Let God's service be the heart's. And go not about begging.

Another bani about true saint is as follows :

With simple food and cloth saint must sleep on grass.

Among other teachings sadhu should return good for evil, should be candid and bold in speech, hard over his passion. Respect for rights and property of other (*Haqq*), calmness (*Sil*) is the ornament of the true sadh. On the true hero who fights and wins is the spiritual battlefield where the coward crouches and regrets.

Laldasis sadhus like Lal Das are family—men and marry with Meos, but do not eat with them. A convert has been known to allow his house to be plundered of all it contained besides maintaining himself by his own labour. (For details see chapter 4, Tradition of Bhakti in Mewat and the Controversy of Sant Lal Das and his Shrine).

Charandas was also a saint from Mewat. He was born in 1703 at village Dehra near Alwar. He founded an order (*silsilah*) at Delhi in 1730. It is believed that Muhammad Shah, the Mughal emperor used to come for his *darshan.* Charandas emphasised on the unity of God, recitation of His name and the greatness of Guru. He denounced idolatory like Kabir. Both men and women were accepted as his disciples. He had been described as a great son and reformer, spiritual sadhu and a poet. He popularized the *Sanskrit* learning and Krishna worship. He wrote many books out of which 20 have been mentioned by modern scholars.[15] He did not follow any specific language. For example:

नन्द के कुमार हौं तो कहाँ बार बार
मोहे लीजिए उबार, ओट अपनी में कीजिए,
काम और क्रोध को काटो जम बेड़ा प्रभु
माँगो एक नाम मौहि भक्ति दान दीजिए।
कहै चरणदास मेरी होय नहीं हँसी
श्याम कहूं मैं पुकारि मेरी श्रवन सुन लीजिए

Churh Sidh was another famous saint of Mewat whose shrine is located in the hills near Alwar where *urs* is celebrated on the fourteenth day of Phagun, month of the Hindu calender. There is a spring near the shrine where both the Hindus and Muslim take bath. It is famous that Churh Sidh was miraculous man and used to take cows in the fields for grazing, remained busy in meditation. It invited the anger of the owner. Then Church Sidh said:

यह ले तेरी लाठी लूगड़ी
यह ले तेरी गाय
हम पे मेहर मदार की
हम कस की घेरे गाय।

Saying this Churh Sidh refused to perform his job as cowboy and turned to be a saint.

VI

The Mewatis played a significant role in the 1857 revolt. Their folk traditions as well as official records prove the point. The revolt attracted the attention of the bards. It is believed that the famous cartridges having pig and cow oil used in the army were manufactured in Mewat. One of the chamars disclosed the secret to the people of Mewat, thus started the revolt. Many battles were fought against the English. I just quote few couplets which are sung by the Mirasis even today to glorify the Meos.

सत्तावन् का गदर की
पड़ी मुल्क मे रल्ल (uproar)
गोरी मारा घेर के
दिल्ली गई दहल (havoc)
अक्ल बड़ी और मन अडर
और गरूरी रूआब

नंदन (London) सू सब नरन (people) पर
गालिब हुआ (appeared) उकाब (eagle)
आयो नंदन सू उकाब
बांधो कलकतो पे रुआब (sway or cowed down)
तय के प्रताप ताउ कौन झेले जंगी की
उत्तर दल्खन के सब भूप दोहे
जदू बिन कौन टोहि ऐह कौन उपंगी की
(sub-division)
दूहल, कुदावा (Pals in Meos) चेतावा ऐसी चटक
रंशी की
कह मन सब कविराय, दीजो दूध पीवन लू गाए
दोहे में टोपी तो राख ले है फिरंगी की।
रायसीना मे मेवों ने
भला जगायो दीन
खक्के मार तीन सौ
कुर्सी खली कर दीन
बंगला में मन न लगे
सूनी दीख सेज
रायसीना के गोर में (around)
देख बना सीस अंग्रेज

Doha is a village just on the border of Haryana, twelve kilometers from Firozepur Jhirka where the Meos fought for Bahadur Shah.

There is a village Raisina in Gurgaon District. The Meos of this village gave much trouble to the English and even forced their ladies to do manual work in the fields with their meonis.

Raisina and Doha, two villages of Mewat (now in Haryana) were placed on *Kachcha* records to punish the Meos of these two villages who fought against the British.

VI

The twentieth century saw the rise of the Meos as a political power under the leadership of Yasin Khan who supported the British. He was an instrumental for the exilement of Jai Singh, the king of Alwar. The folksingers of Mewat used to sing a folksong in praise of Yasin Khan in which he has been described as the hero of Mewat. He was invited by the British to take part in an assembly where many kings were also present. Recently in an article, "History and Society in a popular rebellion : Mewat 1920-33" by Majid Hayat Sddiqui, published in a journal *Comparative Studies in Society and History,* July issue of 1986 (pp. 463-74). The author has also borrowed few couplets from this folksong to support the social conflict between the Meos and the Rajputs and how the rise of Yasin Khan was responsible for the banishment of the prince of Alwar. This legend was told to me my one comrade Mohammed Ahmad of Gumat Bihari a village near Nagina in Firozepur Jhirka sub-division of District Gurgaon (now Mewat).

According to Siddiqi there was no leader in Mewat at that time who could be used against the ruler of Alwar, Jai Singh. Mr. Churchill took advice from Sikander Hayat Khan, then the governor of Punjab who suggested the name of Yasin Khan. Yasin Khan belonged to village Rahna near Nuh. He was well educated and an advocate. As told, Mr. Churchill invited Yasin Khan to Delhi and offered him a chair whereas Jai Singh was kept standing. The folksingers however have confused this event with the conferences of the chambers of princes held in 1918, 1919 and 1933. The British succeeded to win the confidence of the Meos. Yasin Khan as their leader, the Meo rebellions in Mewat in the year 1933 proved successful resulting the decline of Jai Singh of Alwar.* Legend goes as under:

* See also, Shail Mayaram, *Resisting Regimes : Myth, Memory and the Shaping of a Muslim Identity* (Oxford, 1997), chapter 4 entitled 'Construction of the Meo Movement: The written Record', pp. 93–125.

दिल्ली में जलसो जुड़ो सिकरे मेम साब अंग्रेज
जैपुर, उदयपुर, आगरो सबको चिट्ठी देयो भेज।
जब गुड़गॉवा सू चलो, छुटो दिल्ली को धायो,
साहब करां सलोट, चौधरी अब के आयो।
सब राजा या देस का, देखां अपनी-अपनी बाट
कुर्सी दयौ यासीन को, हुक्म चलावे लाट।

Yasin Khan was offered a seat. When Jai Singh reached he got angry over it and said:

कौन कहां का मेव, आज जलसा में आयो
राजा है कि रईस, कहा याने हुद्दा पायो
तोप चढ़ा चरख पे, चलती कर दूँ गंज मशीन
पहले रहणां फूँक दूँ, जब देखूँ यासीन।

Hearing such words Yasin too could not resist his ego and replied in the same manner:

मेरी बारह बावन पाल, दगा न तो सू राखूँ
तेरा लेयूँ राज यह छीन, अर्ज मैं करूँ खुदा सू
रहणा का यासीन की, सुन ले बात खरी
या अलवर के बीच में, तेरी कर दूँ धड़ी-धड़ी

Jai Singh replied:

सुन ले भाई मेवड़ा, अपना दिल में बण रहा खूब
तो सी छोरी मेव की, अलवर में बेचें दूब

The legend is quite a long one having more than 20 couplets in which we find how Yasin Khan united the Meos and directed them not to pay land revenue which, resulted into the rebellion in Mewat. In one of the couplets the queen of Alwar has also been shown advising Jai Singh (when reached Alwar) in this way:

राजा सू रानी कहे, दिल्ली कू जायो
दिल्ली में यासीन खां, वाके पांवन पड़ जायो

Jai Singh replied in anger:

उह हे छोरी मेव की, मैं ठाकुर राजपूत
पावन तो पणसूँ नहीं, चाहे गद्दी जावे छूट

Mr. Siddiqui has used this couplet as under :

इह लड़को है मेव को, मैं ठाकुर राजपूत
चौधरी यासीन के पाव न पड़ूँ, चाहे मेरी गद्दी जावे छूट

From here onwards in the legend there is description of the revenue officials who were sent by the Raja of Alwar for collection of land revenue and how the Meos refused to pay and raised their heads against Jai Singh who sent the army to suppress them. This event is sung by the folksinger as *Yasin Khan ki Baat.**

It is said that during the partition of the country in 1947 AD many Meo families migrated to Pakistan. In the beginning, they were kept in camps. In the morning, they were served tea which was a new kind of dish for them. Later many of them returned back to India and went back to their old homeland 'Mewat'. People wanted to know their experience on the way to Pakistan. They replied that things were alright but serving hot syrup' (tea) was a new experience because syrup or *sharbat* is served cold. This is how the introduction of tea in the sub-continent is reflected in the folklore of Mewat.

*See chapter 6, *Yasin Khan Baat.*

VII

The Meos are known for their laziness and always are in debt. About their laziness M. Darling in his book *Panjab Peasant in Prosperty and Debt,* has given very good description (pp. 94, 101, 102). He compared the Meo peasants with their counter parts Ahir peasants from Rewari. The sandy soils of Rewari produces enough to keep Ahirs in comfort while the comparatively rich soil of the Firozepur valley is heavily mortgaged to meet the extravagance of the thrifty Meos. Almost every Meo is still in the hands of money lender. The Meos of Nuh and F.P.J. are under the burden of heavy debt which goes around 30 times the land revenue while in Rewari is only 6 times of the revenue. Darling analysis this laziness of the Meos in this way. Allied in race to the aboriginal Meenas of Rajputana they have not inherited the qualities developed by the Ahirs in his long patient struggle. The restless life of the camps and jungle has always appealed to them more than the settled life of the farm and the village. Comparing the Meos with the Jats Darling adds that forgetting, too, their humble origin, they modeled themselves upon the Rajputs instead of the Jat. The Jat could at least have taught them to cultivate but the Rajputs with their extravagant ways and contempt for the plough, merely confirmed them in inherited habit. Such blessings, therefore, as nature has given them, instead of being an advantage have only served to make them attractive to the money lender who now has the whole tribe in fee. A folk saying current in the region will suffice:

मेव कमावे भूखा, जाट कमावे धापा

(Meo will work only when he feel hungry and Jat when fully satisfied will go for work).

There are number of folktales regarding the role of village Bania, making the Meo illiterate peasantry fool by using his own arithmetic or sweet tongue. These folktales depicting the exploitation of the Meos by village Bania for centuries till now find place in a separate chapter on "The Village Baniya as reflected in the Folktales of Mewat" is a part of the Book.*

VIII

Dada Heja, Folk Hero of Mewat

Dada Heja is the 'folk hero' of the Meos who had been depicted in the folktales of the region as one of the wisest and clever individual who could compete anyone may be a poet or king. Many folktales have been attributed to him which reflect the socio-religious aspects of the Meo society. He belonged to a village called Kolgaon in Alwar district. This hero is sometimes found having conversation with a thirteenth century poet Amir Khusrau and sometimes in the Mughal court. And recently seen breaking the monopoly of the qazis in performing the marriages or nikah. I shall relate here few anecdotes representing Dada Heja as the 'Hero of the Meo wisdom'.

Once Amir Khusrau was passing through the Mewat and reached Kolgaon. He was very thirsty, and reached near a well where some lady water-carriers were drawing water from the well. Introducing himself to those ladies, made a request for water to quinch his thirst. Amir Khusrau was well known as a popular poet in those days. The water-carriers were happy that such a reputed poet and a knowledgeable person was with them. But he would drink water only when he could compete Dada Heja in wisdom. Khusrau agreed, Dada Heja was invited to test his knowledge. Dada Heja spoke "शाब शाड़ाबड़ शड़ब शूँ" and asked the meaning of this sentence.

Amir Khusrau replied:

*See chapter 3

जब धान कुटे है धुम्मक धूँ
तक छाज करे है फट्टक फूँ
जब हांडिया करे है खदड़क खूँ
तब शाब शाड़ाबड़ शड़ब शूँ।

As a matter of fact, Meos are very fond of a liquid diet called *mahri* or sweet *rabri* prepared with the flour of *bajra* or *jawar* in an earthen pot. When prepared it is consumed in a liquid form, thus giving a sound शाब शाड़ाबड़ शूँ. Dada Heja had actually asked about this sound of drinking *mahri* or sweet *rabri*. In replying the question Amir Khusrau gave full description about this sound from threshing of the paddy till its giving the above sound. All were happy that at least Amir Khusrau answered Dada Heja's question but at the same time unhappy because Dada was just equal to Amir Khusrau in wisdom. Amir Khusrau was allowed to quinch his thirst. Khusrau took little water and thanked the villagers. Seeing the villagers upset over it Dada at the same though not thirsty, drank lot of water. This gave them some relief, at least their Dada drank more water than Amir Khusrau hence he was great.

Once a party of the traders came to the Mughal court to sell some elephants. Dada Heja too happened to be in the court. Being an intelligent hero of his time, he was asked by the emperor to deal with them. Since he had never seen elephant. So when he saw this big animal, came near to it and try to see it minutely. The traders thought that he was some knowledgeable person and expert in elephant trade and might be searching some defects. They offered him ten *asharfis* (gold coins) and requested him to remain abstain from the animal. Dada took the *asharfis*, but continued to watch the animal intently. The traders were frightened now and offered 20 more *asharfis* to Dada Heja and requested him to leave the palace. But Dada was a Dada and showing his honesty threw the *asharfis* and said, "I do not need the money tell me what type of animal is it? Traders were happy at Dada's innocence and taking back their money told him that that was an 'elephant'.

After some years one day at night an elephant just passed through the village Kolgaon and left the traces of its feet. In the morning when villagers saw they went to Dada Heja what were these marks? Dada Heja too wondered but he had to satisfy the folk. Actually he had forgotten the name 'elephant'. But since he was their hero and to satisfy them he replied

कोई पवनचक्की बाँध कर हिरण कूदा होय
कै रात इकट्ठी हो के गई, न तो दिल्ली वाला होय।

Either a deer jumped tieing a wind mill in his foot or the night had gathered or that animal from Delhi had passed through which he had seen.

As we know the qazis have played vital role in the socio-religious celebrations in the Muslim society. When the Meos accepted Islam they were also regulated by the Islamic Law. In Mewat there were few qazis who performed their duties on such occasions. As per the traditions at the marriage feasts no one could take food unless the *nikah* was performed fully.

Once it was the season of marriages in Mewat. A marriage ceremony was to be performed in a certain village. Qazi was busy in other marriage functions in the region and till midnight he did not turn up. The children began crying and weeping as they were hungry. The Meos called their hero to advise them on this occasion. He came and advised the villagers perform this ceremony themselves and do not kill their children. "Let the qazi go to hell". All agreed to the proposal and requested Dada to come forward to perform the rituals. Dada Heja was an illiterate and did not know Quran or *Shariat.* He spoke few words to satisfy the marriage party:

झाड़ फाड़ भाई झाड़ फाड़, काजी न आयो बेटी को काढ।
नीचे शक्कर ऊपर दही, अल्लाह ही निगाह में निकाह सही।
हो गया लाली का ब्याह, चल भई अब खाना खा।

Saying this Dada started eating food and all followed him. Since then it is said that the qazi in Mewat lost his prestige. The qazi who was basically dependent on the surplus of the Meo peasantry how could enforce the law where the people are suffering in his absence.

IX

Women in Mewat are well-known as hardworking at domestic front as well as in the field work. The *Meonies* do not observe *pardah.* The male folk just kill their time in smoking their *huqqa.* They only engage in ploughing with bullocks and digging the soil when required. All the rest of the field work from sowing, weeding, harvesting, thrashing, winnowing to stacking, they leave to their women. Men do only a quarter of the work in the fields while the women do the remaining three fourth. They have to cut the fodder (*dub*) and feed the animals as well.

In the following folksong a *Meoni* has been shown going to the jungle to fetch fodder whereas her husband remains behind at home. He has been requested by the wife to look after the child in her absence. The dialogues show how the Meo husband advises her to be deaf if some ones look at her. Wife also gives some instructions to her husband to take care of the son:

धेरे उठी दूब लू और खुरपा पैनायो
मैं तो जा री दूब लू मेरो छोरो बहलायो
और बीती मेरी जान विकट पर्वत में।

Now the husband gives the following direction :

तू तो जा री दूब लू मेरी सुन जायो
जो कोई आवे मेंड पर तू गूंगी बन जायो
और बीती मेरी जान विकट पर्वत में।

The following song was told by Kunwar Hazari Singh of Faridabad which he used to sing in his childhood. We used to enjoy folksongs in our schooldays during cultural programmes held on every Saturday and other important occasion.

Use of earthen utencils was very common in Mewat in those days. Slowly some of the families according to their economic standard and social status had started buying silver utencils. In this song a housewife is complaining her husband about the attitude of her elder sister-in-law (*jethani*) who refused to give her utencils on loan as her relatives are going to visit her soon. She is requesting him to bring silver utencils to raise the standard of living and to show her *jethani* that she could also afford to posses such items. The song is:

आते जाते तबाक लेतो आयो जेठानी ढमला पे लड़ी
पहल-पहल मेरी बाबा भी आयो, वालू मैं ढुमरी में ख्वायो
जेठानी ढमला पे लड़ी . . . .
पहल-पहल मेरो बाप् भी आयो, वालू मैं ढुमरी में ख्वायो
जेठानी ढमला पे लड़ी . . . .
पहल-पहल मेरो भाई भी आयो, वालू मैं ढुमरी में ख्वायो
जेठानी ढमला प लड़ी . . . .

Here ढुमरी mean a very small earthen pot; ढमला is rather big one and तबाक a silver pot for which wife is requesting.

In this song though we find a jealous attitude of two sister-in-laws on the other hand it depicts the standard of living in Mewat where people could hardly afford to buy a metal pot till recent years. Three kinds of utencils mentioned here are the signs of their domestic standard. Now it had become fashion to have the metal utencils instead of an earthen ones. In such way the housewife desires to have better quality of pots. The folksong depicts the real scence of life in the village society, a historical fact.

In the following song drinking of alcohol instead of milk has been condemned. Interstingly the blame has been attributed to Indira raj. This goes as under :

इंदिरा गांधी तेरे राज में, होय रे · · · ये लोग हुए आज़ाद
दूध का बेला छोड़न लोग, होय रे · · · ये पीने लगे शराब
इतनी कमाई राजा कहाँ गई रे होय रे · · · ·
मेरा कर दैओ हिसाब
दिन छिप जाण दे, सांझ हो जाण दे होय रे . . .
अपना कर लीजौ हिसाब
दिन छिप गयो सांझ हो गई, मेरा दे दो जी हिसाब
पैंट सिलवाई गोरी बुशट सिलवाई, बाकी की पी ली शराब
पैंट सिलवा ले राजा बुशट सिलवा ले, पर पीनी छोड़ शराब
पैंट न सिलवाऊँ गोरी बुशट न सिलवाऊँ, न छोड़ूँ पीनी शराब

To conclude, one can say that if the history is the history of the people as a whole, folklore and memory are its integral parts. There are feelings and attitude, undercurrents of emotions in the masses, which are not recorded in official documents but make profound effect upon happenings. The folklore of a particular period or region is at least as important to the historian as are the newspapers and other sources of information generated by the urbanized societies. More so, an editorial may represent the opinion of one single man, the editor, while a ballad or bard, will certainly express the beliefs of a great number. To write the history of the people, making use of folklare information will definitely give a new dimension to the writing of history. All these questions raised in the chapter need to be re-considered in the context of conteporary debates intiated by the 'post-modernist-challenge.'

REFERENCES

1. *Standard Dictionary of Folklore*, edited by Maria Leach (New York, 1945), pp. 398-408.
2. Ibid, p. 399.
3. Ibid, pp. 402-3. It is important to note that study of Folklore by the Historical Society in America has already been recognized. Homer Caray Macmillan, the author of *Critical Method In Historical Research and Writing* (New York, 1955, pp. 239-40) gives a brief survey, how the folklore found its place in history as its kinship with local history was obvious and tended to draw the two interests together. By the end of 1940s the *Michigan Historical Magzine* had begun to publish a quarterly journal *Hoosier Folklore*, the Minnesota Historical Society helped to start the publication of articles on Folklore in *Minnesota History* and the Department of History at the University of Minnesota and Michigan State College were offering courses in this field. In 1953, a joint session of the American Folklore Society and Mississippi Valey Historical Association deliberated on the way for historians to make better use of folklore.
4. E.P. Thomsan, *The Voice of the Past: Oral History* (Oxford, 1978), p. 88. The value of oral traditions in the context of African societies in the writing of social history has been emphasized by Jan Vansina in his monumental work *Oral Tradition: A case study: Historical Methodology* (Chicago, 1965), pp. 142-82.
5. Vladimir Propp, *Theory and History of Folklore*, Translation by Ariand Y. Martin and Richard P. Martin and others (Manchester University Press, 1984), p. 48.
6. Ibid, p. 51.
7. Richard M. Dorson (Ed.), *Handbook of American Folklore* (U.S.A. 1983), p. 338.
8. For details see *Voice of The Past: Oral History*, op. cit., p. 80.
9. Allan Navin, *The Gateway to History*, Indian reprint (Bombay, 1968), p. 79.
10. *Indian Folklore*, I, edited by D. P. Pattanayak and Peter J. Claus (Mysore, 1981), pp. 1–4.
11. *Subaltern Studies*, VI (Oxford University Press, Delhi, 1989), p. 314.

12. See Appendix VII on "Observation of *Muharram* in Mewat".
13. G.D. Gulati, 'Mewat during Thirteenth Century' published in the *Proceedings of the Punjab History Conference,* (Patiala, 1981), pp. 61-64.
14. For details see author's article '*Hindu Muslim Ekta ke pratik Sant Lal Das*' appeared in the Haryana Edition of Navbharat Times dated 27th November, 1990 published from New Delhi.
15. See *Aravali : Alwar Ank*, p. 72 published by Raj Rishi College, Alwar, 1969.

2

Mewat During Thirteenth Century*

Mewat, the land of the Meos or Mewatis, included in those days most parts of present districts of Gurgaon in Haryana, Alwar and Bharatpur in Rajasthan, Agra and Mathura in Uttar Pradesh. According to the tradition, the Meos claim their origin from the Rajputs. On the basis of the contemporary writings, the region of Mewat was occupied partly by the Jadon Bhatti Rajputs and partly by the descendents of Prithviraj Chauhan of Ajmer.[1]

The physical features of the region played a vital role in the life of the people of Mewat. Because of the hills, deserts, unproductivity and the lack of arable land in those days, this part of the country grew nothing except thorny bushes. The inhabitants were thus obliged to adopt plundering and harass the caravans of traders. They had also extended their depredations to the far off places of Haryana, Siwalik and Bhiana as can be noticed from the chronicles of that period.[2]

Not only they plundered and harassed the traders, but also associated themselves with the disgruntled nobles of the settled Rajputs who had combined together and organized

* The paper was presented at Punjabi University, Patiala at its session held in March, 1982 and was published in its proceedings, pp. 87-93.

a solid block against the Turkish rulers of Delhi. They had developed a special guerilla technique to fight due to the advantageous positions in the hills of Aravallis.[3] Like the Khokhars in the north-west frontier, the Meos also maintained their independence. The boundary of the Sultanate remained fluctuating to the south of Delhi because of the tribal depredations.

The early Ilbari Sultans of Delhi did not have enough time to deal with the Meos, as they were busy in establishing a stable administration and consolidation of their kingdom. They were also faced with the problem of defence in the north-west frontier due to the Mongol invasions coupled with the Khokhars' activities.[4] However, they tried to give their attention towards the activities of the Meos at different times.

The first attempt was made by the Sultan, Iltutmish when he himself took an expedition into the Kohpayah of Mewat. After getting hand over Nasiruddin Qabachah, a powerful governor of the north-west frontier, he marched into the interior of Mewat in order to restore peace and order. This campaign resulted into further recovery of Ranthambhor.[5]

After the death of Iltutmish, his weak successors could not control Mewat and the turbulent Meos began to act contumaciously as usual. The court politics, Mongol invasions and the internal rebellions prevented the Sultans to weaken the pressure of the Mewatis. According to Ziauddin Barani, the author of *Tarikh-i-Firozeshahi,* owing to the weakness of the successors of Iltutmish the Meos in the neighbourhood of Delhi had gained power and multiplied in numbers. They used to come into the city, break through the walls into the houses and molest the people in other ways. The people could not sleep owing to the fear of the Meos. The roads were closed round the capital which prevented the entry of the caravans and traders into the city. Due to the fear of their activities, the southern gates of the city were closed at the time of afternoon prayer and no one could dare to go out of the city after that time. Large number of the Meos used to gather near the *Hauz-i-Shamsi* even before the evening prayer and molested the water-carrier and slave-girls who went to fetch the water after taking off their clothes left them naked.[6] Attempts were made twice to crush the Meos during this period , but it did not bear any result.[7]

Nasiruddin Mahmud, advised by his *vizir* Ulugh *Khan-i-Azam*, showed much zeal in ravaging the region of Mewat. It reveals from Minhaj's account that in 1256 AD the Mewatis had carried off herds of camels, the property of the vassals and loyal followers of Ulugh Khan's household from the skirts of Hansi. He compares Malka, the leader of the Meos, with a gigantic demon and a serpent-hued. The Meos dispersed these articles among the Hindus throughout the Kohpayah of Mewat, as far as the vicinity of Ranthambhor. This act of theirs paralysed the movement of the royal forces which were in great necessity of the camels for their further expeditions to be taken into the various parts of the Sultanate.[8]

After a couple of years the Mongols made their appearance on the north-west frontier. To meet the foreign challenge, it was essential to recover camels from Mewat so that provisions for the armies may be carried. Ulugh Khan mustered a large number of force and marched against the Mewatis. In first advance, the royal forces covered a distance of hundred miles and fell unexpectedly upon the Mewati rebels. The brutality of the soldiers was intensified by the reward of one silver *tanka* (currency of that period like rupee today) for each head and double the amount for a living Meo. The whole of the *maliks, amirs,* Turks and Tajiks with 3000 Afghan horsemen displayed zeal and energy in such a way that the "mention of which will ever endure upon the pages of time," writes Minhaj, "since the standards of Islam were first displayed in the land of Hind, at no time had the Musalmans troops ever before reached that locality and ravaged it."[9] In short, in all directions hunting expeditions were taken. The dwelling places and villages of those mountaineers were captured and plundered.[10]

These expeditions proved a temporary relief but could not bring the required results. The Meos soon recovered from these devastations made by the royal troops and grew in large numbers. It seems that in order to retaliate the royal treatment, they emerged more stronger than before and extended their depredations and did not hesitate to enter the walls of the capital city.

After ascending the throne of Delhi, Ulugh Khan took the royal title of Ghiasuddin Balban, gave top priority to the task of crushing the Meos of Mewat. He undertook hunting expeditions in the neighbourhood of the capital. For a whole year, he was engaged in cleaning the forests and destroying the hiding places of the Mewatis. A fortress at Gopalgir was raised for guarding the capital's south-western approach against the Meos. It was garrisoned with the Afghan troops. Balban lost almost one lakh of his special soldiers in this act.[11] It brought some fruit, as for about a century after this the Mewatis appear to have maintained either cordial relations with Sultans or remained passive in the region. We learn from Ferishta's account that owing to the clearing of the forests the tract of Mewat proved excellent arable land, and became well-cultivated,[12] which perhaps obliged the Meos to become agriculturists from now onwards. However, Badaoni gives the reason of their peace, the appointment of strong governors with orders to put to death the rebels in Mewat.[13]

It reveals from the writings of the chroniclers that the Meos maintained their entity as Hindus. The Meo spirit could not be suppressed, by any of the Sultans till the Khanzadas after embracing Islam controlled the region in the fourteenth century. Later entering the royal services under the Mughals they played important role in the Medieval Indian history.

References

1. The Jadon Bhatti Rajput had settled in Kaman, Tijara and Sarhatta. The descendents of Prithviraj had already occupied the area known as Rath (north-west of Alwar). After the defeat at the hands of the Turks, the Yaduvanshis of Bayana and Thangarh also got settled in Mewat. For details, see *Land Settlement Report of Gurgaon District* (1882), pp. 28-30; *District Gazetteer of Bharatpur* (1971), p. 5; *District Gazetteer of Alwar* (1968), pp. 46-7; *District Gazetteer of Agra* (1965), pp. 33-4 and *District Gazetteer of Mathura* (1968), p. 54. For origin of the Meos and their relations with Minas, see *Vinay: Alwar Ank* published by Raj Rishi College, Alwar, 1969, pp 15 - 21.
2. Minhaj writes, "In this Kohpayah (hills of Mewat) there was a community of odurate rebels, who unceasingly committed highway robbery and plundered the property of the Musalmans and the ejection of the subject peasantry and destruction of the villages in the districts of Harianah, the Siwalik and Bhiana, necessarily followed their outbreaks." See, *Tabakat-i-Nasiri*, English translation by H.G. Raverty, Delhi, 1970, p. 850.
3. They were also good runners as depicted by Abul Fazl. See, *Ain-i-Akbari*, English translation by H. Blockmann, Vol., I Calcutta, 1973, p. 252.
4. For details, see author's article on, "The Tribes in the North-west Frontier during 13th and 14th Centuries", published in *Proceedings of the Punjab History Conference* 1979, pp. 68-76.
5. Hindu Shah Muhammad Qasim Ferishta, *Tarikh-i-Ferishta*, English translation by John Briggs, entitled *History of the rise of the Mahomedan power in India*, Vol., I, reprint, Calcutta, 1966, p. 118.
6. Ziauddin Barani, *Tarikh-i-Firozeshahi*, Ed. Sayyid Ahmad Khan, Calcutta, 1862, p. 56. Hereafter abbreviated as Barani.
7. *Tabakat-i-Nasiri*, op. cit., pp. 760 and 818. Ferishta writes that during the reign of Bahramshah Ulugh Khan procured the government of Hansi and Rewari, in which office he distinguished himself in several actions against the inhabitants of Mewat (Briggs, op. cit., p. 137)
8. *Tabakat-i-Nasiri*, p. 850.
9. Ibid., op. cit., pp. 852-53 and 854.
10. The total number of heads and chiefs of the rebels were about 250. One hundred and forty two horses, sixty bags of silver tankas were extorted from the Rana of Mewat (Ibid., p. 853). For another expendition of same kind see, p. 175. Also see, Briggs op. cit., pp. 135, 142: Abdul Qadir bin Mulukshah Badaoni, *Muntakhab-ut-Tawarikh*, English translation by S.A. Ranking, Vol., I, Patna 1973, p. 134. Also see Nizamuddin Ahmad, *Tabakat-i-Akbari*, English translation B. De, Vol. I,

reprint, Calcutta, 1973, pp. 99-100. In this account we find that the Meos had settled round the city of Delhi.
11. Barani, *op. cit.*, pp. 55-57.
12. Briggs, *op. cit.*, pp. 142.
13. Badaoni, *op. cit.*, p. 185.

3

Village Bania as Reflected in the Folklore of Mewat *

I

In recent years there has been increasing interest among the scholars to study the social, economic and cultural aspects of different societies in India. And the folklore is an important aspect of their culture which needs to be defined here briefly. Since, the introduction of the world folklore in 1845 by William Thoms, there arose a controversy about its definition. In the dictionary of folklore we find more than twenty definitions given by different scholars. However, one may agree that folklore consists of the belief, customs, myths, legends, folksongs, folktales and ritualistic ceremonies of the common people of any society. Folklore or the popular knowledge is the accumulated store of what mankind has experienced, learned and practiced across the ages as popular and traditional knowledge distinguished from so-called scientific knowledge.[1]

While evaluating the importance of folklore as a source of

* Presented at an International Conference on folklore organized by the Department of Slavic Studies, South Campus, University of Delhi in 1990. The revised version of this paper was presented at *Punjab History Conference* at its session held in March, 1996. The same was published in its proceedings (pp. 58-64).

writing history of any society, one can start his argument on the basis of a sound premise. Indian society was non-literate but not uneducated or ignorant. For the masses living in the rural India, the folk tradition has served as a carrier of knowledge and wisdom from one generation to the other. The masses expressed themselves collectively in the folk art forms and folklore, thus assuming the character of 'community memory'.[2]

It is believed that every art including folklore is derived from reality and reflects it. It needs no proof or evidence. Difficulties arise when we attempt to interpret the historical process and decide how history has been reflected. And history, as we know is based on certain sources of information which include written material or record, epigraphy and numismatic. But there are certain areas where no such material is found for historical writing. As has been observed by modern scholars for the social history of any minority group, the limitation of written documentation are such that the use of oral sources introduce an entirely new dimension to the study.[3]

One can plead that the written histories are often motivated and distorted due to the state patronage or become bias due to perceived ideology. The historians' masters are never wrong, their ideologies are full of all virtues and goodness. Their enemies are always villains who are dangerous to the state and society. The folk or local history is the anti-thesis of this tendency. The distortions and motivations are not the part of it. Although subjectivity comes in local and folk history, but it does not mutilate or recreate history intentionally. This is due to the fact that writer or teller of the local or folk history is not the one individual but time and community shape the consciousness which creates history.

It has been pointed out that oral history loses power as time depth increases, it cannot account of the earliest eras. Written history loses its power as social breadth increases as it cannot account for most people. We have more early works from men than women, more from upper classes and the middle classes than the lower classes. Thus it is upto the historians how they are benefited by the folk traditions of any region or society or group.[4]

II

In this regard the scholars working on the Punjab history have made best use of the Punjabi folklore including folk sayings, proverbs, riddles, folktales and oral religious literature. They have made studies about different communities in Eastern, Western, Northern and Central Punjab but ignored altogether the Meo community who gave the region its name in the Southern parts of the state prior to the creation of Haryana and Himachal Pradesh called 'Mewat'. The region is rich in its folklore. The present paper is the outcome of my field work undertaken in the region in connection with my post-doctoral project *Folklore and History Writing : A case study of Mewat.*

The Meos had been the most prominent tribe inhabiting a large area around Delhi. Denzil Ibbetson in his study on the *Punjab Castes* lists the Meos at serial no. 478 who were all Muhammadans (p. 179). Owing to the hills, deserts, unproductivity and lack of arable land, the inhabitants of Mewat took to plundering and harassing the caravans of the traders in pre-Mughal times. Their depredations were extended into the far off places on Haryana and Shivalik, as noticed by the Persian chroniclers.[5] Later, the region remained under the control of the Mughals and the people were obliged to take agriculture as their profession.

The Meos are of the Rajput origin and their claim is universally acknowledged, as they still retain a number of the Hindu customs. The distinctive physical features of the Meos, their dialect, their dress and their cultural pattern all serve to make them a people slightly apart from the rest of the population of Mewat.[6] The Meos are basically a simple people with no acumen for making or saving money. The conception of wealth is limited to land, ornaments and perhaps little silver or gold hidden in some corner. Trade and commerce, being unfamiliar pursuits, are looked down upon. Until a few years ago even the selling of milk was considered to be below the dignity of a Meo who is proud of his Rajput origin. A low standard of living and a high level of pride are the chief characteristics of the Meos and these two together seldom lead to the accumulation of wealth and exploitation of money.[7] The business is the monopoly of the banias or money lenders, rest can only have the wishful hope. A folksaying in the region is common which goes;

> "*banij karenge bania aur karenge rees Banaj liya tha jat ne sau ke rah gaye tees*"
> (Only rich people or bania will do the business, once a Jat did the business and was left with 30 out of 100 rupees).

About the laziness of the Meos, M. Darling in his monumental work *The Punjab Peasants in Prosperity and Debt*, has given a good description. He compares the Meo peasants with the Ahir peasants of Rewari. The sandy soils of Rewari produced enough to keep Ahirs in comfort, while the comparatively rich soil of the Firozepur Jhirka valley was heavily mortgaged to meet the extravagance of the Meos. Almost every Meo was in the hands of money-lenders. The Meos of Firozepur Jhirka and Nuh (then in Gurgaon district of Haryana) were under burden of heavy debt which went around 30 times the land revenue those days while in Rewari was only 6 times of the revenue. Giving the reasons for their laziness the author believed that allied in race to the aboriginal Meenas of Rajputtana they had not inherited the qualities developed by the Ahir in his long patient struggle with the sands of Rewari. The restless life of the camp and the jungle has always appeared to them more than the settled life of the farm and the village. Forgetting too, their humble origin, they modelled themselves upon the Rajput instead of the Jat. The Jat could at least have taught them to cultivate, but the Rajput with his extravagant ways and contempt for the plough, merely confirmed them in inherited habit. Such blessings, therefore, as nature had given them, instead of being an advantage, had only served to make them attractive to the money-lenders, who at that time had the whole tribe in fee.[8] A folksaying is still current in Mewat:

'*Meo kamaye bhookha Jat kamaye dhapa*'
(Meo will work only when he feels hungry and Jat when fully satisfied will go to work).

In the Indian village society, the money-lender is often the one thrifty person amongst a generally thriftless people; and that his methods of business, though disliked, suit the happy go lucky ways to the peasant. He is always accessible, even at night, dispenses with troublesome formalities, asks no inconvenient questions, advances promptly, and if interest is paid, does not press for repayment of principal. He keeps in close personal touch with his clients, and in many villages shares their occasions of weal or woe. And he not only finances his neighbours but frequently keeps a small shop to supply their needs and is nearly always prepared to market their produce. Even with the introduction of the cooperative societies and banks, the money-lender still is a necessity. *Guru bin gat nahin, Shah bin pat nahin* (without a Guru no salvation, without a sahukar no reputation) is an old saying which justifies his role in the village society of Punjab.[9]

Owing to its backwardness and poverty the Meos are still in the grip of village bania. The bania though meeting financial and other needs of his clients could not earn the reputation of an honest and sincere person. In the village folk he is considered a cunning and greedy man. With a number of malpractices, and with his swift and sweet tongue he makes the Meos fool. Following tales testify his above unchallenged positions in Mewat.

III

(1)

With this background we come to the actual title of the paper. As we know the Meos are not much literate and hardly know the tricks played by the village *bania* in the given circumstances.

Once a Meo was to buy cloth for his wife's *ghaghra,* obviously on credit. He went to the market and approached a known *bania* who was also a cloth merchant. The bania readily measured 13 yards of *chint* and at the rate of Rs.3 per yard got his thumb impression on his *bahi* (account book) saying:

तेरह तिया उन्हत्तर, नौ छोड़े लगा सत्तर।

Terah tia unahttar, Nau chhode laga suttar
(Thirteen multiplied by three is equal to 69 and since you are my old friend, a discount of Rs.9, put your thumb impression on the remaining amount only 70).

The Meo just believed him and put his thumb impression in the *bahi* as desired by the bania. So in this tale the village bania is charging Rs.70 instead of Rs.39 that too after a discount of Rs.9 to his client who is happy as he is getting cloth on credit that too with 9 rupees less.

(2)

Once a bania was in need of a servant for his fields. At the same time a Meo zamindar was also searching a labourer for his fields. Both were sitting in a market of nereby small town. Per chance a poor Meo in search of job came there. Now both bania and the Meo zamindar offered him job. The Meo zamindar offered the poor man *Khir* (a sweet dish prepared from milk, rice and sugar) on each Friday in addition to the salary. Bania too offered sweets on each Diwali and *pooa* (a dish prepared from wheat, flour and sugar) on each *amavas* (the last day of the dark fortnight) saying the following very quickly:

"*Aai diwali, khai suhali har amavas ko pua*"
(Come diwali and eat sweets and eat pooa on each amavas)

And about Meo Zamindar's offer he said in a poor and slow tone :

k..a..d.ju..mm..e.r..a..a..ta..a..i
k..a..d.kh..i..r.k..h..a..i..
(When will Friday night come and when will you eat *khir*)

He expressed his word in such a slew tone as if the Friday night will never fall.

On hearing this, the poor and innocent Meo immediately accepted to serve the bania without calculating the better terms offered by the fellow zamindar. Thus the clever tongue of the bania could attract the Meo to his side.

(3)

Once a bania and a Meo were traveling together. The bania was carrying rice and the Meo was having *sattu* (powder of parched grains). Bania wanted to deprive the Meo of his *sattu.* He played a trick. He began praising the rice which he had and condemned the *sattu* saying :

S..a..tt..u.m..a..n.bh..a..ttu
k..a..d.p..i..s..a.k..a..b.g..h..o..l..a
a..u..r.k..a..b.k..h..a..y..a..
(Sattu is liked but it takes long to parch to mix with water and sugar and when to eat, as if you will never be able to

eat).

About the rice he said quickly :

khir pakai, chal mere bhai
(cook the khir and eat it, as if it takes few seconds to prepare and ready to eat).

The poor Meo hearing this, immediately gave his *sattu* to the bania. Now it is well known that *sattu* is a ready—made cooked dish ready to eat. But the sweet and soft tongue of bania reversed the process and ultimately deprived the Meo of his *sattu.*

(4)

In the following tale which was told to Flora Annie Steel a hundred years ago, we find little different from the above tales as in this anecdote a Jat loses his one eye but made the bania full blind and later died. In brief, a Jat farmer asks the money-lender how he got so rich, the money-lender says from Ram (God) and sets the Jat to find him. The farmer sets out and finds a man who calls himself Ram.

Ram, who gives him a conch shall to blow whenever he wants anything, but must blow it in a particular manner. Only have a care of that money-lender, for even magic is not proof against their wiles! The money-lender however, comes to know the secret of the conch except the way in which it was to be blown. He steals it and returns it on the understanding that the bania gets double whatever it brings the farmer. The Jat in his wrath wishes to loose his one eye, on which the bania loses both, and being blind falls into a well and is killed.[10]

Conceived as an aspect of Meo society, the village bania otherwise finds place in other societies. There is ample scope for comparative studies of different groups or societies in which money-lending class has played an important role. The folklore can be one of the important sources of history especially for socio-cultural aspect. This humble attempt is in the same direction but not the final word.

References

1. Maia Leach (ed.), *Standard Dictionary of Folklore* (New York, 1945), pp. 398-408.
2. For details see S.K. Bajaj and Ishwar Dayal Gaur, 'Folklore as source of History' in Ganda Singh (ed.), *The Panjab Past and Present*, Vol. XIX-II (Patiala, 1985), pp. 302-05.
3. Paul Thomson, *The Voice of the Past: Oral History* (Oxford, 1978), p. 88. The value of oral traditions in the context of African societies in the writing of social history has also been emphasized by Jan Vansina in his book *Oral Tradition: A case study: Historical Methodology* (Chicago, 1965), pp. 142-82.
4. For details see *Voice of The Past: Oral History*, op. cit., p. 80.
5. G.D. Gulati, 'Mewat during Thirteenth Century' published in the *Proceedings of the Punjab History Conference*, 15th session (Patiala, 1981), pp. 61-64.
6. Hashim Amir Ali, *The Meos of Mewat* (Delhi, 1970), p. 18.79.
7. Ibid., p. 74-75.
8. M. Darling *The Punjab Peasant in Prosperity and Debt*, Reprint (New Delhi, 1978), p. 91.
9. Ibid., pp. 194-195.
10. Flora Anvie Steel, *Tales of the Punjab* (London, 1894), pp. 137–39. Compare with a popular story in Rajasthan when a peasant goes to a bania merchant whom he has taken a loan. The pen wedged on top of one of the barna's ears fell down—this is where they normally keep their pens. The peasant picks up the pen and returns it to the bania saying, 'Here take your *chhuri* (knife)'. 'Why *chhuri*?' asks the bania, 'it's only a pen'. The peasant says, '*Aap ki chhuri he mere gale pe phiri thi*' (Your knief has cut my neck). See Rustam Bharucha, *Rajasthan An Oral History-Conversation with Komal Kothari*, Penguin Book , New Delhi, 2003, p. 25.

4

Tradition of Bhakti in Mewat and the Controversy of Sant Lal Das and his Shrine*

I

Beginning of Bhakti movement in Tamilnadu in the eighth century is considered as a great event in the Indian history which had deep influence on the contemporary psyche of the people. The imprints of this movement can be witnessed even today in our life. To understand the socio - cultural background of Bhakti it is necessary to know about the saints and their literature available in different languages. Alwar saint Nammalvar and Kamban of Tamilnadu, Vemana of Andhra, Basweshwar and Akk Mahadevi of Karnataka, Namdev and Tuka Ram of Maharashtra, Narsi Mehta of Gujrat, Shaikh Farid and Guru Nanank of Punjab, Lalded of Kashmir. Balram Dass and Jagannath Dass of Orissa, Shankar Dev and Madhav Dev of Asam, Chandidas of Bengal; Kabir,

*This paper was presented at a national seminar on *Sufi Tradition of Rajasthan* held at Jaipur under the auspices of Guru Nanak Chair University of Rajasthan in March 2007. Earlier 'Lal Das as the symbol of Hindu-Muslim unity' (in Hindi) was published in a Hindi daily *Navbharat Times,* New Delhi (November, 1991). A paper on 'Socio-Cultural Fusion in Medieval India: A case study of Lal Das of Mewat' was presented a conference held at Agra College, Agra in March, 1999.

Jayasi, Sur, Tulsi and Meera of Hindi belt of the country, were the great poets of their times whom the millions of the people are indebted for their writings. I am thankful to Dr. Jagmandar Tayal for providing me an unpublished article on *Bhakti Andolan aur Laldas* (Hindi).

The Bhakti movement and its literature was so massive that its impact was felt in the far distant places and backward areas of the country. Mewat is the best example of Bhakti and its saint Lal Das and his sect Laldasi which spread during the sixteenth century. Today thousands of laldasis the disciples of Lal Das follow his teachings.

The region of Mewat takes its name from the Meo community, who are scattered not only in Haryana, Rajasthan and Uttar Pradesh, but also in the remote areas of Madhya Pradesh, Gujrat and Punjab. On the basis of the Persian chroniclers and empirical records it has been established that the Meos were formerely Hindus and take pride of their Rajput origin. The distinctive features of the Meos, their dialect, dress and cultural patterns definitely separate them from the rest of the people of Mewat. The word 'Meo' according to their tradition takes its route from the Meds who fought against the forces of Alexander.[1]

The Meos are divided into two categories of which, the twelve largest are called *pals* and smaller as *gotras,* as a matter of fact showing their Hindu lineage. They had always been the lover of freedom due to their strategic geographical position and disliked the subjugation by any authority. Because of the hills, deserts, unproductivity and the lack of arable land on those days, this part of the country grew nothing except throny bushes. The inhabitants were thus obliged to adopt plundering and harass the caravans of traders. They had also extended their depredation to the far off places of Haryana, Siwalik and Bhiana, as can be noticed from the chronicles of the 13th century.[2]

It is believed that the Meos embraced Islam under the influence of Salar Masud Ghazi, one of the commanders of

Mahmud of Ghazna. According to the Persian sources one Bahadur Nahir of Kotla near Nuh, the district headquarter of Mewat, embraced Islam in the period of Firzoshah Tughluq and was bestowed upon the title of Khanzada by the Sultan. Bahadur Nahir played an important role in the politics of Delhi and Mewat and had become the patron of fugitive princes.

Timur described him a very powerful ruler of Mewat. He refers about two white parrots in his autobiography presented by Bahadur Nahir. When Babur came to India, the rgion was governed by Hasan Khan Mewati who lost his life in the battle of Khanua. He has been described as the patriot of the country who fought for the independence of the country.

After Hasan Khan Mewati we hardly find any reference to any leader of the high rank. Mewat remained under the control of the Mughal governor and later under the states of Alwar and Bharatpur. During the 1857 revolt they took a strong position and fought for the cause of Bahadur Shah. After this the region was brought under the direct control of the British.

II

The Meos though Muslims, hardly gave up their Hindu beliefs. Till recent they were observing both the Muslim and Hindu rituals and were celebrating Diwali, Dussehra alongwith *Id* and *Shab-i-rat.* They still bear Hindu names like, Chand, Suraj, Kundan, Chandan, Moti, Hira etc. The communal harmony among the Hindus and Muslims of the region is the best example of the cultural fusion except a brief period of tension during Babari - mosque episode.

During the medieval period of Indian history, the impact of the socio-religious movement was felt throughout the country and number of sufi *silsilahs* played a very positive role in the life of the people. On the one hand the teachings of Kabir and Nanak and on the other Shaikh Muinuddin Chishti, Nizamuddin Auliya, Shaikh Fariduddin Ganj-i-

Shakkar, Bahauddin Zakariya and others preached love and humanity among the masses. It is in this light that certain regions produced numbers of sufis and saints taking these teaching further in the remote parts of the country. They are well-known and worshipped in their respective regions by the local folk irrespective of their caste, creed and religion.

The region of Mewat near to the capitals of Delhi and Agra too witnessed the birth and growth of different sects among its people. There are numerous shrines of saints in the region which are frequently visited by the Hindus and Muslims both for paying their homage. They hold fairs in their memory and sing songs in the praise of these saints. Among these saints Sant Lal Das, Churh Sidh, Charan Das, Sahjo Bai are famous in Mewat and in the neighbouring regions.

III

Lal Das is most revered among the people of Mewat. He was born in a Meo family in a village called Dhaulidub near Alwar in the year 1540 A.D. His father was Chand Mal and mother Samda, living a very simple life. Lal Das used to earn his living by selling dry stricks a local fuel in Alwar. It may be attested with the following couplet written by Dungarsi in his '*Lal Das Ki Bani*':

जाति कहन को कहिए मेव,
लकड़ी बेचौ, कोई लेव।

(He was a Meo by caste, sold wood, anyone could buy.)

नित अलवर गढ़ बेचन जाये,
उधम करिकर उदर भराय।।

(Daily went to Alwar to sell, by working hard he satisfied his hunger.)

Lal Das died at the ripe age of 108 years in 1648 A.D. His shrine is situated at Sherpur (a village, about 16 kilometers north-east of Ramgarh and 04 kilometers from Naugaon in district Alwar, on the border of Haryana). In his memory quarterly fairs used to be held at Dhaulidub. His dead body was brought to Sherpur from the neighbouring Nangla village in Bharatpur, six months after his death and burial. The tomb is very substantial masonary building hundred feet long, with a high dome, and walls five feet thick. The interior is vaulted and low. The body of Lal Das lies in a crypt, several feet below the surface. Many other members of Lal Das's family were interred at Sherpur, Nangla and Bandoli (here he preached). These are well-attended by the people of all religions and sects. Major P.W. Powlett in the *Gazetteer of Ulwar* gave a very good account of Lal Das and his teachings. His followers are called *Laldasis.* The sect *Laldasi* is very close to Kabir panth. The followers are both married and unmarried. Every *Laldasi* hates begging and believes in hard wor singing Ram's name and rhyms accompanied with music form an integral part of their worship.[3]

The sayings of Lal Das are called *bani* or *gutka,* which are available in the shape of a manuscript in the Oriental Institute at Alwar. Lal Das was a great saint reformer and always spoke for the unity of man and God. He is held as a great Meo and *Pir* among the people of the region. The day before each full moon and every Sunday are kept as *fasts.* The Laldasis are chiefly Meos and Baniyas. They are more numerous in Easterm Rajasthan and parts of Haryana and Uttar Pradesh.

Among the teachings of Lal Das the most important is condermning the begging. The saying goes:

लाल जी भगत भीख न माँगई,
मांगत आते शरम।
घर घर हॉडत दोष है,
क्या बादशा क्या हरम।।

Saith Lal Das. Let not the devotee beg
Begging is shameful

Wandering from home to home is wrong
Even if they be kings or queens

लाल जी साधु ऐसा चाहिए,
धन कमाकर खाए।
हृदय हर की चारी,
पर घर कभु न जाए।
Saith Lalji, The Sadhu should be one
Who earns food he eats
Let God's service be the heart's
Never go far begging.

He pleaded for the respect for the right of property of others and said :

लाल जी हक खाये हक पिये,
हक की करो फरोह।
इन बातों से साहब खुशी,
बिरले बरती कोई।।
Saith Lalji, Eat what is your own
Drink what is your own
And sell what is your own
For these things are pleasing to God
But few observe them.

He further said :

क्या मांगते का मान है,
मांगे टुकड़ा खाए।
कुत्ता जो हांडत फिरे,
जनम अकारथ जाए।
(There is no repect who begs for a morsel. He is like a wandering dog and lives his life meaningless.)

Miracles are important aspects of the lives of the saints. Like other saint Lal Das is said to have also performed many miracles. The questioning whether these miracles are true or not is not imsportant, the main point is that the followers and disciples believe them to be true and this belief strengthens their faith in the greatness of Lal Das. These miracles and anecdotes also reflect popular culture of that period and inform us about popular ways of confronting the authority and ultimately proving the superiority of the saint over the Brahmins and the *qazis*. The Brahmins and the *qazis* are shown fools and villains in the society where as the saint as the Hero.

Once Lal Das came to a village Bahadurpur (in Alwar state) and decided to have rest there. The faujdar heard, that a Meo has become a saint and preaching as guru. Lal Das was asked to be present before him. The faujdar got the water of a well poisoned and compelled Lal Das to drink the same. Lal Das put some sugar into the well, the water turned into sweet. The well became famous as *mithikui* (sweet well) and still survies. The anecdote relates that seeing this the faujdar came and touched the feet of Lal Das. The Dungarsi the disciple of Lal Das says:

फौजदार जब दौड़यो आयो।
दाऊ लर जोड़ा बुलायो।।
लालदास तुम सच्चे पीर।
अब बक्सो मेरी तकसीर।।
जहर कुआं तक मीठा किया।
साँईं भरोसे यह जस लिया।।
जो कोई पिये सो धन-धन करे।
साको अमर लाल को रहे।।

(The faujdar came running and offered him a pair of cloth and said Lal Das, you are a true *Guru*, please forgive me and give your blessings. Poisonous well was made sweet with trust in God. Whosoever drank the water, thanked Lal Das and his fame)

In one anecdote we find Lal Das turning the non-vegetarian food into vegetarian which invited the wrath of the Subedar of Tijara, a historial town in the Alwar state at that time. Later, the hakim apologized for it. Once Lal Das saved a ship owned by a trader of Agra through a miracle.

Kabir and other saints had already created a liberal atmosphere in and around Mewat. Hence, Lal Das got the land already fertile for his thoughts. He tried to identify himself with Kabir who had already won the psyce of the people. One additional point with Lal Das was he did not belong to a lower caste as Kabir. Secondly he was the product of the same region and society and had a great influence on the people of Mewat. That is why he could resist the authority of the faujdar and resist the oppression of the state. He not only opposed the orthodoxy of the Hinduism but also Islam.

Laldasis the followers of Lal Das live a simple life and believe in hard labour. They are, as mentioned earlier Meos, *Banias, Kalals* and *Khatis.* When converted into *Laldasi* sect one has to get his property plundered. In token of his abandonment of world and worldly prides one has to blacken his face, to mount on a donkey with his face to its tail and to hang a sting of shoes round his neck. It is called a '*sawari*' of the *Laldasi.* A cup of *sherbet* is then offered to him and he becomes a member of the fraternity. It is incumbent on a good *Laldasi* to give his earnings to others. *Laldasi* sect of Mewat is one of the most popular sects which practices selflessness and sacrifices for others. (see Appendix regarding an announcement of the '*sawari*').

IV

"On the basis of *Kapatdwara Records* it is evident that the Laldasis were basically Hindus. Sawai Jai Singh of Jaipur (1688-1743) though a liberal in his religious leanings, did nto favour the *Lal Panthis,* the followers of Lal Das, a Meo whose teachings resembled those of Kabir. Lal Das who lived about the middle of the seventeenth century, sought to reconcile Hinduism and Islam. Jai Singh made the *Lal Panthis* living in his state to give an undertaking in writing that they would follow Vaishanva Dharma.[4]

Recently, I have come across an enquiry - report dated 9th June, 1934 conducted by an Assistant Commissioner of Police on the order of the district magistrate Alwar regarding a dispute over the proprietorship of the Laldasi shrine. The said dispute arose when some Meos erected some structure inside the shrine, began performing *namaz* thus challenging the very right of the Laldasis who were residing in the complex for more than three hundred years as claimed by them. The enquiry confirmed that on the whole the shrine has the mixed features of both the temple and a mosque. Since the Laldasis do not follow the teachings of Islam, never celebrate *Id* nor read *kalma* neither observe *rozas* hence the complex where they live, belonged to them. But the Meos converted the *chabutra* into a grave.

It appears from the report that earlier in the year 1914 also an unauthorized attempt was made to perform namaz at the *Samadhi*. Action was taken under P.C.C. 107 and the dispute was settled. Till Meo uprising in 1932-33 no such event took place. In the year 1933 when, one Mr. S.D. Ghasi Ram took over as the District Magistrate he felt concerned about this sect. During an annual fair at Lal Das's *samadhi* he deputed some policemen to maintain law and order. But it seems these policemen alongwith the Meos tried to perform *namaz* and created obstruction in the *bhajans* of the *mahantas.* The *sadhs* reported this matter to the police at Ramgarh but the police officer Amjad Husain did not show any interest in this case and asked his policemen not to involve in this case.

The Laldasi *sadhs* then approached the A.C.P. and showed him the ancient *gazetteer* of the year 1878 which was published from the Settlement Office. They also showed him a hand written *gutka* dated 1829 and other documents which gave details of Lal Das and his life. It is mentioned in this report that Lal Das neither believed in Hindu religion nor Islam. He preached his own teachings. He did many miracles and became famous far and wide. People from Bharatpur, Agra, Mathura, Gurgaon etc. flocked to him and followed his religious beliefs. He died at the ripe age of 108 years and finally buried at Sherpur where the present *math* is situated. Laldasis merry in Meos but do not eat with them. On the basis of the above facts, it was decided that, in future there should be no nuisance in this regard and disturbing the peace may dealt with the action under P.C.C. 107.

This report is a first of its kind, where conflict over a shrine reached the court and the popularity of saint Lal Das was such that both Hindu and Muslims want to own the holy *samadhi*. From the decision it is evident the *Sadhs* or *mahants* have legal right over the whole complex and they are living peacefully since then. (Copy of the decision has been appended in the end as an appendix).

References

1. The Jadon Bhattis had settled in Kaman, Tijara and Sarhatta. The descendents of Prithviraj had already occupied the area known as Rath (northwest of Alwar). After the defeat at the hands of the Turks, the Yaduvanshis of Bayana and Thangarh also got settled in Mewat. For details see Land *Settlement Report of Gurgaon District* (1882), pp. 28 - 30; *District Gazetteer of Bharatpur* (1971), p. 5; *District Gazetteer of Agra* (1965), pp. 33 - 34 and *District Gazetteer of Mathura* (1968), p. 54.
2. Minhaj, a Persian chronicler of the thirteenth century writes, "In this Kohpayah (hills of Mewat) there was a community of rebels, who unceasingly committed highway robbery and plundered the property of the Musalmans and the ejection of the subject peasantry and destruction of the villages in the dustricts of Harianah, the Siwalik and Bhiana . . . ." See his *Tabakat-i-Nasiri*, English translation by H. G. Raverty, reprint (1970), p. 850.
3. Major P.W. Powlett, *Gazetter of Ulwar* (1878), pp. 53-59 and 153.
4. *Kapatdwara Records*, No. 1520 as quoted by V.S. Bhatnagar in *Life and Times of Sawai Jai Sigh* (1688-1743), Delhi, 1974, p. 342 and note 90.

5

Jat-Meos Alliance Against Jaipur: Evidence of *Muraqqa-i-Mewat* *

I

Mewat, the land of the Meos comprises district of Mewat in Haryana, parts of districts Alwar, Bharatpur in Rajasthan and Agra and Mathura in Uttar Pradesh. The Meos had always been prominent in the region and form a majority. The land being near to the medieval capitals of Delhi and Agra, had been an attraction for the ruling classes viz. Turks, Mughals, Pathans and later Jats, Marathas, Rajputs, Sikhs and the British. They changed hands with all the neighbouring powers from time to time.

The role of Meos during medieval period has highly been highlighted by the Persian chroniclers. Due to the advantageous position in the Aravali hills, they always exploited the situation in their favour and hardly accepted any overlordship and successfully maintained their independence.

It was Ghiasuddin Balban, the Sultan of Delhi, who in the thirteenth century took punitive action against them and

* The paper was presented at a National Seminar on *Jats in Indian History* held in January 2001 under the auspices of the Centre for Research and Publication of Surajmal Memorial Education Society, New Delhi.

sent expeditions into the region. They were compelled to give up their depredations and took up cultivation as their profession.

Under the Tughluqs, Bahadur Nahir, the Khanzada and his successors emerged as a political power and played an important role in the court potilics. The fugitive princes of the Delhi court used to take shelter in the Aravalis and sought support of the Khanzadas to succeed the throne of Delhi. Timur too could not ignore their power and had friendly relations with them.

Hasan Khan Mewati proved a powerful ruler of Mewat who fought against Babur (the founder of the Mughal empire in India) in the battle of Khanua sided with Rana Sanga. He sacrificed his life in this battle. After his death, the Khanzadas could not remain organized. It was Akbar, the great Mughal who brought the Meos in the streamline and recruited them as the runners in his army. Under the Mughals the Meos performed as able and obedient servants of the state.

With the fall of the Mughals, there arose many regional powers viz. Jats in Bharatpur and Naruka Rajputs in Alwar. Many parts of Mewat came under their sway but the Meos continued with their trait and allied either with the Jats or with the Rajputs as and when the opportunity came.

II

With Jawahar Singh's coming on the throne of Bharatpur, a new policy of expansion ushered and this gave an opportunity to the Meo Khanzadas to renew their relationship with the Jats. There are scanty references about this new alliance in the contemporary literature. However, the author of *Muraqqa - i - Mewat,* Sharf Alauddin Ahmad throws ample light on this aspect, especially the alliance of Jawahar Singh with Zulfikar Khan of Mewat against Madho Singh of Jaipur, in connection with the Pushkar episode.

Muraqqa-i-Mewat was written in Urdu in the last decade of the nineteenth century in response to *Arjang - i - Tijara* in

Urdu by Shaikh Mohammad Makhdoom Sahib, a Tehsildar of Tijara, to clarify certain controversies regarding the origin of the Khanzadas. The book takes into account the history of India since Mahabharata times till the date of its writing in brief, but in details the political activities in Mewat during seventeenth and eighteenth centuries, describing the role of the Khanzadas. Modern scholars highly speak of the Pushkar episode but hardly about the alliance between the Jats and the Meos against Jaipur state. They speak only about the treaty between Jawahar Singh of Bharatpur and Vijay Singh of Jodhpur against Marathas in which Madho Singh of Jaipur was asked neither to participate nor consulted.

The author of *Muraqqa-i-Mewat* throws new light on this aspect and gives a detailed account of the whole episode. He informs us that Ajmat Khan of Mewat was the Jagirdar of Bhusawal in Govind Garh in Alwar State and was in the service of Raja Sawai Jai Singh and later served his son, Ishri Singh also. When Madho Singh ascended the throne of Jaipur, he accepted the services of the Meos under Ajmat Khan. After Ajmat Khan's death, his grandson Zulifikar Khan was recognized as the Jagirdar of Bhusawal by Madho Singh. He converted the sand castle of Bhuswal into a *pucca* one. When Suraj Mal extended his control over Bahadurpur, the Sayyids and Khanzadas' families took shelter at Bhusawal with Zulifikar Khan.

When Jawahar Singh became the ruler of Bharatpur, he established friendly relations with Zulifikar Khan, who always fought for him against his enemies. On one occasion Jawahar Singh's contingent was about to loose the battle against the Rohillas at Delhi. At this juncture, Zulifikar Khan reached with his men and made a surprise attack on the Rohillas. Jawahar Singh was astonished on this miracle and came to know about this Meo leader, hence friendly relations were established. Zulifikar was offered an elephant and later made the jagirdar of Mewat.

According to *Muraqqa-i-Mewat*, the continuous warfare

between the Marathas and Jaipur state had resulted into the disorder in the region. Jawahar Singh exploiting this situation, made an attempt to control some of the territories. He reached Kama which was under the jurisdiction of Jaipur but could not succeed. Then he thought of Pushkar bath and began his mission. He passed through the territories of Madho Singh. Zulifikar Khan and his brother Sabit Khan could foresee the consequences of this conspiracy of Jawahar Singh. To please both Jawahar Singh and Madho Singh, Zulifikar Khan agreed to assist the former wheras Sabit Khan promised the later so that no loss to Mewat.

Here appears Pratap Singh of Macheri on the scene who was living always under the fear of Madho Singh. Jawahar Singh offered him the Dehra near Alwar and asked him to accompany the Bharatpur armies to Jaipur. Pratap Singh could not decided whether to support Jawahar Singh or not. However, later he alongwith Sabit Khan reached Jaipur on the plea that Jawahar Singh's actions were unjust and moreover Madho Singh stood second to the Maharaja of Udaipur in status.

Madho Singh became alert and invited all his relations and supporters and raised a good number of contingents. Jawahar Singh had already reached Pushkar and sent the message to Madho Singh to be prepared for a battle. He exchanged turban with Raja Vijay Singh, the ruler of Marwar and strengthened his position against Madho Singh. Delay on the part of Jawahar Singh gave enough time to Madho Singh to gather and organize his forces. He was in a position to warn Jawahar Singh not to cross through his territories and sent a threatening letter also. But Jawahar Singh being an arrogant, without paying any heed to this letter decided arbitrarily to return through Jaipur state. Armies of both sides met at a place Mandhauli in the Shekhawat region. The author of *Muraqqa-i-Mewat* provides a list of the supporters of both Jawahar Singh and Madho Singh which follows as under:

(A) Supporters of Bharatpur

(1) Nawab Zulifikar Khan.
(2) Shimru, a Frenchman who had brought his artillery with him.
(3) Madari Khan Meo Barkariye.
(4) Rub Rai Katara.
(5) Nawab Ajmat Khan of Shahbad who was granted the *patta* of 22 villages by Jawahar Singh.
(6) Nawab Najawat Khan, Khanzada of village Machhrauli pargana Kishangarh.
(7) and Jat Faujdars.

(B) Supporters of Jaipur

(1) Nawab Sabit Khan, brother of Zulifikar Khan.
(2) Pratap Singh of Macheri.
(3) Thakur Dalel Singh, jagirdar of Dhola.
(4) Har Sahai and Gir Sahai, advisers to Jaipur State.

In Jawahar Singh's forces, Shimru was in the charge of artillery and Zulifikar Khan was the overall commander of the army. In the first phase, Thakur Dalel Singh and Zulifikar Khan met in the battlefield in which Dalel Singh was killed with his supporters by Zulifikar Khan. His elephant named Badal was made captive. Hearing the news of Dalel Singh's death, Har Sahai and Gir Sahai made an attack on the Bharatpur army. Sabit Khan, brother of Zulifikar Khan also fought with bravery for Madho Singh. The forces of Jawahar Singh had to face a wrath of Sabit Khan and suffered a great loss. Sabit Khan was injured. Excited Zulifikar Khan attacked Jaipur forces with all his might and succeeded in bringing back his brother to his camp. At this juncture, Jawahar Singh without doubting Zulifikar Khan's fidelity generously gave him a warm hug and gifted him his own precious ornament which he was wearing himself.

The Mughals were also in the army of Bharatpur, two wings of which, deceived Jawahar Singh. However, the battle continued in which Zulifikar Khan and Shimru both showed their exemplary courage. They killed Har Sahai and Gir Sahai, two main supporters of Madho Singh. Jawahar Singh was brought safe to Bharatpur by Zulifikar Khan who was made nawab and offered the faujdari of Kama. He remained powerful in Mewat. Jawahar Singh had to face the circastic remarks of the ladies of Bharatpur:

> *"Balghot gayo Pushkar ke nahane se"* which is recorded in *Muraqqa - i - Mewat* by its author.

6

*Yasin Khan Ki Baat**

In Mewati literature *baat* literature has its own significance. It has been carried in the Mewati culture throughout its history by its *mirasis* or folksingers. They take pride in singing *Pandun ka kara, Panch Pahad ki Larai, Ghur Chadi Meo Khan, Darya Khan Sasbadni, Yasin Khan ki Baat* and what not which, are highly enjoyed and admired by the people of Mewat. These are sung in a story-telling form. Mewati feel proud that they have such anecdotes of bravery and romance. *Yasin Khan ki Baat* is told to highlight his career as an advocate and a *masiha* of the Meo peasantry who fought against the tyranny of Alwar state and got relief for his community from high taxes. He was supported by the British in his struggle for the Meos of Mewat against the Alwar State.

Yasin, the Meo leader, is described as being born with unique *rekh,* or lines of destiny, that are drawn by the goddess Bidmata (Bemata) on the forehead. The omens used in the narrative of the bards, are conventional and suggest the influence of the *Sagum Sastra.* (See Shail Mayaram, *Resisting*

*On the basis of a paper entitled "Peasants' Unrest in Mewat as reflected in a Folksong" was presented at a National Seminar on *Peasant Movements* held in March, 1999 at Kurukshetra University, Kurukshetra. Later presented as '*Yasin Khan Ki Baat*' at *Punjab History Conference* held at Patiala in March 2004.

Regemes: Myth, Memory and the Shaping of a Muslim Identity, Delhi, 1997, p. 44). He was born on 4th November, 1896 in a small village of Rahna in Nuh Tehsil of district Gurgaon (now Mewat). His early education was at Nuh and later shifted to the University of Delhi. He joined St. Stephen's College for his graduation and later completed L.L.B. Yasin Khan started his practice in the year 1926.

The Meos those days were considered a backward community and there was hardly any family which could afford higher studies. They were always neglected by the higher castes and were compelled to do hard labour in the fields. They could hardly pay off their debts and had been the victims of the money - lenders as well as of the state. M. Darling in his work on *Punjab Peasants in Prosperity and Debt* has highlighted their miserable conditions.

Choudhary Yasin Khan came into contact with one Munshi Naseeb Ahmed Khan who inspired him to serve the Meo community. Later coming into contact with Sir Saijad Ahmad Khan and other social reformers, Yasin Khan fought against the Meos' backwardness. He pleaded for their education and opening of the schools in the region. For this mission, he made a tour of region of Mewat and collected funds for smooth running of such schools. Motivated by Mr. F.L. Brayne, Deputy Commissioner of Gurgaon, Brayne Meo High School was established in 1923 at Nuh.

Being educated and well - versed in the complications of the Indian law, he decided to fight for justice. He succeeding in getting relief and concessions for the peasantry in Mewat.

It is believed that the chiefs of the Alwar state tried to lure Yasin Khan in their support by offering many favours, but he was a man of integrity and character, he could not think of deceiving his community. Around 1930–31 Yasin Khan began a peaceful movement against Alwar and Bharatpur states to get concessions in taxes and land revenue. It proved successful in Bharatpur but not in Alwar. Hence the struggle between the Meos and the Maharaja of Alwar took an ugly turn and Raja Jai Singh was exiled to London.

The Meos had to face the worst period in 1947. Communal riots broke all over the Mewat. Alwar and Bharatpur states followed a policy of murder, loot and forcible conversion of the Meos. By the efforts of Yasin Khan, Vinoba Bhave, Satyam Bhai and others the peace was restored in the region. After independence on 15 August, 1947, the Meos due to their sufferings in communal franzy began to migrate to Pakistan. But Yasin Khan firmly decided to dissuade the Meos from migration to Pakistan. He convinced Mahatma Gandhi to come and hold a programme at Ghasera on 19 December 1947 to appeal to prevent the immigration and to assure the rehabilitation of the Meos. Yasin Khan served the Punjab hegtalative Council as its member for the years 1926–36 and served as an M.L.A. of the Unionist Party in the Punjab Legislative Assambly for the years 1937–46 but lost election in 1946 to Ahmad Jan of Muslim League. Again he was member of Punjab Legislative Assembly for the period 1952–57 and was re-elected in 1957.[1] He served his community and the region for more than 50 years. He died on 19th February, 1970, at a village Bilaspur in district Alwar. In his memory Brayne Meo High school at Nuh was renamed as Yasin Meo School and now became a college in his name as Yasin Meo College.

After this brief life sketch of Yasin Khan, we come to the *baat* literature. The *mirasis* of the region have been performing a folksong depicting the life story of Yasin Khan and his struggle against the Maharaja of Alwar. It has also been used by modern scholars in their respective researches.

The folksingers always begin their presentation with the praise of the almighty. Hence in this *baat* the same has been placed in the dialogues between Yasin Khan and the Maharaja of Alwar. These couplets describe the happenings during the Alwar movement led by Yasin Khan.

While remembering his *pir* or *ustad* the mirasis begin with:

पहले याद करूँ उस्ताज कू
लगा धणी सू ध्यान।
रियासत अलवर में रूतबो हुयो,
जाका सच्चा करूँ बयान।

First I remember my teacher, then give thought in my heart, I shall truthfully describe the person who earned name in the Alwar State.

सुब्भ घड़ी के बीच, कूख में पैर पसारा।
याको नाव धरो आसीन, मुलक में हुयो जहारा।।

In an auspicious moment, he entered the womb, He was named Yasin and the country celebrated his birth.

याका माता-पिता धनवंत,
कुंवर जी बेद पढ़ायो।।
पढ़गो सारा शास्त्र,
पास एल. एल. बी. पायो।।

His parents were wealthy one and taught him well. He completed his studies and got an L.L.B. degree.

Here the *mirasis* explain the event of the Alwar movement which, brought favours to Yasin Khan under the British. During the conference of the Princes, he was honoured and offered a chair.

दिल्ली में जलसे जुड़ो , सिकरा मेम साहब अंग्रेज।
जयपुर, अलवर, भरतपुर, सबकू कागज दीनो भेज।।

There held an assembly in Delhi, where all English ladies and gentlemen gathered. The invitation was sent to Jaipur, Alwar and Bharatpur states to attend the same.

शिमला के दरबार, औसराय मतवो पावे।
जहाँ ए जनजी अमोज, तार हूँ लू भिजवावे।।
बिस्मिल्ला पहले पढ़ी दिल में पढ़ली कुतुब अमीन।
जिले डाँक में बैठ के, शिमला पहुँच गयो आसीन।।

First remembered the Almighty and read the *quranic* stanzas sitting in horse-cart, Yasin reached Shimla.

In Shimla, like other kings, Yasin was offered a chair. On this occasion the Maharaja of Alwar who was also present became upset and said:

तेरे अजब रेख, आसीन, बड़ो अक्कल में तेज।
तोलू जलसा में कुर्सी पड़ा, तेरो अदब करें अंग्रेज।।

O Yasin, you have strange luck, and have a sharp mind. In the conference you have been offered a chair and the English honour you.

अरज करें जयसिंह, ओसराय सुणयो मेरी।
कहा मेव की जात, कौंण को कुर्सी गेरी।

Viceroy, listen my request, why a chair for a person who is a Meo.

This couplet has its variation and is sung by the mirasis as under:

ये कुर्सी है कौन की, नू पूछें महाराज,
जे आज मेवन लू कुर्सी पड़ा, डूब जाये रजपूतन को राज।।

The Maharaja asked whose chair is it? If the Meos are offered chair like this, the rule of the Rajputs is certainly ending.

This diglogue of the king of Alwar perhaps obliged the Viceroy to justify his actions in these words:

जाकू कलम बड़ो कर देय, कौम को कहा इजारो।
जाने करी विलायत पास, कौन कुर्सी न डारो।।

The pen (education) has made Yasin a big man who cares the community, why not a chair for a person who has received degree.

Yasin Khan was attentive to such dialogues and could not resist himself and ultimately intervened and said :

रियाया कू दुख देयगो, न कुछ याको जाय।
ई पब्लिक सू लेकर भरे, याकू दीजो माफ कराय।।

The king is giving suffering to the subjects, and looses nothing. He is filling his treasure with the public taxes, which need to be exempted.

It follows with these words :

अच्छो खानदान आसीन को, एसोई है आप।
वा मैम्बर आसीन ने, महाराज की बात करादी साफ।।

Yasin Khan belongs to an honourable family and himself also maintains the dignity. Thus the member Yasin made his intentions clear about the Maharaja.

आप कहे आसीन, सुणो महाराज सवाई।
मैं छीनूँ तेरो राज, बात मेरी रहे सदाई।।

Yasin addressed the Maharaja and warned him if he could not acceed the demand, he may loose his throne. Note, my words will prevail.

On hearing this Maharaja got angry and challenged in these words :

तोप किले चढ़ाय दूँ, कर दूँ तेज मशीन।
तेरा गढ़ रहनाय फूँक दूँ, जब देखूँ आसीन।।

A gun fixing on the fort, giving a speed ruining your village Rahna, only then I shall see Yasin.

This challenge of the king provoked Yasin Khan who had to show his strength by quoting his lineage in these words:

मेरे बारह बावन पाल हैं, सब भाई को साथ।
तेरे अलवर को धुंआ कँरू, जै मेरी पलट पड़े मेवात।।

I have the support of fifty two Pals and my folk, I shall turn your Alwar into ruins with the support of the people of Mewat.

दिल्ली का दरबार में, इनकी होग्गी दो दो बात।
तू राजा मैं मेव हू, काई दिन देख हमारा हाथ।।

According to the folksingers both Yasin Khan and the king of Alwar had enough discussion and Yasin Khan challenged him to see in the future.

It seems that song has missed link and directly bring us to believe the conversation between the queen and the king of Alwar where she is seen advising her husband to refrain from the conflict and try to patch up with Yasin Khan.

इक सपना की बात कहे, राजा सू राणी।
तेरी बिचल गई मेवात, कहा तैने न जाणी।।
दिल्ली वाला लाट ने, भरा राव पै रोश।
करी शिकायत मेव ने, जाणे तेरी अलवर लीन खोस।।

The queen relates her dream in which, the king has lost the Mewat region and the Viceroy had shown his anger to the King. He made the king caution on the complaint of Yasin Khan which has resulted in evacuating the throne of Alwar. On hearing this the Maharaja replied :

सुण रे औरत जात, बात मत काढ़ो कच्ची।
ये सपना की बात, कदे न होवे सच्ची।।

O, woman folk, do not speak such words. Dreams never turn true.

धमकी दी मेवात ने, कर उनकी आसंग।
तीन दिन अंग्रेज सू, राणी करणो चाहूँ जंग।।

Mewat has threatened me, after crushing them O queen, I wish to fight the English.

ऊ तो छोरो मेव को, मैं असली रजपूत।
पाँवन जब बी न पड़ूँ, चाहे गद्दी जावे छूट।।

He is Meo boy and I am a true Rajput, therefore I shall never bow before him, let the throne go.

The mirasis praise highly the *Dahngal Pal* of the Meos and sing:

या दहगंल की पाल की, कीरत मुलकन ने जाणी।
पूरी की आसीन ने, जो दिल भीतर ठाणी।।

The people have appreciated the contribution of *Dahngal Pal.* Yasin has fulfilled his goal which he fixed in his mind.

References

1. Nagender Kumar Singh (Ed.), *Encyclopaedia of Muslim Biography,* Vol. V, Delhi, 2001, p. 468. For further details, see Chowdhary Abdul Haye's 'The Freedom Monement in Mewat . . .' in *Kunwar Muhammad Ashraf: An Indian Scholar and Revolutionary* edited by Hors Kinger, P.P.H. Delhi 1969, pp. 291-336
2. A socio-economic survey on the Meos of Mewat was conducted under auspices of the Research programme Committee of the Planning

Commission, Govt. of India in the year 1970. It took the shape of a book entitled *The Meos of Mewat : Old Neighbours of New Delhi* by Hashim Amir Ali, the Director, Rural Institute, Jamia Millia Islamia, New Delhi, (Oxford, 1970). According to this study the first political outburst in recent times was in 1932 when, according to one of the informants, who was himself an active participant in the movement, the British Government had been annoyed with the Maharaja of Alwar. The Unionist Party of the Punjab was therefore used to organize the Meos by religious slogans against the Raja.

Unfortunately the Raja himself had initiated certain policies which injuried the religious sentiments of the Meos. He was fond of hunting and therefore forbade the killing of pigs and even the building of fences as a protection against them! And, as is known, the pigs not only spoil crops but also arouse religious abhorrence. The Meo would have suffered silently if deer or even elephants were to be allowed to graze in the fileds! . . . (pp. 29-30). It is strange the name of Yasin Khan does not figure even once in this whole episode.

Shail Mayaram in her book *Resisting Regemes* . . . depicted Yasin Khan as the leader of the Meos (p. 95) who represented the Muslim League (p. 115). She refers *Yasin ki Baat* in her book (pp. 128-33), Dhamukar ki Baat (pp. 140-48). His role in the communal politics (pp. 151-54), Yasin as a politician (pp. 156-58). She also reflects him as Pro-British (p. 170) whose political advisor was Syed Matalabi Faridabadi (p. 174). The Meo leaders wanted Pakistan and partition (p. 194). The Meo migrated to Pakistan returned back on the appeal of Yasin Khan and Mahtma Gandhi.

7

Babur's Observations of Mewat and the Mewatis *

I

The paper is based on the autobiography of Babur itself i.e. *Tuzuk-i-Baburi* written in Turki and translated into in English by A.S. Beveridge and supported by the contempory and near contempory Persian chroniclers. Babur is known for his pen-writing which he has used in describing the contemporary political, socio-cultural and economic conditions of Central Asia and India. In the preface of *Baburnama,* Beveridge writes that Babur's home-milieu favoured excellence in the quite Arts and set before its children high standard and example of proficiency. He further informs us that his mother Qut-Luq-nigar and grandmother Aisan-daulat had great influence over him who was very learned and full of scholarship of their times. Thus Babur's civilian aptitude, whether of the author and person, the maker of gardens, the artist, craftman or a sportman all nourished in fertile soil of family traditions and example. Babur's intellectual distinction is noticeable throughout his

*Presented at *Punjab History Conference* held at Patiala in 2005 and was pubblished in its Proceedings (pp. 147–50).

writing and observations about the living or dead. His description of Hindustan in this regards is invaluable. He has taken minute notices of things, may be mountains or rivers ; passes or routes, towers or villages, people and their life conditions, flora and fona including the detailed description of his own experiences with the people and places of India. In this small article an attempt has been made to highlight his experiences and observations about the Mewat region and the Mewatis.

II

The region of Mewat roughly includes parts of districts Gurgaon or Faridabad in Haryana; Alwar and Bharatpur in Rajasthan; Mathura and Agra in Uttar Pradesh. From local traditions it appears that the whole Mewat was held by the Yaduvanshi Rajputs continuously some about the eighth century to the thirteenth century. Mahesh, the lord of Mewat, is said it have offered homage to Bisaladeva Chauhan of Ajmer. His descendant Mangal, who had strengthened his position by entering into matrimonial alliance with the Dahya Rajputs, attempted to assert his power against the Chauhans; but Prithviraja III coerced him into obedience. Largely in cooperation with Chauhans or other dynasties in eastern Rajasthan, they engaged in wars against the Turks..[1]

III

The earlier mention of the Mewatis in the Persian chroniclers is found with reference to Illutimash who captured Bayana, Tawangarh and Gwalior. But his success proved temporary. Due to their geographical conditions in the Aravallis and the unproductivity of the land, the Mewatis took to the plundering of caravans and made depredations against the authorities at Delhi. Balban was the first amongst the Sultan who took punitive expeditions into Mewat and rooted out their menace. He first suppressed them and captured their fortreses. The forests in the area were cleared and Afghan soldiers were appointed in the newly built Gopalgir fort. This gave the region peace for about a century or so after which, the Mewatis again became turbutant and made place in the nobility of the Sultan. By Bahadur Nahar's accepting Islam under Firozeshah's reign, the Mewatis became very powerful in the region.[2] His headquarter was in the Tijara hills in which he had erected a fort at Kotila (5 kilometers to the west of a village Bhadas, situtated on the main national highway between Delhi and Alwar via Sohna, Nuh, Firozepur Jhirka in District Mewat).[3] It is needless to mention that the Mewatis became prominent after the death of Firozshah Tughluq and played a significant role in the court politics. The region had become a shelter place for the fugitive princes of Delhi. With the support of the Mewatis many tried their luck to get the throne. When Babur came, Hasan Khan Mewati a descendant of Bahadur Nahir was ruling over the entire region of Mewat.[4]

Babur makes mention that the country of Mewat, near Delhi, yielded revenue of 3 or 4 *krurs.* Hasan Khan Mewati and his ancestors one after another had ruled it with absolute sway for a hundred years or two. In his views "They must have made imperfect submission to the Sultans of Delhi. The Sultans whether because of their own dominions were wide or because their opportunity was narrow, or because of the Mewat hill-country, did not turn in the Mewat direction, did not establish order in it, but just put up with this amount of imperfect submission." He further writes, "For our own part, we did after the fashion of earlier Sultan; having conquered Hind, we showed favour to Hasan Khan, but thankless and heathnish apostate disregarded our kindness and benefits, was not grateful for favour and promotion, but became the mover of all disturbance and the cause of all misdoings."[5]

About the mountain range of the Aravalli, Babur writes, "Hindustan has other mountain range that runs from north to south beginning in the province of Delhi at a building made by Firozeshah called the Jahanuma which is situated on a rocky little mountain. Running from there are patches of rocky little mountain in the vicinity of Delhi. When they reach the province of Mewat, the mountains become larger. Passing through Mewat they go to the province of Bayana and passes on through the pargana of Sikri and Dholpur."[6]

It is through Babur's autobiography that we come to note the Mewati nobles in the court of Ibrahim Lodi who were contributing for the state honestly. Once when the nobles in the service of Ibrahim's mother were convicted for false dealing, were ordered out capital punishment. The details or not known, however, after few days they were pardoned and granted honour. Firuz Khan Mewati was one of them.[7]

During the battle of Panipat with Ibrahim Lodi, Hasan Khan Mewati's son Nahar Khan fell in the hands of the Mughals who was made hostage by Babur in this hope that Hasan Khan Mewati would be kept under watch. Nahar Khan was dressed in a robe of honour, promises were made to him for his father, and later allowed to leave Mewat. But as Babur writes "That hypocritical mannikin Hasan Khan must have waited just his son had leave from me to go, for he came out of Alwar at once joined Rana Sanga in Toda Bhim (Agra District). It must have been ill-judged to let his son go just then."[8] As we know Hasan Khan Mewati sided with Rana Sanga fought against Babur in the battle of Khanua and was killed. He had twelve thousand cavalary man under his command.[9] Hasan Khan was killed by the force of a matchlock which Babur writes as *Zarb-i-Tufak.*[10]

We find in his autobiography how Babur decided to destroy and plunder the region of Mewat and sent Shaikh Jamal to this effect. Mulla Tark-i-ali was also ordered to join him and to neglect nothing of ruin and plunder in Miwat; orders to the same purport were given to Maghfur, the Diwan. They went over-ran and raided many villages and took some Mewatis as prisoners.[11] Babur further writes at a different place that his forces dismounted on the river Manas-ni, 6 kuroh from Alwar, then the seat of the government. He believed that earlier the seat of the government of Mewat must have been Tijara.[12]

After the death of Hasan Khan Mewati we hardly find a leader of that rank. Thus the region was brought under the direct rule of the Mughal nobles. They are seen active in the late half of the 19th century when they fought for the cause of Bahadur Shah Zafar and actively participated in the 1857 revolt and killed number of British officials. We must say that the region of Mewat could not stand for a long as far the state - formation in Medival India unlike Jaunpur, Gujrat, Rajputana and Malwa.

References

1. *Comprehensive History of India*, vol. v, edited by Muhammad Habib and K.A. Nizami, Delhi, 1970 p. 842.
2. For details see chapter 9.
3. *Comprehensive History of India*, vol. V, p. 843. See also Cunnigham's, Reports, xx, pp. 10-30; for the intrigues and counter intrigues in the court of Delhi, see S.B.P. Nigam, *Nobility under the Sultans*, Delhi, 1967, p. 90.
4. Whem Timur invaded Delhi he sent Saiyid Shamsuddin Turmuzi and Alauddin naib-karkari as ambassedors to the city of Kotila. They came back with a letter from Bahadur Nahir in which he had promised to pay his homage to Timur. Bahadur Nahir sent to him as a tribute two white parrots which could talk well and pleasantly. . . . "The sight of these parrorts and the sound of their voices gave me great satisfaction," writes Timur in his *Malfuzat-i-Timuri* "so I gave directions that they should be brought before me in their cages every day that I might listen to their talk. . . ." Bahadur Nahir with his son Kalnash paid their respect personally to Timur. They were honoured with royal favour and bounty. See *Malfuzat-i-Timuri*, Eng. Tr. by Elliot and Dowson, vol. III, p. 449.
5. *Baburnama*, Eng. Tr. A.S. Beveridge, pp. 577–78.
6. *The Baburnama*: *Memories of Babur: Prince and Emperor* Tr. and annotated by W.M. Thackson, New York, 1996, p. 333 and Beveridge, pp. 486–87.
7. Beveridge, pp. 447–78.

8. Ibid., p. 545.
9. Ibid., p. 562. Also see Mohibul Hasan, *Babur: Founder of the Mughal Empire in India* (New Delhi, 1985), p. 91.
10. Ibid., p. 573.
11. Ibid., p. 551.
12. Ibid., p. 578. River Mans-ni means the man-killer. See *District Gazetteer of Gurgaon* (1910), iv A, p. 6. The river is also known as Barah or Ruparel.

8

1857 : Mewat and its Neighbouring Regions*

The imposition of British rule and a ruthless policy of imperialist exploitation created an explosive situation in India around the middle of the nineteenth century. Large bodies of Indian soldiers serving under the British East Company spearheaded an uprising which soon turned to be a popular revolt against alien domination in many parts of the country. The movement received support from several of the dispossessed Indian rulers. Whatever the causes of the revolt may have been, and there were many, then fact remains that during this armed resistance to British rule, thousands of Indians perished on the battlefields and many lost their lives in the massacres that followed. Innumerable patriots were hanged on the gallows or blown to death with cannons, very often without trial. People in District Gurgaon mainly Mewat region too sacrified their lives and raised their head against the British. Irrespective of their cast creed and religion, the

*The paper was presented under the title 'Martyrs of 1857: Gurgaon District' at a National Seminar on *Revolt of 1857 and the Punjab: Historiographical Perspectives* held at Punjabi University, Patiala on 28 November 2007. The Proceedings were published under the title *Rethinking 1857 and the Punjab* edited by Navtej Singh (Patiala, 2008), pp. 28–38.

Meos or Mewatis, Gujars, Jats, Rajputs, Ahirs including Nawabs, Raos, Mirzas, Sheikhs, Pathans, Bilochs, Mahajans, Dhobis and other non - Muslim communities fought actively and were either hanged or shot in hundreds. The massacre beginning in November, 1857 did not stop till May, 1858 and after a gap of five months it again took place in December, 1858.

The chapter is based on the published literature available at various libraries and research institutions in Delhi; Aligarh, Shimla and Kolkata and is a part of my project "Mewat and 1857" which will take its final shape in near future. Needless to state that Gurgaon had been a part of the Mewat prior to becoming a part of the British empire. Therefore its early history is basically the history of the region of Mewat. A brief survey of the region prior to the revolt is necessary to explain why the people of this area thronged together into the revolt?

Mewat, the land of the Meos, comprised parts of districts Gurgaon, Faridabad and full newly created district of Mewat in Haryana, Nuh being its headquarter; parts of districts Alwar, Bharatpur and Jaipur in Rajasthan and parts of districts Mathura and Agra in Uttar Pradesh. The people of the land had always been freedom - loving and did not accept subordination to any authority. They continuously opposed the rulers at Delhi or Agra and tried to maintain their independence. The Meos are among the Jadon Rajput and take their roots from the Mahabharta times and associate themselves with the Pandavas.

The Persian chroniclers are the first who penned down about the Meos or Mewatis. Under the Turks, they created turbulence near the capital, Delhi. The southern gates of the city were closed after the sunset due to the panic created by the Meos. Sultan Ghiasuddin Balban (*c.*1266-86 AD) was the first among the Sultans who as a wazir and later a ruler took hunting expeditions into Mewat and crushed the Meos. But the Meos or Mewatis did not stop their depredations and raised their heads against the ruling authorities as and when got opportunity. Under Sultan Firozeshah Tughluq, their leader Sambhar Pal accepted Islam and became Bahadur Nahir with a title 'Khanzada'.

Babur mentions in his autobiography that Bahadur Nahir and his successors ruled Mewat for about 200 - 300 years. When Babur fought against Rana Sanga, Hasan Khan Mewati Khanzada supported the cause of Rana Sanga and fought against the Mughals and lost his life in the battle of Khanua. The people of Mewat could not stand against the mighty Mughals and joined their services. After the death of Aurangzeb (1707), Rajputs, Sikhs, Jats, Marathas, Rohillas and others revolted against the Mughals and established their indepent kingdoms. Region of Mewat and its people became victims of the Jats and the Narukas of Alwar state. But the British after defeating the Jats and the Narukas became masters of Mewat. Soon the area was given to Nawab Shamsuddin, who was responsible for the murder of William Frazer, the resident of Delhi. He was hanged and the Mewat became under the direct rule of the British. The Mewatis who had joined the British army and the Gwalior regiment always remained discontent. They had already begun their activities even before the revolt of 1857 and had been listed in the British records as notorious, plunderers and what not?

The modern scholars all agree that before the Sepoy mutiny, anti-British waves were already present in the country. The local landlords throughout the country were creating trouble for the British. Near the capital, Aligarh was one of the district where the gangs marauders like Bandhiks and Mewatis infested the surrounding area and their headquarters were in Mursan and Hathras estates (R.C. Majumdar, *The Sepoy Mutiny and the Revolt of 1857*, Calcutta, 1963, Second edition, p. 53). The failure of the British in the Burmese War led to a formidable rebellion in 1824. The insurgents consisting of Jats, Mewatis and Bhattis in Haryana plundered government property and proclaimed that British authority was at an end. (ibid, p. 63). According to William Dalrymple, "Most of Delhi's hinterland was effectively contolled by the Gujar and Mewati tribesmen" (*The Last Mughal: The Fall of Dynasty,* Penguin Books, Delhi, 2006, p. 261).

The British revenue policy in District Gurgaon seems to be very dissatisfying specially the Meo dominated areas Nuh, Firozepurjhirka, Sohna and Tauru. It was main reason for their anger against the authorities. They were just waiting the proper time and opportunity which came soon in the wake of Sepoy revolt at Meerut on 10th May, 1857. The fire of revolt spread soon in the nearby areas and Delhi came under the control of the rebels. From Delhi this spread in the Gurgaon District. Malleson writes, that this district was bounded on the north by the District of Delhi and Rohtak, on the west by the territories belonging to the states of Alwar and Jaipur, on the south by the Mathura district and Bharatpur and on the east by the river Yamuna, and had an area of about 1939 square miles and a population of 6,62,500 persons. The seat of the district administration was located at Gurgaon, then a very small town, little better than a village about 20 miles from Delhi (*History of the Indian Mutiny of 1857-59, volume, vi,* p. 139).

It is well known that Gurgaon had been prominently a Hindu district. The important caste was that of Jats who lived chiefly in Palwal and northern parganas. They were agriculturists like other dominant castes like the Ahirs, the Rajputs, the Gujars who were found scattered almost throughout the district. The artisans and Harijans were solely dependent upon these peasant castes for their subsistence. The Muslims, who formed over 30 percent of the district population and the Meos who were about the one - sixth of the population holding large tracts of land in the southern parts of the district called 'Mewat'.

When about 300 sepoys from Delhi marched into the Gurgaon district on 11th May (afternoon) they found great support from the local populace. Hundreds of peasants from the neighbouring villages and artisans and poor people from the towns of Gurgaon swelled the sepoy's ranks in no time. A few impoverished feudal nobles like Nawab Ahmed Mirza Khan and Nawab Dula Jan also joined them. It is interesting to note that the rebels did not entrust their leadership to the two newly arrived feudal chiefs, but kept it on their own hands. W. Ford, the Collector - Magistrate of Gurgaon tried to check the rebels of Gurgaon at Bijwasan, a small village, 12 kms. from Gurgaon in the morning of 12th May. But he failed. The rebels next attacked Gurgaon, the seat of the district administration. Ford made another attempt to repulse the rebels, but he failed this time also. Demoralized by his successive defeats, Ford fled to Mathura via Bhondsi, Silani and Palwal, taking the European custom officers of all these places with him. The rebels occupied the District headquarters, seized Rs.7,84,000/- from the treasury, destroyed the houses of the Europeans and the loyalists, and released prisoners from the district gaol. (K.C. Yadav, *The Revolt of 1857 in Haryana*, Delhi, 1977, pp. 56-58)

In Mewat, the sturdy and warlike Mewatis came out in large numbers and formed a *dhar* (a crowd turned into a somewhat organized gathering) to finish the British rule. Sadruddin a tall, handsome Meo peasant from Pinnagawa stood at their heads. This peasant leader was a very intelligent and shrewd man, who did his job very seriously. Sadruddin's first attack was on the loyslist elements living in town. His men met with little opposition at Tauru, Sohna, Firozepur, Punahna and Pinnagawa, but they had quite a tough time dealing with the loyal *khanzadas* at Nuh (ibid, pp. 57-58)

A study made on *The Meos of India: Their Customs and Laws* (Delhi 1983) by Shamsuddin Shams shows that "Bahadur Shah II (The titular emperor) gave a stiring call to the countrymen to throw off the foreign yoke in 1857 and he himself became the symbol and the focal point of the hopes of the millions of the drowntrodden people of India. History repeats itself when we find Ali Hasan Khan Mewati raising the banner of revolt against the British rule at the call of last Mughal Emperor of Delhi. A fierce battle was fought between the forces of Mr. Ford, Deputy Commissioner of Gurgaon and Ali Hasan Khan, the acknowledged leader of the Meos in 1857, near Ghasera village situated between Sohna and Nuh (on the Delhi - Alwar road). The Meos fought so valiantly that the British forces were totally routed and the Deputy Commissioner had to flee for safety towards Mathura Cantt. (pp. 31-32)

K.M. Ashraf in an article "Ghalib and The Revolt of 1857" (published in *Rebellion 1857: A Symposium*, Edited by P.C. Joshi, People's Publishing House, 1957, pp. 245-56) informs us that Ghalib was commissioned by Bahadur Shah to write the official history of the Mughal dynasty. He chose to live in Delhi under the rule of the rebels but also kept a diary of the day to day events of this memorial period in Persian, entitled *Dastambo* (included in the collection of Ghalib's Persian works : *Kulliyat-i-Ghalib*, Lucknow, 1872). The entries in this diary begin with the arrival of the Meerut troops succeeded in overpowering the resistance of popular forces in Delhi. In some respects, this diary covers the developments upto the fall of Lucknow (July, 1858). What actually prompted the author to compose this unique document is not very clear. But in any case, it saw the light of day after the British in full possession of Delhi. The record of events in Ghalib's diary is all too brief (See *Dastambuy : A Diary of the Indian Revolt of 1857*, by Mirza Asadullah Khan Ghalib, Translated from the original Persian with a critical Introduction, Glossary and Notes by Khwaja Ahmad Faruqi, Asia Publishing House, 1970. It contains total 96 pages out of which translated pages of *Dastambuy* are only 46). Ghalib writes, "(In the neighbourhood of Delhi) the Meos of Sohna and Nuh (Gurgaon District) have created uproar in such fashion that you would imagine lunatics had broken loose from their chains. Tula Ram is still at large in Rewari and has now joined his forces with those of Devi, the Meo, and operates under him. This group, in those hilly and forest region has its own independent plan of fighting the (British) rulers. In a word you might almost say that the very elements in India are in a ferment" (*Kulliyat,* p. 397) *

The account of hand to hand tough fight between the Mewatis and the British has been given by Charles Ball in his *The History of the Indian Mutiny, Vol. II* (Indian Reprint New Delhi, 1981) on the basis of a letter of an officer attached to the column under Brigadier Short, dated 7th November (1857) Bullumghur (Ballabhgarh). The extract from this letter affords some idea of the operations of this region of Delhi army. The writer says, "I wrote to you last from Kanoond: from that place we returned to Rewaree, where we found a subahdar and a company of the guides in charge of the town, Some report about the Jodhpore legion being at Naud was current in camp, and this was the reason assigned for our looking - up Rewaree. Thence to Goorgaon, twenty miles from Delhi. We were there sent off with the carabiniers, leaving the column halted, to Furrucknuggar. Twenty of the nawab's sowars were shot. After this we entered quite a new style of country. Instead of skirting the hills, we entered them; indeed, crossed a tract of hills running without order and at a range from 200 to 300 feet high, with here and there a peak of 500, until we quitted them again at Sonah. Our object was to punish the wild devils of Mewattees who inhabit these hills, and whose natural trade is plunder. Marwar (Mewat), the district after which they are called, is far away to the west and south - west; but these people cling to this irregular range of hills in all its length

* Khwaja Ahmad Faruqi translates in these words: "In the areas of Sohna and Nuh the Mewatis have run amuck as if crazy ones had thrown off their shackles and rampaged. Under the devil's guidance (devil's should be Devi's), the rebel Tularam, who was fightining in Rewari, joined forces with the Mewatis, and this group has been fightining the British savagely in the plains and on the mountains, the warfare is so bitter that it seems as if the entire land of India is engulfed in whirling storms and flaming fires." (pp. 51-52).

and breadth. As we found every town had been burnt and gutted by these scamps, we returned the compliment by setting their villages on fire; and at Taroo, as I sat smoking my weed in the evening, I counted no less than five huge bonfires, whose lights stretched almost round the horizon. At Taroo, among the ruins of what was a substantial stone—built town, only seven months ago, and which we were ordered to clear, we found and shot thirty fair - skinned Delhi fellows. One day was spent between Taroo and Sonah (five miles) in hunting the hills for Mewattees; we were fired upon by one village— less, I believe, because those gentlemen like fighting, than because they were anxious to cover the removal of their cattle. Here is the only point at which they were are vulnerable; catch them you cannot; burn their villages you may; and in a week they are re-thatched. All this is idle; seize their cows and goats, if you want to bring them to their senses. The guides such active fellows! - beat for Mewattees up the khuds, down the khuds, and over the most dangerous ground, just as we should for chikore, in a way which Europeans could not have done. About sixty of our friends were killed. A hand - to - hand fight took place, which excited a good deal of fun. A Mewattee, a huge fellow, armed with shield and sword, was put up half-way down the khud at our feet. Twenty shots were fired; but no, the bold fellow held steadily on, springing from rock to rock, descending to the bottom of the dell, and then mounting the opposite face. He was so close that we could distinguish the rope fastened round his body, which these people use in climbing about the ravines in which they live. Just as he was reaching the crest of the khud, a man of the guides suddenly came round an elbow of the ravine, and five words explained to him the proximity of the Mewattee. There was not four yards between them when they met. The guide fired-down ducked his friend, the shot missed, but then followed the sweep of the Mewattee's sword upon the guide's head at the same moment the guide giving him the bayonet. A second flash of the sword, and down went the guide, as we thought - a howl of rage rose from the lookers-on. In another minute the guide was seen standing over his foe. His head had been saved by a thick puggree; and the second cut was, thanks to his lungs of the bayonet, of no great strength: when he stooped it was to pick up his puggree. From Sonah we had another day's hunt; such hard work I have never had in the hills. Falls I had at least a dozen. At Sonah we left the Ghoorkas to keep the district quiet, and then came on here. The rajah of this place has been sent a prisoner into Delhi. The fort here is full of sepoy uniforms: uniforms, too, of the poor fellows of the 32nd foot, and officers of the 6th native infantry, have been found. Bullumghur could not hold out against the force, which kept us at bay for months, it is true; but the rajah, with his men and money, ought to have joined us when the outbreak first took place. Twenty fellows, some of them Pandies, some of them Delhi court men, were shot yesterday. The villagers tell us, that when they asked the retreating Pandies where they were going, they answered, 'We have killed all the Feringhees in the north, leaving only one lame man and two boys, and now we are going to *safkur* them in the south.' The word 'attention!' takes our Pandies in most curiously. A fellow, a poor villager apparently, without whisker or moustache, is brought up, and that mystic trisyllable uttered sharply and suddenly, behold the fellow's heels brought smartly together, the hands pressed to the side, and - the individual is taken out - and shot. At Taroo, a Mohammedan padra offered off hand, in the most handsome way, to change his religion: it was changed he was shot through the head." (pp. 58-59)

The Mewatis were fighting not only in the Gurgaon District, but were taking parts against the British in nereby regions and other distant places like Allahabad. For example during the outbreak at Bijnaur the plunder of tahsils, burning, and other usual excesses were committed by them alongwith other tribes i.e. Gujars, Banjaras, etc. (Majumdar,

p. 112). In Agra the kotwal joined hands with the Mewaits and other tribes against the British. A contemporary observer not less than a judge at Agra, Charles Raiken in his, *Notes on the Revolt in the North-Western Province of India* (London, 1858) as quoted by R. C. Majumdar shows the condition in the North - Western Province. It states that the predatory classes, the Gujars, the Mewatis, felt instinctively that their day had come. Their native enemy, the Magistrate, had perished, at the hands of the mutineers or was flying between them, protected only by the people over whom he lately provide. Forthwith they girded on the sword and buckler, sized the matchlock, and sallied forth to pursue their heriditary vacation of plunder. As a matter of course there was an end of police, telegraph, postal communications, and every other symptoms of civilzation, wherever these harpies were found (Majumdar, pp. 119 and 465).

In Barhpura (Etawah) a mob was led by the Mewatis, Julahas and some Thakurs, who rose in large numbers and plundered the sepoy lines. They also carried off the contents of the magazines and bunglows were burnt. The zila and thugi jails were next broken open. The remaining treasure of four lakhs rupees was carried off and records of the collector's office were set on fire (M. P. Srivastava, *The Indian Mutiny, 1857*, Allahabad, 1979, p. 49). Later on, again the Mewatis took up arms against the British and a state of anarchy prevailed in the district of Elawah (Ibid., p. 51).

The secret society organizations of the revolutionary party was active in the city of Allahabad. The Mewatis were the real contrives of the rebellion of the sepoys and the Risala. In mauza Samdabad the Panchayat of the Mewatis was held on 5th June, 1857 at the house of Safikhan Mewati and the plan of the party was to incite the sepoys and the citizens to rise together on the same day (Ibid., p. 69). And the Mewatis of Samdabad and Rasulpur gathered round him (Ibid., p. 74). In the District Gazetteer of Moradabad (1968) we find a reference of plundering of Sambhal by many communities including the Mewatis of Herapur (p. 54). In Pilibhit also we find that the district was threatened by many leaders, one of those leader was Ali Khan Mewati (Majumdar, p. 17). They were also active in Mandsaur in Madhya Pradesh (*Malwa Akhbar,* 9–16 June, 1857).

On 11 July, 2857, Saadat Khan Mewati, a Risaledar in the cavalary of the Holkars made an attack on the residency of Indore and captured the city for three days, later marched towards Delhi. the armies of Mahu and Indore made Saadat Khan as their leader. The joint armies reached Gwalior and after occuping Dholpur came to Agra. By the time the British had already conquered Delhi. Saadat Khan went underground changing his name as Akbar Khan. After seventeen year he was arrested from Banswara and hanged on 2 September 1874 in front of the Central India Prison Residency Indore (*Meo Darpan,* May, 2008, pp. 5-6) Recently Government has issued a postal stamp in the memory of Saadat Khan (*Meo Darpan,* May, 2008, pp. 25-26).

In the border districts of Hissar, Rewari and Gurgaon the Punjabi population also contributed to the rebel strength and some Sikh chiefs joined them with all their heart as suggested by Surendra Nath Sen in his famous *Eighteen Fifty Seven* (Government of India Publication, 1957, p. 334). In the nereby district of Hissar, a palki-bearer who was returning from the city reported that five companies stationed there had mutinied and the hundred Mewatis had joined them. They had murdered the collector, and plundering the treasury were on the way to Delhi (*The Native Narrations of the Mutiny in Delhi,* Translated from the originals by the Late Charles Theophile Metcafe, 1898, p. 113). At another place it has neem reported that a sowar arrived to inform that a company of infantry, bringing treasurer from Gurgaon, had been attacked by the Mewatis (Ibid., p. 114). It has also been mentioned that on 1st June, 1857, orders were issued to clear up quarters at Jhumakpore, and turn out the Gujars and Mewatis who had taken up their abode there and to make room for Luchman Singh, the Vakil of Maharaja of Jaipur (Ibid., pp. 109-10).

On the basis of the lists of the martyrs given by P. N. Chopra and K.C. Yadav one can notice that hundreds of the Mewatis, Gujars, Jats, Rajputs, Sikhs, Pathans and Muslims were either shot or hanged in the Gurgaon District of Southern Punjab. Figures are as follows:

(I) CASTE – WISE

Meos/Mewatis	35
Jats	20
Ahir	09
Sikh	01
Gujar	02
Mirzas	13
Sheikhs	06
Nawabs	03
Rajputs	03
Pathan	06
Biloch	01
Dhobi	02
Mahajan	02
Muslims	86
* Misc.	197
TOTAL	**396**

(II) VILLAGE-WISE DISTRIBUTION OF THE MARTYRS

Nangli	30	Nangal Pathani	02
Rasulpur	08	Rathauj	02
Badshahpur	20	Kasum	02
Palwal	15	Pohora	01
Hussainpur	10	Sauli	01
Hasanpur	07	Balwani	01
Chhajjunagar	06	Hooli	01
Aherowa	05	Bahadurgarh	01
Sohna	04	Jhajjar	01

* Misc. category of persons belong to the Non-Muslims but their actual caste is not established. It needs further investigation. However, there were some soldiers who were in Gwalior Regiment of British Indian army.

Barka	03	Raisina	01
Sultanpur	03	Narnaul	01
Garli Pathi	03	Saral	01
Faridabad	03	Akhera	01
Kasan	02	Dighot	01
Jaginali	02	Kherali	01
Rewari	02	Jharsa	01
Kadurpur	02	Nuh	01
Kanhore	02	Khajuka	01
* Misc.			248
TOTAL			**396**

(III) MONTH-WISE DISTRIBUTION OF THE MARTYRS

October, 1857	01
November	40
December	209
January, 1858	73
February	52
March	08
April	05
May	02
December, 1858	06
TOTAL	**396**

These figures show that the people of Mewat continued to fight against the British and their local supporters even after the restoration of their power in Delhi in September, 1857.

Appendix

The bards used to sing for the bravery of the Meos who played significant role, especially of villages Doha and Raisina.

*Misc. = Villages not known.

It goes : *Sattavan ka ghadar ki pari mulak mein rull*
gora mara gher ke
Dilli gai dahal
Kah man sab kavi Rai
Deeo dudh piwan lu gai
Doha mein topi tou
Rakh li hai phirangi ki
(There was an uproar of 1857 in the country. The whitemen were chased and killed resulting Delhi was shaking. The poet says that we want a cow to have milk for strength since in the village Doha the caps of the firangees have already been kept off).

Regarding village Raisina:

Raisina ke meon ne, bhala jagaya din
Khakke mare teen sau, kursi khali kar din
Bangla mein man na lage, sooni dekhe sez
Raisina ke gorbe, dekh bina sees angrez
(The meos of Raisina rose again the British for the truth. They killed three hundred of them and got vacated the chair of power. Seen the headless English in the neighbourhood of Raisina, the ladies were made to see their palace lifeless).

LIST OF READINGS

(1) Altaf Husain—*Tarikh-i-Zila Gurgaon* in Urdu (Labore).
(2) Ashraf K. M.—*Meo Quam aur Mewat* in urdu (Delhi, 1974).
—, 'Ghalib and the Revolt of 1857' published in the proceedings of a Symposium entitled *Rebellion 1857: A Symposium*, Ed. P.C. Joshi (PPH, 1957).
(3) Ball, Charles—*History of Indian Mutiny, 2 vols* (London 1858-59). Indian Reprint (New Delhi, 1981)
(4) Bhargava, M.L.—*Freedom Struggle in Uttar Pradesh, 6 Vols* (Lucknow, 1957-61).

(5) Chopra, P.N.—*Who is Who of Indian Marlyrs,3 vols* (Delhi, 1992).

(6) Dalrymple, William,—*The Last Mughal: The Fall of a Dynasty* (Penguin Books, 2006).

(7) Ghalib, Mirza—*Dastambuy: A Diary of the* Asadullah Khan *Indian Revolt of 1857,* English Translation from the Original Persian with a critical introduction, Glossay and Notes by Khwaja Ahmad Faruqi (New Delhi, 1970).

(8) Govt. of India—*Proceedings of the Trial of Bahadur Shah II* (Calcutta, 1985).

(9) Gulati, G.D.—"Mewat, during 13th Century" published in the *Proceding of Punjab History Conference,* (Patiala, 1991).

(10) Majumdar, R.C.—*The Sepoy Mutiny and the Revolt of 1857* (Calcutta, 1963) second edition.

(11) Kaye's and Mallson's *History of the Indian Mutiny of 1857-58, 6 vols* (London, 1889).

(12) *Malwa Akhbar* 9–16 June 1857 Natnagar Shodh Samsthan, Sitamau (M.P.)

(13) Sen, S.N.—*Eighteen Fifty Seven* (Govt. of India, 1957).

(14) Srivastava, M.P.—*The Indian Mutiny, 1857* (Allahabad, 1979).

(15) Yadav, K.C.—*The Revolt of 1857 in Haryana* (Delhi, 1977).

(16) *Meo Darpan* (Hindi) Indore, May, 2008.

9

Khanzadas and their Buildings in Mewat *

Region of Mewat is surrounded by the Aravalli hills. Some of the writers in Urdu[1] suggest that the name Mewat is derived from a Sanskrit word 'Mer' which means 'hill', therefore the region in earlier times was called 'Merat' or 'Merwat' which in later days became Mewat in the local dialect. It has also been suggested that the people of Mewat were called 'Meos'after whom the region got its name. There still remains a controversy whether the region gave its name to the people or the people gave their name to the region.[2]

Recently I have come across an old *Gazetter of the Rampur State* printed at Government Press, United Province, Allahabad (1911) in the Chapter III of which deals with the population of the state. Writing about the other Musalmans it says that the Mewatis are the descendants of converted Meos. Their reputation has never been of the best. Nowadays, however they devote themselves principally to agriculture (p. 50).

According to Pandit Jawala Sahai in his *Waqai-Rajputana* (1877) the region of Mewat included tehsil of Alwar, Ramgarh, Bahadurpur, Govindgarh, Pipal Khera,

* Paper was prepared to be presented at a seminar to be held at Sitamau (Madhya Pradesh). Due to the Gurjar agitation, it could not be possible to reach Sitamau.

Kishangarh, Ismailpur, Tijara, Tapukara, Firozepur Jhirka, Nuh, Tauru, Hathin, Gopal Garh, Pahadi, Jurehra and Kaman.[3]

Basically the borders of Haryana, Rajasthan and Uttar Pradesh form the region of Mewat. The Haryana government, few year ago carved out a separate district of Mewat which comprises all villages of Mewat in tehsils Firozpur Jhirka, Nuh, Hathin and Faridabad and Nuh being its headquarter.

It is needless to repeat what I have already mentioned in a previous chapter that during medieval period the Persian chronicles highly speak of the Meos and their turbulent activities which compelled the Turks and the Mughals to take punitive measures against them. Ghiasuddin Balban was the first among the Sultans of Delhi, who waged a war against the Meos and killed more than one lakh of them.

II

It was in the period of Firoze Shah Tughluq that two brothers Sambar Pal and Sopar Pal accepted Islam and were conferred the title of Khanzada. They were given the name as Bahadur Nahir and Chhajju Khan respectively and were assigned the region of Mewat. This is how the word Khanzada came into being. Today all Khanzada families lay claim to the descendants of these two brothers. There is controversy about their accepting Islam and it needs further research. However, some Khanzadas claim their origin from the Jadu Rajputs (Yaduvanshis) and retain the title Khan, which was common among the nobles in the courts of the Sultans of Delhi during those days.

The Khanzadas played a significant role in the court politics especially after the death of Firozeshah Tughluq. Kotila, the capital of Bahadur Nahir had become the shelter-place for the royal princes who used to seek the support of the Khanzadas to gain power. Bahadur Nahir was contemporary of Timur. He presented two white parrots to

Timur and acknowledged his authority over Mewat. Babur mentions in his autobiography that the Khanzadas were ruling Mewat for the last two hundred years. Hasan Khan Mewati the famous Khanzada ruler of Mewat fought against Babur in the battle of Khanua with Rana Sanga.[4]

III

During their rule in Mewat the Khanzadas got constructed a number of buildings in the region, many are still existing, others are in ruined conditions or extinct. General Alexander Cunningham during his tour in the years 1882 - 83 prepared a report on the places, visited in Eastern Rajputana which, included the region of Mewat. He made special reference of the buildings constructed by the Khanzadas in Mewat. The authors of *Murraqa-i-Mewat* and *Arjang-i-Tijara* also give handsome account of various buildings of Mewat including of those built by the Khanzadas. There is a long list of these monuments which, includes tombs, forts, wells, palaces but the chapter incudes only those which are historically important and famous for their beauty and attraction for the tourists.

(A) Alwar and its monuments

Alwar in the lap of the Aravalli range served as a kingdom in the past and now is a district headquarters in Rajasthan. Its old monuments are famous for historical significance as well of tourist interest. Alwar District is known as the 'Gate of Rajasthan', located between the National capital of Delhi and Jaipur, the capital city of Rajasthan on the National Highway No. 08. Hardly 160 kilometers from Delhi, the city is known as the 'Kashmir of Rajasthan' due to its natural location in the Aravalli Hills.

Alwar Ank or Special issue on Alwar of *Vinay* magazine published by Raj Rishi College, Alwar in 1969 AD gives a detailed account of Alwar city and its buildings. There is a lot on its praise due to its location in the Aravalli. The city has a great charm for the tourists from the country and abroad. Bala qila, Silised, Pandupol, Bhartarihari, Sariska, Naraini and Bhangarh are famous for their natural beauty and historicity.

About Bala qila it is believed that in Samvat 1106, Alghuraiji, second son of Kankilji, the king of Ajmer got built a small fortress and founded a city, whose remnants could be seen even today. The author himself has visited this site, which is now a small village inhabited by some Meo families. This very city was named as Alpur. After the death of Alghu Rai, his son Sagarji lost it to the Nikumbha Rajputs who made an extension to the fortress.

The Nikumbhas worshipped a deity called Chaturbhuj, which is still existing in the fort. It is said that the Nikumbhas used to sacrify human beings to please their deity. The people were unhappy over this act of sacrifice. There came the turn of a son of one *domini.* She went to the Khanzada Alawal Khan and made a request to punish the Nikumbhas. When the Nikumbhas were under the influence of liquor and meat, the Khanzadas on the directions of this *domini* made an attack on them. They were killed and the fort came under the control of Alawal Khan. Alawal Khan Khanzada got constructed a big gate and boundary wall around the fort.[5]

During the reign of Salim Shah Sur, the superintendent of the fort got built a tank in the name of the king called Salim Sagar, still exists. Raja Suraj Mal Jat of Bharatpur also got constructed a *kund* inside the fort which is famous as *Surya-kund.* Later the kings of Alwar added some temples and memorials inside the complex. The fort is 1960 feet above sea level. The length from north to south is three miles and breadth east to west is one mile and the total circumference is six miles. It has 15 big and 52 small *burzs* and have 444 holes for the purpose of firing guns. It has 3359 *kanguras* and each *kangura* has two holes. There are eight *burzs,* to protect the fort from outside, one of it is *kabul burz,* second is *naugaza burz* and third one is *hava bangla* and so on. . . .[6]

Cunningham in his report writes: 'The earliest notice of Alwar that I have been able to find is in Ferishta, who states that Hemraj, in A.H. 590, or AD 1193, "issuing from the mountains of Alwar," had driven Gola Rai towards Ranthambhor, and that he retreated to Ajmer on Kutb-ud-din Aibak's advance. (Brigg's Ferishta, Vol. I, p. 193). The fort is said to have been built by the Nikumbha Rajputs, who held the country before the Khanzada occupation. Indor also is said to have been built by the Nikumbhas, but I failed to get any information about them.' According to Major Powlett, they were extirpated by Alawal Khan Khanzadas in Samvat 1549, or AD 1482, near the end of Bahlol Lodhi's regin. Alawal Khan would appear to have been a son of Ahmad Khan and the uncle of Hasan Khan, the opponent of Baber.

'The origin of the name of the city is unknown. Major Powlett mentions that some derive it from *Alpur*, the strong city, and others from *Arbal*, the name of the mountain range on which it is situated. *Arbali* means "higgledy - piggledy," which is descriptive of this broken and confused mass of hills. *Arbali* also is applied to any broken ground. Arbalpur, or Alpur, would therefore simply mean the city, or city, or fort, on the *Arbali* hills. I have a strong suspicion, however, that the old name was derived from the tribe of Salwas, as the early Muhammadan authors mention the capital city of *Salmur*, in the hills to the south of Delhi. *Salwapura* would become Salwar, and as the name is spelt with the palatal S, it might pass easily through Halwar to Alwar. The country of the Salwas appears to have lain between the Saraswati and the Jumna, and adjacent to Matsya.

'There are no old Hindu buildings at Alwar, and there is only one Muhammadan building of any great age. This is apparently a Pathan tomb of early date. It now stands in the heart of the city, and two of the principal streets pass through it at right angles. The walls are very massive, and the dome is very low and flat. Nothing whatever is known about its builder.

'Near the railway station there is a large square tomb of Fateh Jang, who died in Samvat 1604, or AD 1547. He is called a Pathan, and from the date I think he must have been the governor of Alwar under Islam Shah immediately preceding Chand Kai, whose inscription, fixed on the bank of the Salim Sagar in the fort, is dated in A.H. 958, or AD 1550. The inscription of Fatesh Jang is inscribed in Nagari characters in the veranda of the ground-storey. It reads as follows:

Samvat 1604
* * * 55 Phate Jang
Kha waphaiti pai terikh 27 Mah sa ———
Wal lakh do (?) gumatani haini terikh 3 likhita tej (?)

'Here the stange - looking waphaiti must be intended for the Arabic wafat, or "death," which took place on the 27th of the month of Shawal. Fateh Jang is said to have been a relative of the King of Delhi.

'The tomb of 60 feet square, and consists of three storeys of the same breadth, with seven openings on each face of each storey, and fluted octagonal minars at the four angles. The dome springs from an octagonal neck standing on a fourth square storey, of smaller size, or about 40 feet each side. It is crowned by a small square cupola, resting on a foliated base, like those of the Tejara Tombs.

'The tomb stands in the midst of a large square enclosure, with a small masjid on the west side, and a gateway on the south, which still preserves some traces or ornament in blue glazed tiles'.[7]

Arjang-i-Tijara gives a good descriptiom of Alwar. The city is situated in the lap of Arawali Hills with a pucca parkota with five entry gates. Half the portion has one quagmire. The names of the gates are *Ladia Darwaza, Mulakhera Darwaza, Lal Darwaza, Delhi Darwaza* and *Hajoori Darwaza.* Every gate is decorated with a *topkhana* above it. Inside the *Hajoori Darwaza,* lions are kept and properly looked after. The foundation is beautiful with a wide bazaar in the midst of which is located at Tripolia. Above the hill is a fort, underneath of which, is a tank. Near the tank, there is a palace. The fort is known as *Bala qila* having 18 feet high walls. It has four gates named Suraj Pol, Laxman Pol, Chand Pol and Andheri gate. Inside the fort, there were four *kunds* and a tank known as Salim Sagar. Near Salim Sagar, there is a *chhatri* of Maharaja Pratap Singh and a *baoli.* Alwar has all kinds of animals and there are hunting places at Madhogarh, Silveri, Chand pahari, Bhakhera, Kali Khol, Bakhtpura etc. Under Alwar there fall three parganas of Malakhera, Dehra Bahadurpur and Dehat. The fort of Malakhera was built by Maharaja Pratap Singh in the samwat 1732. The city is famous for fairs which are held at Bhartihari, Siliser dam, Shahpur, Vijaygarh and Rupbas.[8]

Near the Railway station, there stands an old structure. It is known as Fateh Jung Gumbaj. It has five storeyes with doors and long windows all around. Arabic and Persian verses are inscribed on the roof of the first floor and a floral lining on the third floor. On the top, a small dome has been constructed in an umbrella shape with four supporting pillars. On the corner of first floor, the inscription of Fateh Jung Khan, a Khanzada, is inscribed in Dev Nagiri script. It was constructed in his memory in the year 1545 AD[9]

(B) Tijara and its buildings

The fine old town of Tijara is presently situated at a distance of 55 kilometers from Alwar and 95 kilometers from Mathura. It had been an old historic and one of the chief towns of the Khanzadas of Mewat.

At the time of Alexander Cunningham's visit it was surrounded by number of magnificent trees—the banian, *nim, pipal,* mangoes and others and till today maintains its old glory. Its site was then marked by one good-sized Muhammadan tomb, Idgah, and a well, and a number of sati canopies or domed *chhatris.* Alexander counted sixteen of these sati monuments, which, were said to have belonged to the Hindu wives of Khanzada chiefs, but now only the remnants of these can be witnessed. The town of Tijara stands on high ground, some portion being apparently mounds of accumulated ruins. The site had been very heathy. The principal buildings include the following:

> A great Pathan tomb to the south of the city called 'Bhartari Ka Gumbaj' because the land on which, it stands formerly belonged to one Hindu saint of this name. It is one of the largest tombs in Northern India. It was said to have been built by Alauddin Alam Shah, the brother of Sikandar Lodi, who was for a long time governor of Tijara under Sikandar.

About the best and beautiful description of the tomb and other buildings of Tijara one can only quote Alexander Cunningham's account given in his report :

> "The tomb is an octagonal building of the style that prevailed during the hundred years' rule of the Sayids and Lodis from A.H. 830 to 930. But it is much larger than any of the Delhi tombs of that period. Its outside dimensions are 128 feet in breadth, by 115 to 120 feet in height. The centre room is 48´feet in diameter, with walls 17 feet thick, beyond which is an open verandah, of 9´ feet, with walls 9´feet thick.(1) The terrace plinth, which is 13 feet high, extends for 3¾ feet beyond the walls, thus making the whole breadth of the basement 128 feet. At each angle outside, attached to the up-rights walls, there is a sloping buttress, which is one of the characteristic features of the style of the Sayid and Lodi architecture. There are three doorways, 6´feet wide, on each side of the outer walls, and only one doorway, of the same width, on each side of the inner walls. These inner walls thus form eight great blocks of masonry, each of which contains two small rooms, 5´feet long by 4 feet broad.
>
> "Externally there is a second storey, 15 feet broad all round, with a battlement parapet 4 feet thick, and an octagonal cupola 7´feet in diameter in the middle of the terrace on each face.

"Above this there is a third storey, which occupies two-thirds of the thickness of the inner walls, the innermost third being the wall of the dome, which is 5 feet thick. On the terrace there is a small cupola, 5 feet square, at each angle, and another in the middle of each face, or altogether sixteen small cupolas.

"Externally the lower part of the dome is octagonal, with a small semi-circular minaret at each angle, above which it rises in hemisphere. The spring of the dome is 65 feet above the floor. Externally the dome is quite plain; but it is crowned by a handsome octagonal cupola, which stands on a spreading floriated base. There are several other examples of this ornamental style of cupola at Tejara. The dates of the buildings are not quite certain, but I see no reason to doubt the belief of the people that one of them is the tomb of Ala-ud-din Khanzada, the son of Bahadur Nahar, who died between 840 and 850 A.H. Some, however, say that it is the tomb of Ala-ud-din Alam Shah, the brother of Sikandar Lodi, who was governor of Tejara for many years. The tomb of Mubarak Sayid, in Mubarakpur Kotila at Delhi, has a similar style of cupola, but in a much less developed form. Mubarak was assassinated in A.H. 837. There is also an example of the same form on a great Tomb at Alwar, which bears the name of Fateh Jang, and the date of Samvat 1604, or A.H. 954.

"This grand tomb at Tejara stands in the middle of a small earthen redoubt, with a ditch and ramparts all round. It is now used as a barn by the Hindu proprietor."

"At a short distance to the south-west of Bhartari there is a very pretty stone masjid, standing on an earthen terrace, raised to feet above the fields. It is 77 feet long by 25 feet broad, with three openings in front, but only one dome is visible from the outside. In front of the entrance, at a distance of 21 feet, there is a neatly built tomb, 32 feet 10 inches square, resting on a stone plinth 35 feet square. This is said to be the resting-place of the last of the Khanzadas, named Hasan Khan, the opponent of Baber, who fell on the fatal field of Khanwa in A.H. 933 (16th March AD 1527). Inside the tomb is 25 feet square, with a door-way on each side. The building has the usual wide-spreading caves and battlements, with a hemispherical dome, sur-mounted by an octagonal cupola, on a spreading foliated base. There is no inscription of any kind, but the people are unanimous in assigning the tomb to Hasan Khan.

"At a short distance outside the town on the east there is a well-built stone mosque which is simply known as the Lal Masjid, from its red colour. It is 115 feet long by 40 feet broad outside, with fluted minars at the four corners. There are arched doorways in front, opening into a long room, 100 feet by 25 feet, which was once covered by three domes, of which the middle one was taller and larger than the others. The south dome has now fallen. The centre dome is hemispherical, with the remains of a spreading foliated base of a pillared cupola on the top. The date of the building is unknown.

"Near Hasan Khan's tomb there is a well-built tomb standing in the midst of a raised courtyard, with a ruined gateway on the east side. Both tomb and gateway are inscribed with verses from the Koran in well-formed letters generally in good preservation. Nothing is known about the owner of the tomb."[10]

Major P.W. Powelt in his *Gazetter of Ulwar* furnishes a detailed historical account of Tijara since its foundation by one Tejpal. He acknowledges Tahsildar Makhdum Baksh for providing more information of the town.[11]

(C) Sarhata

It is situated four miles to the east of Tijara. At the time of Alexander's visit it was merely a village situated under the hills of Aravalli. Nowadays it is a large village near the old one as told by Mohd. Ibrahim of Mewat. Inspite of its ruined condition Alexander Cunnigham obtained twenty eight old coins at Sarhata of which three were Indo-Scythian. At his time of visit the only building of some importance was a stone mosque called *Mahal*. It was a long pillared hall of three aisles, with seven arched openings in front, supported on double square pillars. The dimensions were 65 by 30 feet outside, and 54' by 26" feet inside. The building stood in a highly raised courtyard, upwards of 80 feet square, pierced with eight openings on each side. Its roof of twenty-one small domes formed a conspicuous object at some distance. The minars at the back angles were sloping. Access to the roof was obtained by staircases in the thickness of the side walls. The back wall had the usual *mihrabs*, or niches, as well as the usual projection outside immediately behind the central mihrabs. The date of the masjid was not known, but from its general correspondence in dimensions and details with the masjid at Kotila, Cunningham thought that it could be assigned to the time of Bahadur Nahar who held Mewat under Firoz Tughlak and his immediate successors at the end of the 8th century of the Hizra. He is said to have made Sarhata his capital.[12]

(D) Bahadurpur

The old city of Bahadurpur is situated 13 miles to the north - east of Alwar, near the end of a low range of hills. On the basis of Major Powlett's Rajputana Gazetteer vol. III, p. 279, Alexander Cunningham believed the foundation of revival of the town by Bahadur Nahar or one of his successors. But as the name was written Bahaduravyapura in a Jaina inscription, Cunningham attributed its foundation to Hindu period, and the name changed to Bahadurpur during the rule of Bahadur Nahar between 1375 AD and 1400 AD. Major Powlett described it as:

> "extensive and flourishing, with large bazaars and numerous fine houses, temples, and tombs."

The inscription just referred to is fixed in the wall of a

ruined Jaina Temple on the east side of the town. Cunningham read it as follows:

1. Sam 1573 varse, Ashadha badi 4 dine Sri Bahudravyapura Sri Sri
2. Mala Sanghenam Adinatha chaityam karitam Pratishthitam Sri kha * * *
3. Sri Jina Hansa Suri vijayarajye, acharya Sri Punya Ratna Suriti.

"In the year 1573 (AD 1516), on the 4th day of the waning moon of Ashadha, in Sri Bahudravyapura, this temple of Adinatha was built by the fortunate Mala congregation under the prosperous pontiff Sri Jina Hansa Suri, and the teacher Sri Punya Ratna Suri."

In an old well, there was an Arabic inscription of many lines; but the whole text was so much worth away as to be generally illegible. The usual opening of Bismillah, & c., could be traced.[13]

(E) Firozpur Jhirka

Seventy-five miles to the south of the national capital Delhi, Firozpur Jhirka is situated in the southern end of the district Mewat. It is a very old town named after a *jhir* or spring. It is situated at the mouth of a ravine which, forms a narrow but easy pass leading towards Tijara, 14 miles to the north. According to Cunningham "The old Hindu name of Jhirka, or Jharka, was derived from the springs of water which spurt from the rocks in the pass, and form a perennial stream, with numerous clear and sparking pools. There are many pretty nooks in the pass, with remains of fortifications in two or three places. The town itself is fortified, but its strength lies in the position at the mouth of a narrow ravine, which could be easily defended by small numbers. In early days the position was, no doubt, covered by thick jungle. Here the

Mewatis always sought safety when hard pressed by the Delhi troops. Thus, in A.H. 795, or AD 1393, Bahadur Nahir, when attacked by Tughlak II, abandoned Kotila, and fled to *Jhirka.* Again, in A.H. 828, when Mubarak Sayid ravaged Mewat, the people took refuge in *Jahra* (read Jharka, and not Tejara, as suggested by Major Powlett). Here also Sher Shah's famous general, Khawas Khan, retired from the persecution of Islam Shah, and here he defeated the king's army. Near Firozpur-Jhirka, the famous prince Sangram Sah of Mewat was, joined by the Khanzada chief Hasan Khan, before marching to oppose Baber. This junction of his enemies' troops at Jhirka most probably brought the place to Baber's notice, as he mentions that "he had heard much of the fountain of Firozpur, and of the great tank of Kotila." On Sunday, (14th April 1527) he records his visit thus—

> "I mounted and rode out from the camp, for the double purpose of seeing the country, and of conducting Humayun to some distance on his way. That day I went to visit Firozpur and its fountain, and took a Maajan. In the valley from which the water of the fountain flows, the Kanir flowers were all in full bloom. It is very beautiful, though it will not support the high praises lavished upon it. Within this valley, where the stream widens, I directed a reservoir to be made of hewn stone, 10 feet by 10 feet. We halted that night in the valley, and next morning rode to visit the tank of Kotila."

"A small tank, about 20 feet square, still remains in the bed of the Jhirka stream.

"On all sides of Firozpur, there are tombs and mosques or *masjids,* the relies of former greatness; but, as they neither possess inscriptions nor are of any importance architecturally, which could not impress Alexander Cunningham while to describe them.

"Under the hills to the west of the town there is a large

Hindu building called Bhond-ka-Deora, or simply Deora, which is curious from the novelty of its plan. In front there is a large hall of 56 feet square. It is divided into five aisles each way by six rows of stout octagonal pillars, 2 feet 3 inches thick. The middle aisles are 8 feet 8 inches wide, those on each side of the centre are 8 feet wide, while the outer aisles are only 4 feet 2 inches. The whole space is thus divided into twenty-five bays, of which the central one and four others in the corners of the next aisles are roofed by hemispherical domes, the largest being ribbed melon-fashion. The other bays are roofed with flat vaults.

"The temple is dedicated to Mahadeva. In front these three central, aisles have arched doorways, but two narrow side aisles are closed. The projecting caves rest on brackets, between which are panels ornamented with sculptured flowers and elephants. Over the middle of each doorway, there is a large flower, and on each side of it, there is an elephant. On the bases of the two central elephant, there are short Nagiri inscriptions, consisting of a single line: each is dated in Samvat 1578=AD1521, during the reign of Ibrahim Lodi.

"At first view the building looked very much like a masjid, but it may be more aptly compaed with many of the Hindu temples in Bengal which,are usually square, with either five or nine domes, called respectively *panch-ratna* and *nava-ratna.* The heavy octagonal pillars are also after the *Bengali* style, as seen in the mosqe of Gaur and Hazrat Pandua. The whole of this pillared hall is *bedi.* The actual temple is, a three storey building at the back, around which perambulation is made."[14]

(F) Indor

"The old fort of Indor, one of the strongholds of the Khanzada chiefs of Mewat, is situated on the hill range which forms the boundary between the Alwar territory and the British district of Gurgaon. It is 6 miles to the north of Kotila and about 70 miles to south of Delhi. The old ruined town lies to the east in the valley below, and has now shrunk to an "insignificant village." The foundation of the fort is ascribed to the Nikumbha Kings of Alwar, about whom nobody seems to know anything but the name. All, however, admit that they preceded the Jadonvansi ancestors of the Khanzadas.

"The fort of Indor stands on the western edge of the hill range, and is quite invisible from the east. This part of the range is called *Kala-pahar,* and is about 4 miles in diameter. On the east side, there is no means of access except by a very bad rocky foot-path. The fort is frequently mentioned in medieval Muhammadan history. It follows :

> "In A.H. 829, or AD 1425; Jallu and Kaddu (the grandsons of Bahadur Nahir) "took up a position in the mountains of *Andwar.* They were attacked for several days by the royal forces, who drove thaem out of Andwar, and then they went to the mountains of Alwar. Next day His Majesty destroyed the fortified post of Andwar, and marched against Alwar. When Jallu and Kaddu posted themselves there the royal forces followed them. At length they were reduced to distress, and were compelled to surrender. His Majesty granted them quarter, and afterwards graciously gave Kaddu a reception."[15]

"In A.H. 832, or AD 1428, Mubarak Sayid marched into Mewat to the palace of *Hindwari* (read Indor), when Jalal Khan (Jallu) submitted, and paid tribute as usual.

"In A.H. 836, or AD 1432, Jalal Khan shut himself up in the fort of *Andaru* (read Indor), which he afterwards burnt and deserted.

"In all these three instances Professor Dowson has failed to recognize the name of Indor, which was the favourite residence of the Khanzada Jalal Khan. His tomb also is at Indor, and his name is connected with all the traditions of the place. In my account of the family of the Khanzadas I have referred to the traditions still current about Jalal Khan.

"The dargah, or tomb, of Jalal Khan is an oblong building, 95 feet by 34 feet outside, with three rooms inside, each 22 feet 3 inches square. The long walls are 6" feet thick, and the end walls are each 7 feet 10 inches. The roof consists of three massive hemispherical domes. In the middle room is the grave of Jalal himself, with three others. In the eastern room there are eight large and one small grave, and in the western room are eight large and two small graves. All these, no doubt, belong to members of his family. There are about twenty other domed tombs in the neighbourhood, but they are small, and without inscriptions, except the Kalimeh. To the north-west there is a tank called Chanda-tal ; and to the west there is a khangah, or shrine, of Chandan Shahid, or the "Martyr."

Major Powlett states that

> "the present Khanzadas of Indor are poor, but they hold the proprietorship, and maintain a *Mulla* to call the *Azan*, or summons to prayers, and to educate their children. They do not yet plough with their own hands, and they preserve the records of better days. One document they produce dated Rabi-ul-Awal, Hijra 970, and bearing the Emperor Akbar's seal, directs the Chaudhari, Kanungo, and Mukaddams of 'Sirkar Alwar' to assist certain Khanzadas of the Indor family who had been commissioned to put down insurrection in that Sirkar".[16]

(G) Sohna

Sohna is famous for its hot spring, as well as for the *masjid* and tombs of the holy saint Hazrat Shah Najm-ul-Hak. It is situated on the national highway between Delhi and Alwar at a distance of 57 kilometers from Delhi and 98 kilometers from Alwar. Cunningham on his visit at Sohna met an old man named Rahim Baksh, the descendant of Hazrat Najm-ul-Hak who had a *farman* of Akbar who had granted a sum of Rs.100/- annually on the anniversary of the saint's death and

01 rupee daily for lamps. He was also told that nine generations of the saint had passed since the death of Najm-ul-Hak. The *farman* of Akbar dated the month of Isfandiar Ilahi, and Jalus 50, or A.H.—1012-13, or AD 1603-04. Some Arabic inscriptions on the entrance gateway of the enclosure contained certain verses from Koran. He also saw a short Nagiri inscription dated in Samvat 1561, or AD 1504 equivalent to AD 910. He suspected both pillars and trellis might have belonged to some earlier buildings. The whole style and plan of the mosque, with its tomb and gateway was so like that of Bahadur Khan at Kotila. According to Cunningham the date must be at least a century earlier than the time of Akbar. Perhaps 1481 AD represented, the period of its erection, while the pillar inscription of Samvat 1561, or AD 1504 must have been added afterwards.

To quote Cunningham,

> "The mosque is 73 feet long by 32 feet broad outside. The courtyard in from is 108 feet long, and the domed gateway projects 14 feet beyond the walls of the enclosure, making a total length of 154 feet. The gateway itself is a fine building, 28 feet 3 inches square, with a lofty flight of steps in front. The tomb in front of the masjid is 18 feet square. Each of the side walls of the enclosure is pierced with ten arched openings. The mosque consists of three long aisles, with seven arched doorways in front, the whole supported on stone pillars, the outer row of pillars being a double one. There are only three hemispherical domes over the alternate bays of the middle aisle. They are all melon-shaped outside.
>
> "On a second high mound just outside the town on the north there is another masjid, 69 feet long, which is said to be older than that of Najm-ul-Hak. It is fitted up as a dak bungalow. Close to it, on the south side, there is a small twelve-pillared tomb, 21 feet 4 inches square. Twenty feet further to the south there is a large tomb, 40 feet

square. It is divided into three aisles each way, making nine bays, of which the middle and four corner ones are covered with hemispherical domes. Nothing whatever is known about the owner of the tomb.

To the east of this tomb there is a large masjid, 95 feet 9 inches long by 27 feet 2 inches broad, which bears the name of Kutb Khan-ki-Masjid. Kutb Khan is said to have belonged to the Khanzada family. The mosque is very substantially built of grey stone from the neighbouring hills with slightly projecting ornaments, of various patterns, in different coloured stones. The whole style, as well as the plan of the building, reminded me strongly of the fine Kila-kohna mosque of Sher Shah at Delhi. I think, thereore, that it may be ascribed to the middle of the 10th century of the Hijra, or about AD 1550".[17]

On the basis of *Tarikh-i-Zila Gurgaon* (in Urdu) by Sayyid Altaf Husain the author of *Murraq-i-Mewat* supports Cunningham and informs us that Sohna is located on the foothills of Aravali and was an ancient city of the Khanzadas. Inside the city there were strong beautiful building and a mosque. Friday mosque was constructed by Shah Nazm-ul-Hak which is located in the midst of the population on the North and is a double storey structure. Inside it are the trellis and doors. Each door had three yards in high pillars of black stone and the roof is red. Number of verses from the Koran are engraved on the mihrabs and doors. . . . The mosque was built during the Khanzadas' rule. According to the author it has been supported by Mr. C.A. Hacket who wrote Alwar Gazetteer.[18]

(H) Bhondsi

'Bhondsi or Bhonsi', as Cunningham writes, "is a large village at the foot' of the hill range just halway between Sohna and Gurgaon. It possesses an old stone mosque, with a tomb in the middle of the enclosure and a fine entrance gateway, standing on a high platform. The builder's name is unknown, but he is said to have belonged to the Khanzada family of Mewat."

"The masjid is a substantial stone building, 74 feet 8 inches long by 27 feet 4 inches broad. It consisits of three domed apartments, the middle one being 18 feet 8 inches square, and the side ones 17 feet 9 inches by 17 feet 3 inches. The walls are 6 feet thick, and there is a staircase in the thickness of each of the end walls, giving access to the roof.

"The tomb in front of the masjid is of the usual square Baradari plan, 22 feet square, with the corners cut off, to form an octagon for the support of a hemispherical dome.

The gateway is 27 feet 10 inches square. It stands completely inside the courtyard, its outer walls being flush with the east wall of the open enclosure. At each of the two eastern corners of the courtyard there is a projecting turreted room, 12 feet square, the object of which I could not discover. The ornament and inscriptions from the Koran are all raised in stucco, like those which prevailed from the time of Firoz Tughlak to the end of the Lodi rule. In one place the date of Samvat 1691, or AD 1634, was found written in ink. The date corresponds with the reign of Shah Jahan, but I think that the masjid must be at least one century earlier."[19]

(I) Kotila

Kotila had been the capital of Bahadur Nahar Khanzada, where he received the envoys of Timur. At the time of Alexander Cunningham's visit it was only a small village of about a hundred houses. The site was chosen for security, as it was protected on the east by the large lake named Dahar, which is from 4 to 5 miles in length by upwards of 2 miles in breadth.

The village occupied high ground at the mouth of a ravine, which probably contained a running stream a few centuries back. There are traces of walls with earthen mounds or ramparts covering the village, from which the occupants could escape up the ravine, and over the hill, on the appearance of a large force. In fact, the Mewatis used to retire from Kotila as soon as the enemy appeared before it.

The lake of Kotila was visited by Baber, who calls it "the tank of Kotila." He described it as follows :

> "One of its banks is formed by the side of a hill, and the river Manisni flows into it. It is a very large take, but does not look well from either of its sides. In the midst of the tank is a rising ground; around it are a number of small boats. The inhabitants of the towns on the banks of the tank, when any alarm or confusion occurs, embark in their boats, and make their escape. When I arrived there, a number of people got into their boats, and rowed into the middle of the lake."[20]

"The fort still exists, but is unoccupied. The northern wall, with its gate at the north-east corner, is still standing. It rises about 600 or 700 feet above the village, and the only approach from the east is by a narrow foot-path, as the rocky hill is generally very precipitous.

"On a high mound in the middle of the old town there is a very fine stone *masjid* (mosque), with a tomb standing in front of it in the middle of a large enclosure. These buildings are the Jami Masjid and the tomb of Bahadur Khan Nahir, when I visited the site few years ago, it housed few families of the Meos. The Jami masjid was begun in the reign of Muhammad Shah, son of Firoz Tughlak, when he occupied Kotila during his campaign against the Mewatis in A.H. 795. The building was not finished until A.H. 803, Muhammad Shah having died in 796."[21]

I myself took a tour of the region and visited more than half of the places in person. Many of these monuments are maintained by the Archeological Survey of India and the concerned state Governments. The monuments and other buildings are of historical as well as of tourist attraction. Many are on the tourist map as well. But it is painful to note that mostly these monuments are in bad shape and need proper care from the concerned agencies. The local residents feel free to visit and use these buildings as they desire. They deface the walls writing slogans, names and what not just making these monuments dirty and filthy. Hence the proper care is needed urgently.

References

1. *Murraqa-i-Mewat* by Sharf Alanddin Ahmad in Urdu, Hindi translation by Anil Joshi under the title *Mewat Ka Itihas* (Alwar, 1989), pp. 51-52.
2. For details see chapter 2.
3. *Murraqa-i-Mewat*, p. 53.
4. *Baburnama*, p.573. Highly controversial view given by modern sholars on the origin of the Khanzadas that they were originally Gujars . . . and are said to have teken their rise from the issues of the Pathans' intercourse with Gujar women. Khan is the title which every Pathan (or Afghan) assumes; hence Khanzada, the Khan's offspring, or litterally sons. See *The People of Hindustan* edited by J. Forbes Watson and John William Kaye, Vol. 7, reprent Delhi, 1987) at serial No. 347.
5. *Alwar Ank*, p. 58.
6. Anil Joshi, *Alwar Darshan* (Alwar, 2004), p. 33.
7. Cunningham, pp. 120–21. See Powlett pp. 155-57 for more details.
8. *Arjang-i-Tijara*, pp. 52–53.
9. Anil Joshi, *Alwar At A Glance* (Alwar, 1988), p. 17.
10. Cunningham, pp. 115-17. There is a controversy about the tomb. tomb which is incorrect. The author has argued ari's tomb, it could have the resting places of the Hindus not the Muslims. Secondly, Bhartihari was the brother of the king Vikramajit of Ujjain who never ruled Mewat and never visited Tijara. Moreover his regime is much older than the Khanzadas. There is folksay that there was a saint named Bhartari who worked as a labourer for this tomb and never accepted wages for his labour as per his guru's order. Since he was doing all this without any money, hence the name of the tomb was called after his name. See *Murraqa-i-Mewat*, p. 137.
11. Powlett, pp. 129–32.
12. Ibid., pp. 118–19. *Arjang-i-Tijara* makes mention of a well which was famous for its sweet water far and wide (p. 49). The writer of *Murraqa-i-Mewat* too highly speaks of this well and informs that this well was constructed by Nahar Khan Khanzada. Suraj Mal Jat, the ruler of Bharatpur had great admiration for this well. About this well he said that if this well could be shifted to Bharatpur he could have unearthed it and taken to his capital. The well is located enroute from Tijara to

Nagina (pp. 130-31).

13. Cunningham pp. 119-20. According to the author of *Murraqa-i-Mewat* the *qasba* of Bahadurpur was populated by Bahadur Khan son of Bahadur Nahar and gave his name to the city (p. 141). The fort of Bahadurpur been very strong and famous in the past. See *Arjang-i-Tijara,* p. 53.
14. Ibid, pp. 127–29. The author of *Murraqa-i-Mewat* informs that Firoze Khan son of Bahadur Khan son of Bahadur Nahar populated it and gave his name to the city. Since near to the city there is a spring or jhir, hence it is called Firozepur Jhirka (p. 141). Recently a small book in Hindi *Firozepurjhirka: Itihas ke jharokhe se* (2002) by Tara Chand Bansal on the basis of the local miyth tells us that the earliest city Firozepurjhirka was actually located in the west in the hills and was called Bhond, two kilometers from the present walled city. Bhond in Mewati language means remnants. During Aurangzeb's period it was destroyed and the population shifted in side the walled area (p. 11)
15. Cunningham, pp. 133–34.
16. Ibid., pp. 134–35 and Powlett, pp. 134-35. According to *Murraqa-i-Mewat* the fort was built a fresh in the period of Jalal Khan where he used to oppose Saiyyad Mubarah Shah. There were about 14-15 tombs of the Khanzada chiefs. It is believed that earlier the fort was like the fort of Alwar built of stones only, p.
17. Cunningham, pp. 135–37 and Powlett, p. 7.
18. *Murraqa-i-Mewat,* p. 130.
19. Cunningham, pp. 137-38.
20. Ibid., pp. 129–30 and *Baburnama,* p. 580. Also see *The Baburnama: Memoirs of Babur, Prince and Emperor,* Translated and annotated by Wheeler M. Thackston (Oxford University Press, 1996), p. 389.
21. Ibid., p. 130.

10

Lesser—Known Sources of Regional History: A Case Study of *Arjang-i-Tijara* *

Being near to the seats of government viz. Delhi, Jaipur, Agra, Bharatpur, the region of Mewat has always been important in the Indian History and had a great influence over the political activities of the country. There is hardly any coherent history of the region available to us however, some references to the region can be noticed in some historical writings.

Arjang-i-Tijara by Shaikh Muhammad Makhdum is perhaps the first in this direction which deals with the regional history from the Mahabharata's time till the year of its writing in 1878 AD. Anil Joshi has made the Hindi translation of the book and I have used the same for my purpose of writing this paper.

It was written keeping in view to know about our ancestors

*Presented at a National Seminar on "Historical Sources and Historiography of Rajasthan : New Perspectives" organized by the Centre for Rajasthan Studies, University of Rajasthan, Jaipur, held on 11-12 February, 2011. Revised version of this paper was presented again at a National Seminar on "Sources of Medieval India: Chronicles, Literature, Architecture, Paintings, Epigraphs and Coins" (12-14 March, 2011) organized by the Centre of Advanced Study, Department of History, Aligarh Muslim University, Aligarh.

and their lives, relations among other castes and their living standard in the past. Since the history is the medium to seek such knowledge, hence, the tahsildar Sahib made an attempt to record the historical events of Tijara region i.e. Mewat on the basis of his own experiences, available some historical literature and the prevailing traditions among its people. Major P.W. Powlett seems to have borrowed information mostly from Tehsildar Sahib and gives a detailed historical account of Tjara in his *Gazetteer of Ulwar* (pp. 129-32).

In the beginning of the book Tehsildar Sahib on the basis of the Hindus' belief talks about the foundation of the *qasba* Tijara in the year 5000 B.C. To support this belief the people refer one Susharmajit a king of Sarhatta in Duryodhana's period, whose successor Tej Pal happened to be in this area during his hunting venture. Seeing the region fertile and useful for settlement, he made it his capital, giving the name *targajnag* which means the place of three forts. Later the place became famous as Tijara.

The author questions this theory in the light of one *Tarikh-i-Mirat-i-Masudi* and argues that since no ancient remains are found, in or around the city. It was founded by one Tej Pal, brother of Tahan Pal, the ruler of Rewari. He accepted Islam during the campaigns of Shihabuddin Muhammad Ghori in the end of the 12th century and was renamed as Jalal Khan with the title Khanzada. Hence the foundation of that city of Tijara could be placed in the 11th century.(p. 2).

Next follows the description of the Khanzadas, who had been a very powerful race to be reckon with by the Sultans of Delhi during medieval period till Babur's establishing the Mughal Empire in the country. The account seems to be on the basis of the medieval Persian chroniclers which deal with the role of the Khanzadas in the then politics. The author on the basis of the *pothis* of *Jaga Khanzadas* makes us to understand that Sambhar Pal was given the title of Bahadur

Nahar by Firoz Shah Tughluq, as he had killed a lion (*nahar* in Mewati language) in a single attempt of his sword.

The word 'Khanzada' invites the attention of the author on the basis of other theories which need to be verified from the contemporary literature if available. The account about the origin of this race is interesting. According to the author the conversion of Sambhar Pal into Islam is based on two grounds. First, that Sambhar Pal voluntarily accepted Islam by Nasiruddin *Chirag-i-Dehlawi.* Secondly, on the basis of one *pushtnama Khanzada,* he was a plunderer and for the fear of to be made captive by the royal army, he turned into Islam. Here author gives a statement whosoever was converted into Islam, was given the title of Khanzada. He refers *Tarikh-i-Ferishta* makes mention of one lakh Khanzadas under Firoze Shah Tughlak who were converted into Islam and were given this title. (p.3) But it needs further investigation as *Tarikh-i-Ferishta,* hardly refers to such an event.

Bahadur Nahar became very powerful during the fourteenth century in the Mewat region having the fort of Kotila under his control. There are references of princes of Delhi seeking shelter at Kotila and to seek his support for gaining the throne of Delhi. There is also a reference of presenting two white parrots to Timur by Bahadur Nahar. The author does not mention his sources of information. But it, seems to be based on the Persian chroniclers of this period including the autobiography of Timur.

Hasan Khan Mewati did not attract much attention of the author who mentions him in just a passing reference. According to the author he supported Rana Sanga against Babur with 10,000 cavalary-men. (Babur in his autobiography rather mentions Hasan Khan Mewati in some details). *Arjang-i-Tijara* describes the Afghan rule in India. There is an anecdote of Bahlol Lodi's birth that how he was born after the death of his mother due to a wall-collapse. Later how he was blessed by a *faqir* to become the ruler. He annexed the Mewat region and gave it to Tatar Khan including Tijara. The tomb of Tatar Khan was located to the east of Tijara. When Sikandar Lodi succeeded the throne, Tijara was granted to Alam Khan. He founded the city of Alawalpur in the middle of the hills. He got constructed a dam, *baoli* and a bridge over a stream in the north of the city. It is believed that he also got built Bhartari's tomb. There are other buildings in his memory located around the city (9-10).

Under the account of the Timurid, the author makes a mention of Mewat which was granted to Hindal by his brother Humayun, the son and succeesor of Babur. He got built a palace and a mosque. The mosque remained incomplete due to Sher Shah's revolt. In this work many references to different buildings are found. A brief account of the conflict between Humayum and his brothers is also mentioned (12-13).

The author mentions that Akbar the great Mughal ruler married the daughter of Hasan Khan's brother which is not correct (see chapter 12). The emperor organized the land and introduced many reforms. He appointed different officers at different level. Tijara was divided into 18 parganas which were registered as *sarkars.* According to the author Tijara was under Suba Delhi. Seven *havelis* which were given to Mirza Hindal have been registered as *Haveli* Tijara in the Mughal records.

Arjang-i-Tijara gives us a very interesting account of the *mazar* or tomb of one Ghazi Gaddan Sahib who was very miraculous person. Akbar used to visit his dargah. He had granted a land free grant for the maintenance of this dargah and 1 1/4th paise for lightening the lamp. There used to be held a fair in his memory as '*Shah Gaddan Sahib ka mela*'. The account of the Mughals is highlighted only when the references of Tijara or Mewat occur. Hence the book reaffirms that book is basically a history of Tijara or Mewat. The author refers to Peshwa Baji Rao who had reached Mewat and made a plundering. The same way Churaman

Jat of Bharatpur also plundered the region. He destroyed Alawalpur and Tijara including good old buildings. However, the efforts of Muhammad Shah brought back the peace and prosperity of Tijara and Mewat. After his death we witness the decline of the Mughals and no law and order in Mewat (pp. 14-15).

The author provides, a list of the rural villages under five heads :- name of the real *mauza, mauza dakhili* and other three (without entry). There were 118 *mauzas* in total recorded under the Mughals (15-19). With the decline of the Mughals, the Jats of Bharatpur became powerful and made their expansion towards Mewat. Suraj Mal got constructed a fort at Kishan Garh. He was a true follower of one Malik Mian Muradshah Sahib of Hasanpur near Tijara and believed in his miracles. Therefore he got built a palace for him and made Hasanpur tax free village. After the death of Muradshah his seat was held by his successor Mian Dayamshah (p. 19).

In between Najibudaula Rohilla with the support of the Marathas had succeeded in bringing Nawab Najab Khan on the throne of Delhi. He got hold over Mewat by evacuating the region from the Jats. Afterwards Marathas by defeating the Mughals made their control over Mewat. Reference of black grams to be used in the battle after some religious ritual making miracle, is of interest which shows how, the superstitions were prevalent among the people (p. 21).

After the Marathas, the British controlled the region of Mewat. A brief discussion about the origin of the Meos has been made. Tehsildar Sahib agrees to the theory of their Rajput origin and believes that they also originated from Meenas whose gotras and Pals are common. However, some Jadon Rajput mixed with the Meos had created a separate gotra 'Gotwal Meo'.

"The region took 'Mewat' its name from the Meos. They are divided into 12 *gotras* and 52 *palas.* Those do not figure among those twelve pals they are called Nepali. The Meos follow Hindu customs and do not merry in their own pal. They are Muslims only in the name and there is no prohibition for *namaz* and observing *rozas.* They also get their body tattooed like other communities in the region" (pp. 24-25).

The following pages deal with the kings of Alwar from its founder Partap Singh till the period of Maharaja Sheodan Singh when British appointed their political agent in the Alwar state. In the beginning the author tells us how Maharaja Pratap Singh with his statesmanship got hold of different areas of Mewat and established his control over the Alwar fort which was earlier the seat of Nikumbha Rajputs and taken over by the Khanzada Alawal Khan who got built this fort. After the death of Hasan Khan the successor of Alawal Khan, the Mughals took over the control of the fort. With the decline of the Mughals, the Jats came into power and got hold of the fort. They failed to pay the salary of the *qiladar* for about a year. They handed over it again to Pratap Singh who paid them the dues. The city of Alwar was founded and Tripolia was constructed during his reign with a big bazaar with roads on the four sides. A palace was also built inside the fort. Pratap Singh had no issue hence he adopted Bakhtawar Singh as his son who succeded him after his death.[1]

Maharaja Bakhtawar Singh had to face certain difficulties while establishing his claim over the throne. He had to sacrifice some parganas to the Jaipur State and had to be satisfied with the title of Maharaoraja which was conferred on the imperal nobels. The sheikhs who were supporting Pratap Singh, raised their heads against Bakhtawar Singh under their leader one Ilahi Bakhsh who was later killed in a battle. And this juncture we witnessed the rise of Ahmad Bakhsh Khan as a *vakil,* who with his statesmanship brought Bakhtawar Singh and the British together as friends. This friendship resulted into the ouster of the Marathas from Mewat in the year 1803 AD. The Maharaja is known for his love for constructing palaces and forts at different places.[2]

Bakhtawar Singh had one daughter Chand Bai and a son

Balwant Singh from his queen named Musi who belonged to a Meo family. After his death his son Balwant Singh was to succeed to the throne but some nobels wanted to bring his brother Banne Singh to succeed. It resulted into a struggle for power between the nobels and the Meo community who were Muslims. With the intervention of Nawab Ahamd, both were declared equally succeesors. But this agreement could not work for more than three years. It led conspiracies which made Bakhtawar Singh merely as a pensioner and was decided that whosoever died without a mail child the second would succeed the whole territory. Though Bakhtawar Singh was blessed with a son, but died after thirteen months. Bakhtawar Singh too died soon and it paved way for Banne Singh as an undisputed ruler in the region. He made attempts for the welfare of the state and its people. Criminal courts were opened and judges were appointed. Separate civil judicial courts were established. In between the assets and jagirs of late Bakhtawar Singh were included in the Alwar state.

In his period the palace of Alwar took a majestic look with the construction of *Diwan-i-Khas*. The *Dungri* too was beautified. Siliser dam with a canal was constructed for the irrigation purpose. In addition *Vinay Vilas* palace, *Lal darwaza, Hazoori darwaza, Peel khana, Rath khana* and a number of *chhatries* were erected which made Alwar as one of the beautiful cities of Rajputana and could be compared with Kashmir. The Maharaja had the galaxy of renowned wrestelers, dancers and artists in his court. It is through *Arjang-i-Tijara* that we come to know that the Maharaja of Alwar was with the British during the 1857 revolt. He sent an army to assist the Britishers towards Agra. They met with a great loss on their way because of the Meos creating havoc in the region. Later on he sent one Munshi Ammujan to Firozepur Jhirka for maintaining law and order. In result of such actions of the Maharaja the burden on the financial exchequer increased. In the meantime the Maharaja had a paralytical attack and succumbed to it. He was succeeded by his son Sheodan Singh.

Sheodan Singh seems to be a poor administrator who could not control the local feuds and ultimately Britishers had to appoint one Mr. Nixon Sahib who was their political agent at Bharatpur to inquire into the affairs of the Alwar state. After submitting the report, Captain Impti was appointed as political agent of Alwar. He proved to be a successful administrator and introduced various reforms in the state. He is known for the construction of the court complex, hospital and a road between Alwar and Tijara.

The author of *Arjang-i-Tijara* gives a detailed account of the celebrations on the occasion of a male birth in the royal family of Alwar. He states that on the birth of his son, Maharaja Sheodan Singh remained busy in throwing his wealth through donations to the poor both Hindus and Muslims and also holding frequent banquets. In the court dancing and music parties became the main feature of these ceremonies day and night. Nobody needed any permission to attend such parties. The passage between the palace and the Moti Dungri palace was decorated with lights. The city was full of fair and festivities. The Maharaja invited the Prince of Duke of Eden from Calcutta. The lavish expenditure on such functions and on the stay of the prince brought bankcrupcy. Mr. Thomas Cadel was appointed to take the stock of the situation who later stopped these celebrations and took law and order in his hands. The Maharaja once again became a pension-holder and whole state-affairs came under the British agent.

The book gives a brief description of Mr. Cadel and his administration in the Alwar state. The Maharaja was sanctioned Rs. 50,000 per month as his pension. The author of the book admires the action of Mr. Cadel and credited him for bringing back the prosperity of the state. He admires him for completing many projects in the state which include road construction, postal system and hospitals (pp. 25-44).

In the end, Tehsildar Sahib describes famous places of the region including the places of interest i.e. palaces, forts, temples, mosques, tombs, dams, bridges etc. The list of these places contains the details of the cities and *qasbas* Tijara, Alwar, Ram Garh, Govind Garh, Laxman Garh, Raj Garh, Thana Ghazi, Bahror, Mumdawar, Kishan Garh, Bansur etc.

References

1. Partap Singh spent his life on the back of horse fighting various enemies and was successful in expanding his kingdom. He was well-read in Hindu classics and politics. For more details, see a special issue of *Vinay's Alwar Ank* published by Raj Rishi College, Alwar, 1969, pp. 26-27.
2. The Britishers in lieu of the support granted the region of Rath, Neemrana, Haryana, Kishan Garh and Tijara to Bakhtawar Singh. He consolidated the Alwar State and also took to its expansion. For details, see *Alwar Ank*, p. 27.

11

Alwar Ank of *Vinay*: A Survey of History and Culture of Mewat

More than forty year ago, Rajrishi College, Alwar in Rajasthan, made a plan to prepare and publish an exclusive Alwar issue through its annual magazine *Vinay*. Ultimately it saw the light of the day in 1969. This special issue contains the heritage of Alwar through out its history and culture since ancient times. It is significant to know the past and present both of the Alwar state and the city. The editorial page of the book highlights its importance for the readers.

The *Alwar Ank* is divided into three parts : History, Art, Literature and Culture, Political and Economic issues. More than thirty scholars have contributed invaluable material on these aspects which are really significant as far as their nature is concerned. These papers are based on the well-researched minds and experiences of the writers and are useful for the scholars working on the history and culture of the Alwar state and Mewat region. I have gone through the pages of this issue, and the quality of the papers compelled me to write a note on the contents of the book.

The book contains three sections. First section. *Itihas ka dard* has seven articles with two to four sub-sections each. The second section has five chapters some carrying sub-sections also. The last part of the book has nine chapters without sub-sections. There is an appendix showing important dates, a bibliographical survey and exclusive list of Alwar literature.

The first part of the book begins with a map which looks like a mustard-bag. Mohar Singh Yadav therefore titles his paper, 'Geography and mustard-bag'. The chapter seems to be an introductory one. In this article the author gives very briefly the geographical features of Alwar state which includes Aravalli ranges, steppes and deserts, scattered all over the region. The dense forests are the dens of wild animals, birds and trees. Ruparel, a rainy river, is the only river of the state. The main crops of the region are wheat, barley, maze, *bajra, jawar* and mustard (pp. 9-12).

Second chapter deals with three main communities of the region viz. the Rajputs, Meos and Minas, written by Jagner Singh, Ilyas Khan Gorewal and Bhawani Singh Pankaj. There had been hundreds of communities in the region but these three remained prominent because of their role in historical times.

Jagner Singh while dealing with the Rajputs claims their origin from the Raj-putra or son of a king who associated themselves with the *kshatriyas.* In Alwar state there were three main branches of the Rajputs which remained dominant-Badgujar, who were predominant under the Gurjar-Pritiharas rulers of Kannauj in Macheri (Matsya), Raj Gargh (Vyaghraj), Rajorgarh (Paranagar) and Devti during 9th to 16th centuries. The famous Ishwar Mal refused to accept the suzerainty of the Mughals hence their power was destroyed by Akbar and now almost non-existence.

The author briefly surveys the Chauhans who had been prominent in many villages of Mundawar, Behror and Bansur tehsils of Alwar. The Chauhans had been more dominant during Prithviraj Chauhan's period who ruled the vast region between Delhi and Ajmer (pp. 12-14).

The author in the last, touches the Kushwaha Rajputs who traced their origin from the Suryavanshi Kush, son of Lord

Rama. Their successors were called Narukas, Rajawats and Shekhawats. The Kushwahas appeared on the scene in the Alwar region during 13th century. As far the Alwar state is concerned the Naruka branch of the Kushwahas Rajputs had been significant, as they successfully ruled over the regions about two centuries (pp. 14-15).

Iiyas Khan Gorewal's essay on the Meos is important as it deals not only with the origin of the Meos, their role in the region as a ruling class but also showing their dominance in the present day-to-day socio-cultural and political activities. The author on the basis of Alexander Cunningham's account provides a list of their twelve *pals*. He agrees with Cunningham on the issue of Meo-Mina as one community who had adopted agriculture and plundering as their profession. The Meos still feel proud of being one of the ancient communities of the country though Muslims. It is really appreciable that the author highlights the contribution of the Meos in building of various temples in the region. They also donate on certain occasions for mosques as well as temples. They are real carriers of Hindustani culture (pp. 15-21).

Bhawani Singh Pankaj in his essay on 'Minas' informs how they had been dominating certain areas of Dausa, Amer and Khoh in Rajputana before 11th century. They lost their control over this region during medieval period and were compelled to adopt plundering as their profession. The author hints upon the Shashbadni, the daughter of Bada Mina who was married to the son of a famous Meo Todar Mal to show how the Meo-Mina were one community. There prevails a full folksong *baat of Sasbadni*, sung by the folksingers and rejoiced by the Meos and Minas both in the region. After independence in the year 1947 the Minas adopted agriculture as their profession and took interest in educating themselves. They had been dominant in Thana Ghazi Tehsil of Alwar district till Akbar's time who later crushed them and destroyed Kyara, the capital of the Minas. To this date

'Kyara poora hua' a saying applied to any destruction or calamity. Hence Rajputs, Meos and Minas had been very prominent in the historical period of Alwar or Mewat required such attention (pp. 21-22).

Pinaki Lal Joshi's article seems to be a part of his book *History of Alwar* (in Hindi). The chapter describes very briefly the history of the region under the sub-sections Ancient period, Medieval period and Modern period. The Ancient section explains that on the basis of *Puranas* the region was under the rule of Hiranyak or Hiryankshipu whose grandsons on Daityaraj gave the region in charity to one of his commander Madhu. The successors of Madhu lost it to the Suryavanshi which later came under one Mastil before Mahabharata's time who gave his name to the region as Matsya and constructed a town Macheri as his capital. The king Virat, the grandson of Matsya built another town and gave his name as Viratnagar. The Pandavas spent their exile in the deep forests located in between Birat and Matsya. During this period one Susharmajit founded Sarahatta near Tijara or Trigart which also belongs to Mahabharta's time. Hence during the ancient period, region had three important towns, Tijara in the north, Matsyapuri in the south and Virat in the west, from where the governance was done.

The reports of *Archiological Survey of India,* part XX, give a brief survey of the early medieval period under the Yaduvanshis and the Gurjar-Pritihara rulers. The southern part of Alwar came under the Badgujars and western part under the Nikumbhas. Later Prithviraj Chauhan annexed the Nikumbha's territories and assigned to his family.

Around thirteenth century Alwar region came into contact with the Muslims and according to the author compelled the people to embrace Islam. Firoze Tughlak got converted number of communiies into this new regligion. Meos who were earlier Hindus, became Muslim.The Yadav as of Tahangarh became Muslims in large number and were known as Khanzadas who played important role in the history of Alwar. Alawal Khan Khanzada took over the Alwar fort in his hand and got built a boundary around the fort. His son Hasan Khan became very famous person.

The author very briefly surveys the Mughal Era and begins the modern period with the foundation of Alwar state by Pratap Singh who carved out his kingdom from the states of Jaipur and Bharatpur. In the year 1770 Rajgarh was made as the capital, Mughal emperor Shah Alam gave him the title of Rao Raja with a mansab of 5000 horsemen. Rao Raja diplomatically dealt with the Marahattas, Mughals and the Jaipur state and spent his whole life on the horse back.

Pratap Singh was succeeded by his son Bakhtawar Singh at the age of twelve years. Supporting the cause of the British against the Marhattas, he was well rewarded and the Alwar state extended its boundaries. After his death Rani Musi, a Meoni queen became *sati* with him for his son's right as a legal successor whose *chhatri* is still worth noticing in the Alwar palace.

Vinay Singh succeeded at a time when Mughal empire was in the process of its decline. Balwant Singh son of Rani Musi had a conflict with Vinay Singh for the throne. With the intervention of the British, Balwant Singh got the northen part of the state and made Tijara as his capital. Vinay Singh proved a good administrator and established a court which disbursed justice on the basis of religion. Till 1838 Hindi dominated in the day to day administration. Many officers from Delhi joined the services of Vinay Singh who promoted Persian language. The Maharaja supported the British during 1857 revolt and after few days, he died. Due to his interest in art he spent largely on the palace and constructing *Vinay-Vilas.* The economic conditions of the people of the state became poor.

Vinay Singh was succeeded by Sheodan Singh who was famous for his love for music. His court became a centre of musicians and dancers. He led a luxurious life which resulted into the economic crisis. It gave the British to intervene in the state affaris. Major Cadel was appointed as the political agent who took certain measures to improve the economy. British currency was introduced during this period. Maharaja died in 1874 AD.

Sawai Mangal Singh succeeded Sheodan Singh at the age of 15 years. He studied Hindi as well as Urdu and English. In 1877 there was a nation-wide famine, and the Raja liberally helped he victims. He was lover of conversing with the scholars and the Brahmins. Viveknand came to Alwar in his period. The Raja spread education and did welfare for his subjects. He died at the age of 33 years.

Jai Singh succeeded the throne of Alwar on 10th December, 1903. He became famous for declaring Hindi as state-language and establishing Raj Rishi College in the city. He brought many social reforms including banning child-marriage and old age-marriage. Heavy tax was imposed on the antoxicated items. The economic condition of the state improved. After the death of Jai Singh, Sawai Tej Singh succeeded him and ruled the state till its amalgamation in the Indian Republic (pp. 23-30).

The fourth chapter deals with the major towns of the state which witnessed the history under the title "*Nagar Jinko Itihas ne Dekha*". It includes four towns viz. Matsyapur, Raj Garh, Tijara and Alwar. These are dealt by Jeewan Singh, Narain Singh Dewan, Luxmi Narain Jain and jointly by Narain Singh and Jai Singh Neeraj respectively. The authors make attempts to highlights the historical and cultural significance of these towns (pp. 30-42).

The next chapter relates to the rock-edicts of Tasai by P.L. Chakrovarti and Rajor Garh by Brahm Datt. Tasai is located on the Alwar-Bharatpur road and now is a modern village. According to the author this edict belongs to V.S. 182 which could be of 8th century AD. As far as the Rajor Garh edicts are concerned, one of the edicts is preserved in the National Museum, belonging to the period of Maharaja Mahipal Dev of Gurjar-Pratihara dynasity dated 922-23 AD. The second edict is significant which furnishes information regarding the destruction of a temple due to an earthquake (pp. 42-47).

Sixth chapter contains the biographical sketches of historical personalities of the state. Among the schlolars, Akhtar Husain deals with Hasan Khan Mewati, Dr. Jai Raj Neeraj writes about Sawai Vinay Singh, Narayanvir Singh about Sawai Jai Singh and Ramesh Arya with Alabande Khan Saheb.

Out of these four personalities the last one is about Alabande Khan who was a famous musician of his times and had great respect in the court of Jai Singh. His elder brother Zakiruddin Khan Saheb was a court musician at the court of Udaipur (pp. 47-58).

Chapter-VII 'In the lap of nature and history' contains the description of the famous Bala Qila, Silised, Tal-tree, Bhartrihari, Pandu Pol and Narain ji etc. written by Mohan Lal Vijay Vargia, Raghuvir Singh and Shikhar Chand Jain. These places are important for their historical background as well as a tourist attraction (pp. 58-66).

Second part of the book is entitled 'literature art and culture'. This includes chapters on Literature, Paintings, Music, Architecture and Culture. Chapter I of this part includes twelve sections on various titles like: Bhakti tradition, *Riti Kalin* and *Arvachin* tradition, period of *shairi*, folk literature, languages and the speeches, literary institutions, Oriental Institutes, State Museum, *Sirjun and Singim, Din ke Ujale mein Alwar, Raat ki bahon mein Alwar.* This chapter is in full length of 87 pages providing the scholars almost all the details regarding the culture of Alwar by different authors.

Chapter-II deals with the Alwar style of painting which originated in the state under the Naruka rulers during 19th century. Jai Singh Neeraj has taken pain in describing this aspect of the region and also added some pictures of this style depicting the court dancers, one *Haveli* and dancers doing their make up. The temples and *chhatris* of Alwar contain number of paintings, depicting the characters of Rama and Krishna. These paintings are on subjects like court's *mehfils*, natural environments in which Sufis and Saints, religious congregations are shown. They also depict *Rag Ragini*, pictures from *Mahabharta, Geeta, Ramayana, Brahamanas* etc. Alwar style is the best example of Irani, Mughal and Rajasthani style in a balanced manner. Oily and bright colours are the chief features of Alwar style of paintings. The author refers Shri Ram Sahai Nepalia, Vishnu Sharma, Shri Ballabh Das Verma, Dr. P.L. Mathur in connection with the modern painting (pp. 150-158).

Chapter-III entitled 'Music', contains two sections viz. tradition of folk music and feudal music by Dr. Jai Singh Neeraj and Prof. Prakash Chand Jaiuran. Both these music traditions have made recognition at a national level. Folk-music can be divided into (A) Alibaksh *Khyal*, (B) *Ratwai*, (C) *Turra Kalangi*, (D) *Dhapli Raag*, (E) *Rane Doom, Mirasi, Natni-Berari, Koli* and songs of *Kalbelias*. Alibaksh was born in the 19th century and was a lover of music. His music was full of devotions. He created nine *khyals*. His manuscripts of *khyals* are preserved in the Alwar museum.

Ratwai belongs to the Meo-community and has its own cultural significance. *Turra Kalangi* belongs to folk-play music which was promoted by the English. It is believed that *Turra Kalangi* tradition belongs to the saints Tukungiri and Shah Ali of Agra who used to sing throughout the night. *Turra* is a symbol of Shiva and *Kalangi* of Parvati. This tradition could be witnessed in the stage-dramas of Bhakt Puran Mal, Rao Raja Kevat, Raja Risalu, Harish Chandra etc.

Dhapli Raag is very common in Alwar, sung by a musical group in a competitive form. It is basically a copy of the classic music in a village form.

Rane, Doom, Mirasi etc. are the product of some communities of Alwar and adopted as their profession. Due to the influence of feudal Rajput culture they perform their music on certain occasions like birthday, marriage etc. Dancing and music as a profession among the Meos is on decline which oblige them to sing on the filmy tunes.

The feudal music tradition is based on the tradition of

the court music of the Mughal court and adopted by the Indian states. Vinay Singh had in his court classic music signers who enhanced the beauty of the court during various festival like Holi, Dushehra, Diwali and the marriages, birthdays in the royal families. This tradition of patronizing music was followed by successors kings of Alwar. It resulted into the establishment of *Kala Bharati* in 1943 to promote such arts (pp. 158-166).

The fourth chapter is on art and architecture divided into four sections viz. medieval art by Jai Singh Neeraj, Pathan and Mughal art by Vallabh Das Verman, Rajput art by Jeevan Singh. The Modern architecture has been dealt by Narain Veer Singh. Medieval period witnessed the main architectural movement of Alwar at different places. These include mostly Jain and Shiva temples including the edicts of Rajor Garh or Para Nagar. A good number of idols also find reference. The photos include 16 feet high of Jain *Tirthankar* at Naugaza, *Lachho ki Deori* or the artistic gate of Neelkanth, *Sheesh Mahal* of Rajgarh fort and *Sheesh Mahal of Dewan ji ki Haveli.* The places like Tal Vriksh, Saithali and Bhangarh are also famous for their temples.

Under the Pathan and Mughal period, tomb of Tripolia, Fatehjang and *Khan-i-Khana* (now only ramnants) and many buildings were constructed by the then rulers which are rich heritage of Alwar.

A small note on Rajput Architerture by Jeevan Singh throws light on various forts, *baolis, daris, chhatris* with special reference to *Musi Rani ki chhatri* which, are good example of this period. Same way a note on the modern Architerture includes the modern building viz. Vijay Mandir, Sariska-palace, which have influence of the western architecture (pp. 167-173).

The fifth chapter on 'Culture' by Prof. Om Prakash Dargan concerns with the communities viz. the Rajputs, Meenas, Meos and Ahirs who migrated during the partition but highlights the last one who contributed in the mixed culture of Alwar. Contemporary king Tej Singh did a great task in rehabiliting the migrants from the North-West and encouraged them to settle in the Alwar State. He got established number of camps and provided all facilities at Ram Garh, Kishan Garh, Khairthal, Tijara and Mundawar. The author provides a list of places where the migrants from Punjab, Kashmir and Sind settled permanently. But he has great appreciation for their contribution in various fields like trade, commerce and agriculture (pp. 174-80).

The last section is about the political and economic conditions of Alwar which have been dealt mostly by Prof. Jugmandir Tayal and rest by Prof. Shadi Lal Gupta and one by Jai Pal Singh. The chapter is basically a statistical one and provide various figures on different aspects of political and economic life of the people of Alwar. Nine tehsiles of Alwar on the basis of area and population make the district holding fourth position in the state. The figures have further been divided into male and female numbers in the district on the basis of religion, rural and urban areas. The daily life in the district during day time and evening has been dealt with full interest in which fairs and festivals of the districts are referred as the occasion of celebrations and recreations. A small section deals with the newspapers and magazines of the district which added to the awakening of the people. Some of these magazines earned reputation in the country. These were *Vinay, Arawali, Mahila Jagriti, Nishant, Kamla Sahtyki, Tej Pratap, Alwar Patrika, Sawatantra Bharat, Kisan Sathi, Naujawan, Aage Barho, Pehchan, Hira Moti* which, really reflect the people as lovers of literature.

Among the public institutions '*Arya Samaj*' was the first which was established in 1892 AD. Followed it *Sanatan Dharm Sabha* was founded in 1895 which, received financial support of Rs.300/- yearly from the government. In 1920 *Hindi Sahitya Samiti* was established which is now unknown. *Som Vanshiya Kshatriya Sabha* founded in 1922, played its role for the cause of the people during 1925-26 plague. *Hari Kirtan Samaj*, Jain Hospital, *Jain Mitra Mandal, Jat-Kshtriya Sewa Sangh* and many more caste-based institutions were created.

Many could not be registered and disappeared untimely. Others are still functional under different names.

The next section is on the political activities which began after the death of Jai Singh in 1937, on the issue of succession. In between the Congress has also established itself in the same year whose first President was Pandit Salig Ram and Inder Singh Azad. The party led some movements in the state. In the year 1939 Praja Mandal was also founded. Pandit Hari Narain Sharma became its first secretary. There is a continuous series of movements in the state till its merger in the federation of the country on the persuation of Sardar Patel who came to Alwar in Feb., 1948. Bharatpur, Alwar, Karauli and Dhaulpur were made the 'Matsya League' and Alwar as its capital. It became the part of Rajasthan in March 1949.

In the middle of the twentieth century Alwar witnessed many rise and falls. Many political parties played their role and governed the district. Alwar made many developments in the field of agriculture, education and other fields. In the field of education, the role of Raj Rishi College has well been discussed. There are detailed informations about 'Sariska Wild-life Sanctury' and mineral products of the region. After independence Alwar has contributed more in the agriculture and industrial developments.

In the end, an appendix provides important dates since the establishment of Alwar state by Maharaj Pratap Singh in 1775 upto the year 1968, when the postgradute courses were restored in Raj Rishi College. In the last we find a very informative list of the books and literature on Alwar for the benefit of the scholars (pp. 232-36).

With such valuable contents of the *Alwar Ank*, there is a need to revise it further with the latest findings. The scholars working on the history and culture of Mewat can very-well depend on it for their basic knowledge of the region.

Appendix I

लाल दास की सवारी का पोस्टर

दोहा श्री लाल दास की सांची बात।
रिजक मौत साहिब के हाथ।।

श्री लालदास धर्म प्रचारक संघ
अलवर द्वारा प्रसारित
"वसवारी निकालने के उपलक्ष में'

सर्वलालदास प्रेमी सज्जनों और अन्य साधारण को सूचित किया जाता है कि बाबा लाल जी महाराज के मन्दिर ग्राम बांधोली में एक सवारी (मृतावस्था के समय लालदास जी के नाम पर जीवन दान मांगने के लिए बोली जाती है) का आयोजन दिनांक 9-3-1974 शनिवार प्रातः 10 बजे रखा गया है। यह सवारी लगभग 10 वर्ष पूर्व किसी लाला दास प्रेमी ने निकाली थी।

अतः आप लोगों से करबद्ध निवेदन है कि सवारी के महत्व को देखने के लिए अपने इस घोर कलियुग में बाबा लाल दास की महत्वत्ता जानने के लिए सादर आमन्त्रित हैं। आप लोगों से प्रार्थना है ज्यादा से ज्यादा लोगों में प्रचार करें तथा पधारने की कृपा करें।

प्रार्थी
रामचन्द्र नारेडिया
श्रीलालादास धर्म प्रचार संघ
अलवर (राज.)
मोदी रंगबिहारीलाल (ठाकुरिया)

मुकटलाल अग्रवाल
श्रीलालदास धर्म प्रचारक संघ
अलवर (राज.)

Appendix II

हिन्दु-मुस्लिम एकता के प्रतीक 'मेवात' के संत लाल दास (1540 ई.-1648 ई.)*

अरावली पर्वतमाला के पूर्व व पश्चिम में वे क्षेत्र जो हरियाणा व राजस्थान की सीमा बनाते हैं, मेव जाति का निवास है। मेव जाति के नाम पर ही इस इलाके को मेवात कहा जाता है। इस क्षेत्र में गुड़गावां अलवर व भरतपुर ज़िले के अनेक छोटे-बड़े कस्बे व गांव शामिल हैं। मेव लोग धर्म की दृष्टि से इस्लाम के अनुयायी हैं और अपने गैर इस्लाम भाइयों के साथ मिल-जुल कर रहते चले आ रहे हैं। भारत के इतिहास में हिन्दू मुस्लिम जातीय एकता का 'मेवात' एक अनूठा उदाहरण है।

हमारे देश के इतिहास में मध्यकाल सदा ही इतिहासकारों के लिए चर्चा का विषय रहा है। हमें यह नहीं भूलना चाहिए कि इसी काल में हिन्दुस्तान में अनेक सूफी व संत पैदा हुए थे जिन्होंने अपने प्रयत्नों व वाणी से भारतीय समाज में हिन्दू-मुस्लिम साम्प्रदायिक एकता पर बल दिया। इसमें मुख्य थे शेख मुइनुद्दीन चिश्ती, शेख निजामुद्दीन औलिया बाबा शेख फरीद, अमीर खुसरो, गुरू नानक, संत कबीर, दादू, मीरा आदि। इन सूफी संतों के प्रयास से ही प्रेमपूर्ण व उदार समाजिक वातावरण तैयार हुआ था जिसकी नींव पर अकबर जैसे महान शासक को सुलह कुल व राष्ट्रीय एकता का सपना साकार करने का अवसर मिला।

*भारत डोगरा द्वारा संगृहित एवं प्रकाशित *राष्ट्रीय एकता के पोस्टर*, नई दिल्ली, 1991

सूफी संतों की श्रेणी में अनेक ऐसे संत भी हुए हैं जिन्होंने हिन्दुस्तान के अनेक भागों में इस देश के निवासियों के बीच उन्हीं की भाषा में जातीय एकता का पाठ पढ़ाया। दिल्ली के दक्षिण में मेवात के संत लाल दास का नाम इस सम्बन्ध में विशेष रूप से उल्लेखनीय है। इनका जन्म 1540 ई. में अलवर के निकट धौली दूब गांव में एक मेव परिवार में हुआ। इसके पिता का नाम चांदमल व माता का नाम समदा था। ये बचपन से जंगल से सूखी लकड़ियां इकठ्ठी करके अलवर शहर में लाकर बेचते थे और अपना निर्वाह करते थे

जाति कहन की कहिए मेव,
लकड़ी बेचै, कोई लेव।
नित अलवर गढ़ बेचन जाये,
उद्यम करिकर उदर भराय।

लाल दास ने विवाह कर गृहस्थ जीवन व्यतीत किया। वे भीख मांगना बुरा मानते थे बल्कि लकड़यां बेच कर जो धन प्राप्त होता था उसमें से आधा निध र्निों में बांट देते थे।

जो कोई मांगे जाकौ देय
हिन्दू तुरक की भेंट न लेय

ऐसा विश्वास है कि लाल दास को 50 वर्ष की आयु के बाद ज्ञान हुआ और वे समाज के सभी वर्गों के लोगों की सेवा में जुट गए। उन्होंने बिना जात-पात व भेदभाव के दुखियों के दुख दूर किए। उनके आश्रम में दूर-दूर से लोग चाहे वे अमीर हों, चाहे गरीब, बड़ी श्रद्धा से आने लगे।

जात जो छत्तीसों धावै
राजा राणा सभी आवै
उत्तर तौ दक्खन धावै
पूरब व पच्छम आवै

लाल दास का देहान्त 108 वर्ष की आयु में 1648 ई. में शेरपुर नामक

गांव में हुआ जहां उनकी समाधि आज भी मौजूद है। लाल दास के अनुयायी लालदासी कहलाते हैं जिनमें हिन्दू व मुसलमान दोनों शामिल हैं। इनके अनुयायी अधिकतर अलवर, भरतपुर, मथुरा व गुड़गावां जिलों के रहते हैं जिनमें मेव, बनिया, जैन, कुम्हार, बढ़ई तथा अन्य स्थानीय समुदायों के लोग शामिल हैं।

हिन्दू तुरक दोऊ आए दारे
दुविध करै जो मूरख हारे

संत लाल दास की स्मृति में शेरपुर, धौली दूब व बांधौली नामक स्थानों पर समय-समय अनेक मेले लगते हैं जिनमें दूर-दूर से लोग सपरिवार शामिल होते हैं। इस अवसर पर एक बहुत बड़ी रोटी बनाई जाती है जिसे 'लालदास का रोट' कहते हैं। सभी धर्म, जाति व समुदाय के लोग इस रोट का प्रसाद बड़ी श्रद्धा से ग्रहण करते हैं।

संत लाल दास के शिष्य व भक्त 'साध' कहलाते हैं जिन्होंने लाल दास की शिक्षाओं का संग्रह किया। यह संग्रह 'लाल दास की वाणी' अथवा 'लाल दास के नुक्ते' कहलाता है जो हस्तलिखित पोथियों में अलवर, जयपुर व नागरी प्रचारणी सभा, वाराणसी के संग्रहालयों में सुरक्षित है। इनकी भाषा सीधी व सरल 'मेवाती' बोली है जिसमें बृज व राजस्थानी बोली का मिश्रण है। लाल दास के भक्त व शिष्य अपने गुरू की भांति गृहस्थी हैं और सादा व परिश्रम का जीवन व्यतीत करते हैं। भिक्षा मांगना अपना अपमान समझते हैं:

भगत भीख न मांगई
मांगत आवे शरम
घर घर हांडत दोष है
क्या बदशा (राजा) क्या हरम (राज परिवार)

इसकी अपेक्षा लाल दास के शिष्य रूखी-सूखी खाना और जमीन पर सोना बेहतर सयझते है।

साधू ऐसा चाहिए, रूखा खाये गरास (ग्रास)
ऊपर ओढ़े कामली, तले बिछावे घास

लाल दास केवल इन्सानी धर्म को मानते थे। उनके लिए हिन्दू व मुसलमान दोनों समान थे। यही कारण है कि लाल दास के शिष्य यानि साध न तो हिन्दू होते हैं और न ही मुसलमान। उनका विश्वास था कि यद्यपि हिन्दू व तुरक अलग-अलग धर्मो को मानने वाले थे, फिर भी दोनों का ईश्वर या साहब एक ही था:

हिन्दू तुरक को एकहि साहब
राह बणाई दोय अजायब

लालदासी पूर्ण शाकाहारी हैं और किसी प्रकार का तम्बाकू व मदिरा आदि का नशा नहीं करते। ये लाल दास की प्रशंसा में गीत व भजन गाते हैं और उनके बताए हुए मार्ग पर चल कर बिना किसी भेदभाव के साम्प्रदायिक सद्‌भावना से मिल-जुल कर रहते हैं:

लाल लाल सब बनत है दास बने न कोय,
दास बने जो लाल का लाल दास सम होय।
लाल दास सम होय जगत की माया जाने,
भेदभाव नहीं तनिक सभी को अपना जाने

अंत में लाल दास की एक सूक्ति प्रस्तुत है जो आज भी उतनी ही औचित्यपूर्ण है जितनी लाल दास के समय में थी:

कहै लाल साई को प्यारौ
श्रावण सुनो इक सबद हमारौ,
हिन्दू तुरक एक सो सूझै
साहब सब घठ एकहिं सूझै।

Appendix III

लाल दास की समाधि की जाँच रिपोर्ट

[illegible]

[illegible] (वे मन्दिर [illegible] [illegible]
[illegible] [illegible] [illegible]
हुये महाराज [illegible] और [illegible] मन्दिर [illegible] मुख्य [illegible]
[illegible] मसजिद के [illegible] और मुख्य मन्दिर के बाहर [illegible]

(यह सब [illegible] और [illegible]

और महंत [illegible] [illegible]
[illegible] के पश्चात [illegible] यह हिन्दू मुसलमान [illegible]
के बनाये हुये हैं [illegible] महन्त और [illegible] के [illegible]
तरफ [illegible] और [illegible] [illegible] (मैं वहां पर [illegible]

[illegible] (तो मैं [illegible] देखने में [illegible] बनाये हुये [illegible] और
[illegible] (यह [illegible] कोई मुसलमान ने [illegible]
[illegible] के पश्चात बनाया है [illegible]
[illegible] मसजिद का [illegible] क्योंकि [illegible] मसजिद का [illegible]
[illegible] मन्दिर [illegible] ([illegible]

[illegible] [illegible] [illegible]

[illegible] [illegible] [illegible]
[illegible] [illegible] [illegible]
[illegible] बना दिया ([illegible] मुख्य [illegible]
[illegible] (सीढ़ी) बना दी है ([illegible] मसजिद के [illegible]
[illegible] [illegible] मन्दिर की [illegible] है

[illegible] [illegible]
[illegible] [illegible] [illegible]
[illegible] (और [illegible]
[illegible] [illegible] है ([illegible]
[illegible] [illegible] [illegible]
([illegible] सन् [illegible] दफा [illegible] सी. पी. सी. के अनु
सार [illegible] [illegible]
[illegible] [illegible] ([illegible]
[illegible] [illegible]

[illegible] आदेश [illegible]

[illegible] और किया गया। जिसका उत्तर यह कहा गया कि यह स-
म्बन्धी फाईल जो केस नं० [illegible] ता० [illegible] रद्द कर दिये गये
हैं। यह हवाला इस मुकदमे को लिये पूरा है तमगढ़ थाने से भी
इस सम्बन्ध को कोई लेखा अभी तक नहीं है। जो मैंने वादी से

यह प्रश्न किया, हमने उसी समय [illegible] लालदासी कबसाकर

[illegible] तक उन्होंने कहा कि हमने डरके मारे
और [illegible] कागज में न समझकर [illegible] क्योंकि उस समय सासन
प्रबन्ध कमजोर था। यह बात नाकाफी होगा कि यह मठ न तो हिन्दुओं
का है और न मुसलमानों का है। बल्कि लालदासी अनुयाईयों का है।

चाहे वे कोई भी कौम के हों। [illegible] जो कोई इस्तापित [illegible]
गये हैं यह लालदासी पंथ के धर्म उपदेश और स्वतंत्रता के बिलकुल
इसलिये इनमें [illegible] करना पसन्द आवश्यकता है
इन [illegible] इनसार तो औ[illegible]

~~[illegible]~~ [illegible] जाती है।

आज्ञा अनुसार थोड़ा समय लेकर दोहराने में
निम्नलिखित बातें प्राप्त हुईं। सम्बन्धी जगह न तो हिन्दुओं की है
और न मुसलमानों की। [illegible] लालदासी अनुयाईयों की है।

यह [illegible] के मध्य में होता है और इसी तरह से दूसरे [illegible]
[illegible] अनुसार होते हैं और [illegible] पुलीस प्रबन्ध के लिये पुलिस पुर[illegible]
[illegible] जाती है। यह इस[illegible] कार होती है। इस [illegible]
[illegible] इस[illegible] तहसील [illegible] एक [illegible]
[illegible] आज्ञापत्र कागज[illegible]
[illegible] सब इसपेक्टर पुलीस [illegible]
[illegible] ३-३-३४ई० थाने [illegible] ने बरामद करने को लिखे जो आजाता है।
[illegible] ने यह [illegible] कानून प्रारम्भ [illegible]
[illegible] खां [illegible] ४-४-३४

[illegible]

[illegible] किया गया था। [illegible] उत्तर में [illegible]
[illegible] [illegible]
[illegible] [illegible]
[illegible] कोई [illegible] नहीं है। [illegible] वादी से

[illegible] हमने उसी [illegible] दस्तावेज [illegible]

[illegible] हिन्दू [illegible] नहीं थी [illegible] हमने [illegible]
और [illegible] में न [illegible] क्योंकि [illegible]
[illegible] कमजोर [illegible] नहीं होगा। कि [illegible] हिन्दुओं
को और मुसलमानों के है। कि लालदासी [illegible]
[illegible] कोई भी [illegible] है। [illegible] कोई [illegible]
[illegible] लालदासी [illegible] और स्वतंत्र [illegible] है।
इसलिये [illegible] है
[illegible] और [illegible]
[illegible] होती है।

आज्ञा अनुसार [illegible] लालदासों [illegible]
[illegible] प्राप्त हुई। [illegible] हिन्दुओं की है
और मुसलमानों की भी [illegible] लालदासी अनुयाइयों की है

यह [illegible] में होता है और इसी तरह [illegible]
[illegible] होते हैं जो [illegible]
[illegible] होती है। इस [illegible]
[illegible]
[illegible]
[illegible] [illegible] [illegible]
[illegible] [illegible]
[illegible] [illegible] कानून [illegible] है
[illegible] [illegible] –38

Appendix IV

लाल दास की समाधि के उत्तराधिकार के मुंसफी फैसले की फोटो कापी

(६) रहीम खाँ वल्द मौ... [illegible]
मेव उम्र करीब ५६ साल
रिटायर्ड फौजदार साकिन
फिरोजपुर जि॰ अलवर
मुद्दायलेहम

दावा बाबत इजराय हुक्म इम्तनाई
दवामी इस अमर का कि मुद्दायलेहम
लाल दासी सम्प्रदाय के धर्म के खिलाफ
मन्दिर श्री लाल दास जी वाके धोली दूब
में नमाज इबादत ~~कौम~~ व अजान
पढ़े जाना या दीगर तरीके इसलाम से
कोई काम न करे और लाल दासियों को
लाल दासी धर्म के अनुसार नित्य प्रति
की सेवा। पूजा पाठ करने में वो इससे-
सम्बन्धित उत्सव इत्यादि मनाने में किसी
किस्म की मजाहमत न करें।

निर्णय

वादी अपने प्रोक्सी सहित उपस्थित है प्रतिवादी
गण में से [illegible] नहीं है। [illegible] रेकार्ड [illegible] मुसा
मौजूद है पत्रावली को अवलोकन किया। [illegible]
नुवाद को अध्ययन किया जा चुका - आर्डर १ रूल ८
ज़ा॰ दी॰ के सिद्धान्तों पर भी विचार कर लिया गया।

२ - वादी गण का इरशाद यह है कि ग्राम धोली दूब निजामत
अलवर में प्राचीन काल से श्री लाल दास जी का एक
मन्दिर स्थित है जिस में लाल दास जी के माता पिता
की समाधी हैं, इस मन्दिर में सम्प्रदा से लालदासी

/ [illegible] सम्प्रदाय के अनुयायी अपने धर्म के अनुसार सेवा पूजा
आरती इत्यादि करते आ रहे हैं। मंदिर [illegible]
[illegible] की [illegible] अक्षर [illegible]
[illegible] पत्थरों में [illegible] हुआ है। लालदास
[illegible] दिया जिसके
अनुयायी हिन्दू व मेव मुसलमान दोनों जाति के [illegible]
हुए हैं। और मन्दिर श्री लाल दास जी [illegible]
[illegible] धर्म के अनुयायी [illegible]
[illegible] में सेवा पूजा पाठ आरती [illegible] करते चले
आये हैं जो हिन्दू धर्म की प्रणाली से मिलता जुलता है

(१) प्रातः [illegible] इत्यादि [illegible] सेवा [illegible]
[illegible] आरती गाई जाती है और [illegible]
[illegible] बजाया जाता है

(२) मध्यान्ह में १० बजे से १२ बजे तक भोग लगाया जाता है

(३) संध्या समय भजन व आरती गाई [illegible]
[illegible] घड़ियाल, नगाड़ा बजाया जाता है।

[illegible] प्रकार नित्य होने वाले सेवा पूजा के अतिरिक्त [illegible]
[illegible] इत्यादि होते रहते हैं वार्षिक
[illegible] इत्यादि उत्सव मनाये जाते हैं।

मन्दिर श्री लाल दास जी में [illegible] नमाज का पढ़ना, [illegible]
[illegible] व कुरान शरीफ पढ़ना या पढ़वाना [illegible]
[illegible] इबादत करना या दीगर इसलामी तरीके [illegible]
[illegible] करना [illegible]

नए मंदिर रखवाले पक्षों से अन्य वादियों पक्ष को
[illegible] इस्लामी ढंग से नमाज न पढ़ें आदि न लगावे।
इस्लामी [illegible] से ज़्यादा न करें अलावा
दोनों धर्म के अनुसार [illegible] की सेवा पूजा पाठ
आज्ञों के साथ करने में व उत्सव आदि मनाने में किसी
प्रकार मजाहमत न [illegible] मंदिर मजकूर की इमारत
में ख़लल अन्दाज़ न हो और [illegible] का अपना मंदिर
से हटाना नाजायज़ दावा मय ख़र्चे दिलाया जाए। इसके
अलावा [illegible] को मुद्दइयान ने [illegible] पृथक
प्रार्थनापत्र भी मुद्दइयान को दीगर [illegible] को
प्रतिनिधित्व के रूप में दावा दायर करने व मुद्दालेहम के
इन्हीं मजाहमत करने वालों के प्रतिनिधि के रूप
[illegible] दावा दायर करने की इजाज़त चाहते हुए और जिसपर
न्यायालय ने इजाज़त दी और आर्डर 1 रूल 8 [illegible] के
अनुसार दीगर सम्बन्धित जन की सूचना हेतु नोटिस [illegible]
[illegible] में प्रकाशित कराये और कोई ऐतराज़ किसी प्रकार
न होने पर दावा बतौर of Representative Suit
[illegible] मुद्दइयान भी Representative
Capacity में भी [illegible] भी दावा कर सकते थे अतः
[illegible] और [illegible] आवश्यकता ही है [illegible]
नहीं रहती है।

जवाब दीगर का उजर यह है कि मुद्दईयान लालदासी नहीं मजाज नालिश नहीं कोई मन्दिर लालदास धोलीदूब में वाक्ये नहीं है। मुद्दायलेहम जहाँ नमाज पढ़ते हैं अजां देते हैं वह इबादात मसजिद है और उन से मिले हुवे दादा चाँदमल व बादी समद की मजार आल व दीगर आम कबरिसतान इसलामी है जिन पर गैर इसलामी हरकात धारऊत व कानून मनाई— तो भी लालदासजी गैर मुसलिमान थे और उन्होंने इसलामी इबादात को बेजा आबरी रोका इस लिये लालदासी— इसलामिया उद्दामात [को बेजा] आबरी के माने होने के मजाज नहीं न गैर इसलामी हरकात करने के मुस्तहक है दावा बेरून मयाद है और मुद्दईयान का हलफनामा इन्कार है— दावा मय खर्चा खारिज किया जावे।

(२) दावे के बाद ही मुद्दईयान ने जेर आर्डर ३९ रूल १ व दफा ९४ [illegible] एक दरख्वास्त दौरान पेश करदी कि मुद्दायलान के खिलाफ आम जो हुक्म इम्तनाई इस— मन्शा से जारी कर दिया जावे कि वह मुद्दईयान की आरती सेवा पूजा में मजाहमत न करें और कुरान नमाज [illegible] [illegible] दौरान तहकीकात मुकदमात नई बात न करें— उसपर मुद्दायलान को नोटिस दिये जाकर ब— हस्स सुनकर ता० १८ [illegible] को न्यायालय ने जो आर्डर ३९ रूल २ आदि [illegible] प्रार्थना स्वीकार करते हुवे हुक्म इम्तनाई आरजी जारी किया— उसके अपील के

मैं व गिरधारी के दरम्यान मिसल अपील व हाई कोर्ट में
चली गई और इतना समय लग गया। – अपील से
हुक्म आखरी में कुछ तरमीम की गई और हाई कोर्ट से
कोई निगरानी मौजा दखल नहीं हुवा / ता. 3-3-68 को मिसल
वापिस लौटी तब से न्यायालय के अध्यक्ष का चार्ज लिया
था – उस रोज फरीकैन को अपने २ दस्तावेजात जो कब्जे में
हो पेश करने की आज्ञा दी गई ताकि बयानात फरीकैन जेर
आर्डर 10 रूल 1 जा. दी. लेने में आकर तनकीहात बरामद
हो सके और केस आगे समाअत किया जावे/

उभयपक्ष की प्लीडिंग्स व बयानात जेर आर्डर 10 रूल 2
जा. दी. पर पूर्ण विचार होकर निम्नलिखित निर्धारणीय
विषय स्थिर किये गये /:—

1. क्या लालदास जी ने एक नया मजहब चलाया —
जिसके मानने वाले हिन्दू व मुसलमान दोनों फिरकों-
में से पैदा हुवे और लालदासी कहलाये ॥

2 क्या मुद्दईयान लालदासी मजहब के मानने वाले है
और मजाज नालिश है ?

3 क्या जायदाद मुतनाजा वाके धोली दूब लालदासी
फिरके का पवित्र धार्मिक स्थान या मन्दिर (
Religious Shrine) है जहाँ लालदास जी के माता पिता की
समाधि है और जिस स्थान पर लालदासी फिरके मजहब
मत के मानने वाले लालदासी मजहब
उसूलों के मुताबिक सेवा पूजा आरती करते हैं

-क्योंकि लालदासी फिरके के मानने वाले हस्ब जैल तरीके से इबादत करते हैं और अपने पवित्र धार्मिक स्थान (Religious Shrine) मुतनाज़ा पर हस्ब जैल तरीके से जो हिन्दू धर्म के तरीकों से मिलता जुलता है सेवा पूजा पाठ आरती उत्सव वगैरा करते व मनाते आये हैं जिस तरीके को कायम व जारी रखने का उनको हक हासिल है।

(1) सुबह व शाम भोग, मंजिरे इत्यादि बाजों के साथ भजन के रूप में आरतियां गाई जाती हैं और उस के बाद घड़ियाल व नक्कारा बजाया जाता है

(2) दोपहर को भोग लगाया जाता है

(3) सुबह शाम की तरह रोजाना सेवा पूजा के अलावा सप्ताहवार जागरण, कीर्तन होते रहते हैं और वार्षिक मेला, श्राद्ध इत्यादि उत्सव भी मनाये जाते हैं

क्योंकि लालदासियों के इस धार्मिक स्थान (Religious Shrine) मुतनाज़ा में नमाज पढ़ना अज़ान लगाना कुरान शरीफ पढ़ना या पढ़वाना इस्लामी ढंग से इबादत करना दीगर तरीके इस्लाम से कोई काम करना लालदासी धर्म के खिलाफ है जिससे लालदासी मज़हब मानने वालों की तौहीन नुकसान व तकलीफ है और लालदासी ढंग से सेवा पूजा उत्सव में रुकावट पड़ती है और मुद्दालेह को ऐसा करने का हक नहीं है।

क्या मुद्दायलान लालदासी मजहब को मानने वाले हैं [illegible] इस्लाम मजहब के मानने वाले हैं और इस लालदासी धार्मिक स्थान मुतनाजा में उन्होंने बेजा तौर पर दावे से 2/6 माह पहिले से बचन व [illegible] मांग व दीगर लालदासियों को नुकसान पहुंचाने [illegible] करने को इस्लामी ढंग से नमाज पढ़ना इख्तियार करना शुरू कर दिया है जिससे मुद्दई का मुद्दायलान को कोई हक हासिल नहीं है

1 क्या लालदासी स्थान मुतनाजा के लालदास जो [illegible] कहलाता था। और मुद्दायलान ने अनुचित सम्बन्ध से जबर्दस्ती तौर पर लालदासियों की हक तलफी व नुकसान [illegible] ... [illegible] झगड़े को हटाकर इस्लामी [illegible] [illegible] का [illegible] है [illegible] [illegible] उनको हक नहीं है और वह वहां से हटाये जाने के काबिल है।

क्या जायदाद मुतनाजा जहां मुद्दायलान नमाज पढ़ने का दावा देते हैं वह मकान मस्जिद है और उससे मिले हुये दादा [illegible] व [illegible] और [illegible] व [illegible] व आम कब्रिस्तान इस्लामी हैं और लालदासी गैर मुसलमान नहीं थे और न उन्होंने — इस्लामी खिदमत की वजा आबादी को रोका इसलिये लालदासी इस्लामी अरकान की बेजा आबादी में मानी होने के मजाज नहीं है

[illegible] [illegible] [illegible] [illegible] है

10 [illegible] [illegible] [illegible] के मुताबिक है

६ मुद्दईयान ने अपना [illegible] [illegible] P.W.1
[illegible] P.W.2 शिवप्रसाद P.W.3 [illegible] P.W.4
[illegible] P.W.5 [illegible] P.W.6 किशोरी[illegible]
P.W.7 [illegible] P.W.8 [illegible] P.W.9 महेन्द्र[illegible]
P.W.10 [illegible] P.W.11 [illegible] P.W.12 सुरजन[illegible]
P.W.13 [illegible] P.W.14 [illegible] P.W.15 [illegible] P.W.16
[illegible] P.W.17 [illegible] P.W.18 [illegible]
P.W.19 उन्नीस गवाहान के बयानात [illegible]
[illegible] लिखाये हुये और [illegible] मुद्दईयान ने और बयान
छोड़ दिया। तहरीरी सबूत में मुद्दईयान ने [illegible]

[illegible] by Major P. W. Powlett in the year [illegible]
page 53 Religion [illegible] EX.P.A [illegible]
नकल EX.P.A, है, [illegible] त्रिपाठी की सम्पादित
[illegible] [illegible] EX.P.B [illegible] EX.P.C
[illegible] की नकल EX.P.C। है, [illegible]
[illegible] में छापा हुआ है EX.P.D
[illegible] नं. [illegible] EX.P.E
नकल [illegible]

[illegible] EX.P.F नकल बयान [illegible] EX.P.G
[illegible] EX.P.H नकल बयान [illegible]

EXP9 पर ता॰ १३ [illegible] सिफुस्टी प्राई मिनिस्टर

EXP J, [illegible] श्री मसनलाल मिताब EXPK सा

सम्बन्धी [illegible] EXPK1 जिसकी नकल EXPK2 है

जी की मिताब EXPO सफे १२ से १६ तक दाय की

[illegible] हुई है जिन मे खास २ बाबी EXPO1-19 है

जिनकी नकलें मिसल मे EXPO 13-25 है - एक मिताब

[illegible] के सफा [illegible] श्री है वह EXPP है सम्बन्धी [illegible]

मिताब मे EXPP1-2,3 है जिन की नकले मिसल पर EXP

6 है जोग योग अभ्यास [illegible] मे [illegible] दास

व [illegible] दास का संवाद है वह EXPQ है / इस तरह अस

मिताबे भी है और उनके साबित आदि [illegible]

नकले भी बाद मिलान मिसल पर शामिल हुवा है

EXPW [illegible] संघ श्री (नकल [illegible]

6 [illegible] ने कोई जवाब नहीं दिया बल्कि [illegible]

को लिखवा दिया कि उन्हें कोई सबूत देना नही

है मुद्दईयान [illegible] है देखलिया जावे - इसके —

अतिरिक्त [illegible] और [illegible] मुद्दायला ने ता॰ १०

को दो दरख्वास्ते दी है व [illegible] मंजिल इकबाल

[illegible] जवाब दावे के साथ नकल शामिल अर्ज EXL

किया हुवा है - [illegible] मुद्दईयान ने [illegible]

फैसले [illegible] मजिस्ट्रेट [illegible] जारी

कि नक़ल हुक्म सीरश्तेतुफ्तय अलवर वादी/ख
पेश किये है जिनकी असल मिसलें नहीं मिल
सकी है बाकी PWD मुहकमे ने हलफ़ से उनको
सही बतलाया है और कहा है कि मिसलें मिलजाय
तो देखलीजे [illegible] नक़्शा मौक़ा स्थान चौकी दुबजी
कमिश्नर उस्ता से बनवाया है वह अक्षर वादी/ग है
२ — नम्बर है नं. १— EXPA जिसकी नक़ल EXPA1 —
मिसल पर है Gazetter of Alwar by Major
P. W. Powlett in the Year 1878 (Page
53) Religion ~~Lal~~ Lal Dasis.
में दिये हुवे लालदास जी के चरित्र व सिद्धान्तों
को देखा गया। तो पाया जाता है कि लालदासी
एक अपनी भांति का पृथक ही मज़हब है जिसके
[illegible] लिखा [illegible] मुसलमान व फ़कीर से हिन्दु धर्म
के से है बाकी मूर्तिपूजा नहीं मानते सच्चाई व
परमात्मा का सब के लिए एक ही रास्ता मानते
मांगना बुरा, खुद कमा कर खाना, बुराई के लिये
भलाई करना [illegible] को बुरा बताना प्रीति रखना
राम का नाम लेते ~~रहना~~ करना और ताल मृदंग नक्कारे
वगैरा से भजन गाना वैराग्य प्राणायाम आदि
उसूल इस मज़हब के पाये जाते हैं और लालदासजी
के अनुयायी भी हर क़ौम के मनुष्य हुवे जैसे
कबीरदास जी का पंथ है वैसा पाया जाता है।

बाणी लिखित में मिलती है। EXP 10 व EXP P
दोनों बाणियों भी पुस्तकें हैं उन में दो बाणियां
EXP 01-12 हैं। जिसकी नकल EXP 013-25 मिसल में
है - इसी तरह EXP P में EXP P1, P2, P3 जिनकी नकलें
EXP P4-5-6 मिसल में है इन सब बाणियों से भी
यही नतीजा निकलता है कि अच्छी उपदेशों
नीति और हिन्दू शास्त्र वाणी से मिलती जुलती है
यह सब बाणियों में दर्ज मिलती है नकल EXP K
में सफा 110 पर EXP K1 पाया जिसकी नकल EXP K2 मिसल
में है उससे भी यही परिणाम निकलता है कि लालदास
जी अपने तौर पे और अनुभव रखा में प्रीति
रखते थे। मुरक्का अलावा EXP E जिसकी नकल EXP E
मिसल में है उससे भी यही नतीजा है कि लालदासी
[illegible] मजहब अलहदा बना जिसके पालने वाले
लालदासी कहलाये। EXP B का भी यही नतीजा है
जो [illegible] का संग्रह है अलावा शहादत जो मुद्दई-
यान की पेश हुआ है वह भी यही कहती है कि लाल-
दास जी ने एक लालदासी मजहब चलाया जिसके
मानने वाले हिन्दू न मेव मुसलमान दोनों थे पाये
जाते वाले [illegible] जाते मानने वाली हैं PW
जैसे - PW1 कहता है [illegible] जात मानने वाली है PW
ताईद करता है PW [illegible] बताई है दोनों खबर
[illegible] साहब खां से जो कहते लाल मेव और
मुसलमान, हिन्दू [illegible] बताई [illegible]

13

[illegible] पढ़े लिखे, चूंकि वे [illegible] होना कहे न [illegible]
[illegible], [illegible] [illegible] के यहां के राम व मुसलमान [illegible]
p.w.6 का कहना है कि मुसलमानों में सिर्फ मेवई
लालदासी मजहब को मानते है p.w.14 ने भी बताई
है "कि ऐसी कुटि लालन को ओढ़ी, गाल
छेरी सो सब ही मूड़ी। नीच रमा और सताया नाद
मूड़े साधु तीन सो साठ। कुल बाबू आल को देखते
हुवे इस तनकीह का फैसला मुद्दईयान के हक में —
निकलता है। ExPB ने मु. अमदल शकूर ने पाली के
तारीख मेवात में भी रसा ही लिखा है।

4 तनकीह नं. 2 - p.w.10 का बयान व नकल रजिस्ट्रेशन
सर्टीफिकट Ex.pw1 बताते है कि श्री लालदास मे
धाम दुधारिका सेंथा अलवर जो कि अलवर गवर्नमेंट
के Alwar Registration of Public Societies
Act — [illegible] रजिस्टर्ड संस्था कर दी गई है। जिसके

[illegible] pw10 है मुद्दई हीरालाल प्रेजीडेंट है और p.w.10 ने
बयान में बताया है कि प्रधान सुन्दरलाल मुद्दई Vice

President संस्था है और दीगर सारे गवाह
मुद्दईयान यहां तक कि मुदायला [illegible] p.w. [illegible]
pw15 भी बयानों में मानते है कि मुद्दईयान लालदासी
है पस तनकीह मुद्दईयान के हक में तय होती है।
कि वह लालदासी मजहब मानता है।

निष्कर्ष न 3 — EXPA1 नकल Gazetteer of Alwar
by Major P.W. Powlett — में अलवर से दूरी
धौलीदूब में लालदासी shrine है और नवम्बर
नवम्बर में साल भर में मेला होता है जहाँ लालदासी
यात्री इकट्ठे होते है EXPB श्री लालदास नामक संत
पुस्तक श्री लक्ष्मण प्रिय पाठी ने [illegible] से प्रकाशित करायी
[illegible] लालदास जी की हिन्दू उत्पत्ति धर्म उनके —
सिद्धान्त वाणी के सम्बन्ध लिखी है चूंकि यह संग्रह
Collection है और authority असल नहीं है
अतः इन मसालों इकट्ठा किया है उसमें EXPB2 अलवर
राज्य के हिस्सा तुर्कों अलवर का है जिसकी किताब EXPC
है और नकल EXPC1 जिसका पा. है इसमें धौलीदूब के
स्थान का वर्णन है EXPB के सफा 112 पर दर्ज है कि
चांदमल लालदासजी के पिता व समदा उनकी माता
[illegible] को [illegible] धौली दूब में है जहाँ वह मरे थे
और दफनाये गये थे — इस किताब EXPB के सफा
पर लालदासजी मजहब के निकाय का आली उत्सव
मेलों के तरीके Alwar Gazetteer by Major
P.W. Powlett [illegible] पा. दिये हुये है सफा 120 पर
EXPB अब्दुल कादिर [illegible] का लेख है कि इस विषय
में गवाहों प्रहलाद को अवलोकित किया गया तो PW1-14
[illegible] से नहीं कहना है कि [illegible]
[illegible] जो [illegible] में दिखलाई हुयी है।

न नानकदासी फिरके का पवित्र धार्मिक स्थान है Religious
Shrine है जहाँ पर नानकदास जी के शिष्य बाबा चौद
[illegible] बाबी रामदास की समाधि था है वह तो मुख्य
स्थान है उसके सामने तिबारे में सेवा पूजा आरती
आदि मजीरे नगारे घडियाल आदि बाजो से होती है
उसके मुकाबले के तिबारे में हिन्दू देवताओं के चित्र
[illegible] रामायण की लड़ाई दिखाई है और तिबारे भी सब पवित्र
धार्मिक स्थान का जुड़ा अंग है कोई स्थान ऐसा नहीं है
जो मसजिद हो या कब्रिस्तान हो या जहाँ नमाज वगैरा
इबादत के तौर पर पढ़ी गई हो या पढ़ी जा सकती हो — बाबा
[illegible] गुलाल दासी जी स्थान के पुजारी थे जो मेरे बड़े उनकी
समाधि व चरण पादुका है गर्ज यह है कि कुल स्थान
मुद्दई नम्बर [illegible] नानक दासी सम्प्रदाय के धार्मिक [illegible]
pwlp का विख्यात कथन है — और उस स्थान पर नानक
दासी सम्प्रदाय के सिद्धान्तों के अनुसार नानकदासी सेवा
पूजा करते आये हैं अतः तनकीह मुद्दईयान के हक में तय
होती है। EXD1 में भी दरगाह नानकदासी फकीरों की दर्ज है
[illegible] भी मतलब नहीं है दरगाह शब्द का अर्थ ——
Shrine [illegible] कोई मतलब से नहीं है क्योंकि उस—
जमाने में उर्दू फारसी के अलफ़ाज इस्तेमाल होते थे इस
लिये दरगाह शब्द का प्रयोग हुआ है/
११— तनकीह नं० 8 EXPA जिसकी नकल EXPA1 है

ने लिखवाई है [illegible] तेईस [illegible] निशान लगाने वाले
लालदास के वाले [illegible] खैरथल करके आजे राम जी सेवा भये
रामपुर द्वारा कर रहे हैं [illegible] कर सकता / PW 6 ने
अपना पहिला बयान EXP 9 भी माना है PW 8 ने भी
आरती लिखवाई है PW 9 ने भी आरती बताई है और
बातें भी लिखवाई हैं PW 9 लालदासी साधु है PW 5
खैरथल के स्थान पर नक्कारा बजाते हैं और लालदासी
स्थानों पर आरती सेवा पूजा का [illegible] बताता है PW 6
[illegible] पुर में ; [illegible] लालदासी साधु है PW 8
[illegible] के लालदासी स्थान का नक्कारची है
[illegible] की आरती सेवा पूजा का [illegible] बताता है / शहर
लालदास जी के पवित्र स्थान [illegible] है [illegible]
[illegible] के [illegible] आरती सेवा पूजा होती है EXP A में

major [illegible] ने [illegible] है Repetition of
Ramnam & singing [illegible] seem to be the
only form of worship but [illegible] Gods
[illegible] is [illegible] held essential

[illegible] PW 17 के बयानात [illegible] इन सब बातों
[illegible] कि [illegible] व सबूत को देखते हुवे
[illegible] के [illegible] साबित है [illegible]
[illegible] / EXP F व EXP [illegible] बयानों से व [illegible]
EXP [illegible] EXP D से भी [illegible]
का [illegible] स्थान से होना उसको चोरी [illegible]

व नक्शा पर जुमीता होता काफी है, ला.टि.
पाया जाता है जिससे भी धाड़पानी वगैरह वाला
व्यर उमारती होना पाया जाता है पस नतीजा निकार
क़ाईम ४ नकला गया है। दर्ज रहे कि मस्जिद मर
जया इसलिये व गुलशनों दरख्त याद नहीं हुवा
इसलिये मैं बाकी [illegible] न महकमे [illegible]
[illegible] को [illegible] मैं [illegible] सेना [illegible]
[illegible] [illegible] को जाता है इसलिये Ex.P.F.,
Ex.P.G., Ex.P.H., Ex.P.I. [illegible] शहादत हुई है।

12- [illegible] जैसे तो [illegible] मुद्दईयान
कहते हैं कि लाल दास आरामिक पोलिस इस्मान
वाले चौकी हुवा मैं कभी नमाज नहीं पढ़ी गई
इस के तौर पर न अजां [illegible] न [illegible]
पढ़ी गई हमेशा से लाल दास आर्य
से सेवा पूजा आरती बाजों के साथ होती
रही आरती भजन भी कबीर की साखी
व गुरु नानक जैसे बड़ों को व हिन्दु
वैष्णव मजहब के [illegible] को लिये हुए
है हरीक राम के नाम का जाप इत्यादि
[illegible] व भजन [illegible] बाजों के

साथ न जाते वहाँ / तीर्थ स्थान
के हैं। इस लिये ख्याल कीया तो
मानना पडता है कि राम रहीम खुदा
ईश्वर सब एक बात है। और मन्दिर
मसजिद गिरजा सब पवित्र स्थान हैं।
मगर यहाँ पर तो कानूनी हक देखना
है; नैतिक धार्मिक तौर पर जिम्मेदारी
बाद / कानूनी हक यह होता है कि
एक धर्म के धार्मिक स्थान पर दूसरे
धर्म के तरीके से कोई काम नहीं
किया जा सकता क्योंकि वह सिद्धान्त के
विरुद्ध पडता है और एक समुदाय
के मनुष्यों के जिनका वह पवित्र स्थान
है तमाम को दुख पहोंचता है और

मैं आवश्यक/ मजहब के उसूलों के खिलाफ

इस्लाम/नोर से इबादत की रीति तो

कोई नहीं बना सकते। लाइनम बड़ी

हकूलवाव/ होती यह साफ है।

क्योंकि लालदास मेव थे, इसलिये मेव

लोग जो मुसलमान होगये थे, परन्तु

उनके रिवाज रस्म हिन्दुओं से मिलते

जुलते थे। वह लोग लालदास जी आपके

मजहब के साधू व महात्मा के अनुयाई

होगये। और हिन्दुओं की तरह आरती

सिवा पूजा करते रहे। जब कोई

इस्लाम ने मेवों को पक्का मुसलमान

बनाने को मस्जिद में इबादत करना

सिखाना शुरू किया तो बहुत से मेव

मुद्दई ने ऐसा मुबाहसात नम्बरी दावे को एक प्रकार से तहलील कर दिया है। देखिये मिसाल पी.डब्लू.14 व पी.डब्लू.15 जिनका मुबाहसात पर मुताल्लिक पहले पर हो चुका है। जैसे लिखा लालदास जी कहा जाता है मन्दिर वह जायदाद मंदिर में मजाहर थी, और न मात्र चन्द जो लिखे ही शुरू किया और मोहल्ला इसलाम के बहुतों से नाका-न्याय का ज्यादा जो उसके हो गया, रहीम रामानन्दी का साथी है। जो यह रामानन्दी सम्प्रदाय के खिलाफ है। बाकी Ramlal Dass रहे हैं इसलाम मजहब में ज्यादा खुश-फहम थे। जबतक बाकी हिन्दू लोग कोई और नन्द लालदास जी का दीगर मुद्दई ने अहकाम से ज्यादा का शामिल होना जाहिर किया है, उनके तनकीह नं. 2 के कब्जे में दखल किया गया है कि मुद्दई का इसलामी तरीके से इस्तेमाल करने का हक इस लालदासी सम्प्रदाय के ... में कोई नहीं है और तनकीह मुद्दईयान के हक में तय की जाती है।

५८. तनकीह नं. 6 – पी.डब्लू.14 व पी.डब्लू.15 व पी.डब्लू.16 के बयानात से तो यह माना जाता है कि मुद्दालेह लालदास जी को अक्तूबर सं. ४५ के करीब महंत लालदास जी को हटाकर ... का नया लगाया है बाकी दीगर मुद्दईयान की शहादत बताती है कि लालदास जी का महंत लालदास जी का हटाना है लेकिन उपर लेकर दिखाकर बदलता है और उसमें नं. 3 में ... लिखा हुआ है। महंत ... और

Ex.P.o. व Ex.D.D. [illegible]

[illegible] है।

P.W.-14 ने अपने बयान [illegible]

[illegible] Gazette [illegible] point out

करके बताया है। जिससे Ex.6.0. व Ex.6.6.।

[illegible]

[illegible] Major P.W. [illegible]

[illegible]

[illegible]

[illegible]

[illegible]

[illegible]

[illegible]

[illegible]

[illegible]

[illegible]

[illegible] है।

13- [illegible]

में [illegible]

[illegible]

[illegible]

[illegible]

[illegible]

नात: यह तनकीह भी मुद्दईयान के हक में तय की जाती है। और का मसला [illegible] है। जिससे [illegible] [illegible] [illegible] [illegible] [illegible] है। [illegible] होती है।

१५ - तनकीह नं० ८ - यह तनकीह नं० ५ व ३ दोनों को मिलाकर [illegible] Counter [illegible] है - चूंकि [illegible] सबूत [illegible] तनकीह का मुतअल्लिक [illegible] और उन्होंने कोई सबूत नहीं दिया और तनकीहात ३ व ५ के फैसले में पाया गया है कि यह कुछ स्थान [illegible] सम्प्रदाय के [illegible] स्थान है। कोई मजार न कब्रिस्तान है न कोई हिस्सा मस्जिद है जहां नमाज व कुरान शरीफ पढ़ी जा सके या [illegible] और [illegible] हिन्दू या न मुसलमान कबीर व गुरु नानक [illegible] पंथ [illegible] सेवा पूजा हिन्दू सिद्धान्तों व सनातनी [illegible] उपासना का तरीका [illegible] के साथ [illegible] इस लिए वह Non Muslim थे, क्योंकि [illegible] कोई भी तरीका उन्होंने मुसलमानों का नहीं किया, also [illegible] Exh [illegible] EXPB [illegible] Ex [illegible]

[illegible] का [illegible] Ex [illegible] व Ex [illegible] व शहादत [illegible] १ - १४ इस मामले पर साफ है कि वह कुरान, नमाज, रोजा न [illegible] न रखते थे, मांस नहीं खाते थे। [illegible] Ex [illegible] में मिलता है कि [illegible] ने उन्हें मांस खाने को दिया [illegible]

जाता है. जवाबदारी/समझदारी के आरम्भिक स्थान में कोई किसी दीगर मजहब को फायदा/नुकसानदायी धर्म कैफियतों के खिलाफ इबादत नहीं कर सकता - यह ख्याल दूसरा है कि इस्लाम मजहब वालों को मस्जिद में कोई इस्लामी [illegible] से/नमाजी में शोर नहीं हो सकता. जो भी/जो लोग हिन्दू के खिलाफ मन्दिर. या धार्मिक आरम्भिक स्थान में वह ऐसा नहीं कर सकता / तनकीह मुतअल्लिका के खिलाफ तय होती है /

२९. तनकीह नं. ९ कोई सबूत नहीं मिलता कि दावा बेजा मियाद हो, बस तनकीह मुतअल्लिका के खिलाफ तय होती है। कानूनी मियाद का आर्टिकल १२० लागू होता है /

तनकीह नं. १० कुल तनकीहात को देखते हुये व ऊपर लिखी वजूहात की बिना पर दावा मुद्दईयान काबिल डिक्री है मय खर्चे के / आदेश.

आदेश है कि

दावा मुद्दईयान बर खिलाफ मुद्दाअलैहम बहैसियत नुमाइन्दा / दीगर [illegible] के [illegible] कि मन्दिर धार्मिक स्थान में [illegible]

[illegible]

लालदासी और लालदास मतावलम्ब के अनुयायी थे। इन्होंने उनका पाठ करके नमाज पढ़ना शुरू किया। [illegible] और लालदासी मतावलम्ब के हिन्दुत्व विरुद्ध हैं। इस विषय में [illegible] का बयान व उसमें जो कुछ बातें [illegible] Ex.C.A.1 Ex.C.B. में भी मिलते हैं [illegible] हैं।

[illegible]

[illegible] को [illegible] हुए [illegible] राम हरि के नाम का भजन ही लालदासियों का [illegible] है।

[illegible]

Appendix V

लाल दास की समाधि से सम्बन्धित प्रधानमंत्री को ज्ञापन

सेवा में,

दि० : 26-7-86

श्रीमान् प्रधान मंत्री महोदय
भारत सरकार,
नई दिल्ली

अलवर जिला शाखा विश्व हिन्दू परिषद के जिला मंत्री श्री प्रकाश राम गांधी ने शेरपुर के सम्बन्ध में दि० 26-7-86 को राजस्थान पत्रिका के जिला प्रशासन से निराधार मांगें करके गुमराह किया है। तथा जिलाधीश महोदय के ऊपर पक्षपात पूर्ण रवैया अपनाने का आरोप लगाया है।

वास्तविकता यह है कि ग्राम शेरपुर में लालखां उर्फ लाल शाह की दरगाह (दरबार) है। लाल खां जाति से मेव मुसलमान थे। वह मेव समाज का पहुँचवान सूफी दरवेश था।

लाल खां पुत्र चांदमल खां का जन्म ग्राम धोलीदूब (ननिहाल) में हुआ। उनकी मां का नाम समदा था। लालखां का ताल्लुक मेव मुसलमानों की पाल दूलौत से था। जिन के अलावा भरतपुर में तीन सौ साठ गांव आबाद हैं। लालखां के पिता का गांव टोंडी है बास कौत गांव तहसील फिरोजपुर जिला गुड़गांवा (हरियाणा) में आबाद है। जानों के अनुसार लाल खां की कई शादियां हुई बड़ी बीबी का नाम चौमिठी गांव आीन था, उससे सात बेटे पैदा हुए जिनके नाम ये हैं :-

1- पहाड़ खां 2- नौरंग शाह 3- आलम शाह 4- शेर खां 5- गरीब खां 6- कुतना खां 7- कुतुब खां।

लालदास के मजार में उनकी तुरबत के साथ साथ एक मस्जिद दो मंजिली और कुटुम्ब कबीले का कब्रिस्तान मौजूद है। इसके अलावा एक और मस्जिद इसी चारदीवारी से लगी हुई है। जिसमें मुसलमान नमाज पढ़ते आये हैं।

इस मस्जिद में तीन कुलाबे की एक बांदी में बैठे जाने की तरफ से एक लाउड स्पीकर मय माइक के अजान देने के लिए मस्जिद में लगाया गया था। जिसको मुद्दा बनाकर नमाजियों के ऊपर झूठे मुकदमें बनाये गये तथा पुलिस की बेरोंसा कर शामिल मुसलमानों को अनुचित रूप से परेशान किया गया व दिनांक 7-7-86 को जुहर की नमाज पढ़ते हुए नमाजियों को पुलिस ने मारापीटा और नमाज न पढ़ने के लिये पाबन्द किया और मुसलमान समुदाय की औरतों व बच्चों के साथ अभद्र व्यवहार किया गया तथा पंखे, मुसल्ला, व लाउडस्पीकर व चद्दरा आदि सामान को उठाकर ले गये।

लगातार....2

[illegible] बाद [illegible] अधिकारियों [illegible] [illegible] के मुताबिक [illegible] ने इस संबंध में प्रशासनिक अधिकारियों को अपनी शिकायतें अवगत कराया। [illegible] दिनांक 15-7-96 को जिलाधीश महोदय व पुलिस अधीक्षक महोदय ने मौके पर आकर जांच की। तत्पश्चात् जिलाधीश महोदय ने यथा स्थिति बनाये रखकर शान्ति पूर्वक मस्जिद में नमाज पढ़ने/पढ़ाने रहने के लिए अस्थायी आदेश दिए।

[illegible] [illegible] में [illegible] [illegible] [illegible] [illegible] की [illegible] में [illegible] [illegible] उन्हीं के आन्दोलन के जरिये को आ रहे हैं। और उनकी [illegible] के बीच इस बारे में अफवाह है। इस समय बल्लू व मल्लू का [illegible] [illegible] [illegible] रहते हैं। उन्हें यह काम विरासत में मिला हुआ है। [illegible] [illegible] [illegible] और [illegible] [illegible] को [illegible] जा रहा है।

अतः [illegible] हिन्दू परिषद के [illegible] [illegible] मन्त्री ने तथा उन्हें आरोपियों ने प्रशासन की [illegible] पर अनुचित कार्यवाही करने के लिए प्रेरित किया है। ऐसे व्यक्तियों के विरुद्ध जांच कर उनके खिलाफ कानूनी कार्यवाही [illegible] जावे।

प्रार्थीगण

(बल्लू व मल्लू पुत्र मोहम्मद [illegible])
ग्राम हैदरपुर तह० रामगढ़
एवं
[illegible] [illegible] समाज
जिला – अलवर (राज०)

प्रतिलिपियाँ :-

[illegible] ——————————
——————————
——————————

Appendix VI

मेवात में जंगे आज़ादी (1857)*

मेवात अपने पुराने ज़माने से भारतीय इतिहास के पन्नों में अपना स्थान बनाए हुए है। महाभारतकालीन मथुरा, बैराट आज भी पुरानी कहानी 'पंडुन का कड़ा' के ज़रिए हम याद करते हैं। मेवात की भूमि जहां सालार मसूद गाज़ी को याद किया जाता है वहाँ आज भी संत लाल दास और शाह चोखा की मज़ार पर माथा टेका जाता है। यहाँ के लोगों में जहाँ इन साधु-संतो के प्रति आदर है वहाँ सबसे बड़ी बात है अपनी आज़ादी की। मेवातियों ने शुरू से ही आज़ादी पसंद जीवन जीने की कला का प्रदर्शन किया है। चाहे वह दिल्ली के तुर्क शासकों का ज़माना रहा हो या फिर मुगलों या मराठों का, जाटों का या फिर अंग्रेज़ों का। 'पाँच पहाड़ की लड़ाई' और 'घुड़चड़ी मेव खाँ' की कहानियाँ हमारे मेवाती लोकगीतों का अभिन्न अंग हैं जो मेवों की शूरवीरता का उदाहरण हैं। 1857 की जंगे आज़ादी के पीछे भी हम मेवातियों की यही आज़ादी की परम्परा जुड़ी है। मुगल बादशाह बहादुर शाह ज़फर तो सितम्बर 1857 में रंगून भेजा गया था लेकिन मेवाती दीवाने उसके बाद भी अंग्रज़ों से टक्कर लेते रहे। आखिर क्या था इस दीवानगी में? चलो हम उनकी आज़ादी की जंग को तारीखी ढंग से देखें।

फारसी इतिहासकारों ने पहली बार लिखित रूप से हमें मेवात से रूबरू कराया है और बताते हैं किस तरह से महमूद गज़नवी के खिलाफ उन्होंने अपनी

*Delivered at Doha village in Mewat, on the occasion of the celebration of the 150th year of 1857, as *Jashn-i-Azadi* on 10th May, 2007.

आज़ादी बरकरार रखने के लिए उसके खिलाफ जंग लड़ी और इसी तरह जब राजपूतों को हराने के बाद दिल्ली में तुर्की शासन स्थापित हुआ, मेवातियों ने दिल्ली के दरवाज़े तक दिल्ली के सुल्तानों की नाक में दम कर रखा था। यहाँ तक कि उनका नमाज़ पढना भी मुशिकल कर दिया था। सुल्तानों की हिम्मत नहीं थी कि दिल्ली के दक्षिणी दरवाज़े सूरज ढलने के बाद खोले रखें। नहीं तो यह रही दिल्ली और इनके शासकों की सेना, मगर किसमें ताकत थी इन आज़ादी के दीवानों को रोकने की। सुल्तान बल्बन ने आखिरकार अपने सैनिकों में इनामी घोषणा की, कि हर ज़िन्दा मेव पर दो सोने के तनके और मुर्दा मेव पर एक सोने का तनका सरकारी खज़ाने से दिया जाएगा। बस फिर क्या था, शाही घुडसवारों ने पूरे मेवात पर कुफ्र ढाया और एक लाख से भी ज़्यादा मेवातियों को मार गिराया। पूरा एक वर्ष तक यह संषर्ष जारी रहा। बलबन ने गोपालगिर का किला बनवाकर वहां अफगान फौज रखी ताकि भविष्य में मेव सिर न उठा सके।

दिल्ली की शाही सेनाओं का मुकाबला निहत्थे मेवाती कब तक करते। सांभरपाल ने फीरोज़शाह तुग़लक को अपनी बहादुरी का नमूना पेश किया एक नाहर (शेर) को अपने हाथों से मार के, और बन गया बहादुर नाहिर खां खानज़ादा, और तब शुरू होता है मेवात में खानज़ादों का इतिहास। लेकिन एक बात हमेशा याद रखने लायक है कि मेवात में हिन्दू-मुस्लिम भाई-भाई की तरह साथ साथ जीये और साथ-साथ मरे। जब बाबर ने राजपूताना के शासक राणा सांगा के खिलाफ लड़ाई लड़ी तो हमारे मेवातियों ने हसन खां मेवाती के आध ीन राणा सांगा का साथ दिया जो खनुआ के युद्ध में शहीद हो गया।

मुग़लों की ताकत के सामने बड़े-बड़े नहीं टिक पाए। मुग़लों ने इस मुल्क को अपना लिया और इस मुल्क ने मुग़लों को। फिर तो इस मुल्क का हर शख्स मुग़ल सत्ता की प्रजा बन गया। मेवातियों ने भी मुग़लों के दरबार को सुशोभित किया। उन्हें बड़ी-बड़ी जागीरें मिलीं और मुग़ल सेवा में गुप्तचरों का काम बाखूबी निभाया। अकबर महान ने हिन्दू-मुस्लिम एकता को सराहा और दरबार में बिना जात पात के सभी को आमंत्रित किया। बड़े-बड़े राजपूत शासकों ने मुग़लों से वैवाहिक सम्बंध स्थापित किए। हसन खां मेवाती के खानदान से यानि ज़माल खां मेवाती से मुगल बादशाह हुमायूँ व बैरम खाँ का वैवाहिक सम्बन्ध स्थापित हुआ था। अब्दुर्रहीम खाने खाना जो कवि 'रहिम' के नाम से मशहूर हुए वह मेवातियों का नाती था।

मुग़लों का पतन औरगजेब की मौत के बाद (1707 ई.) शुरू हो गया था। राजपूत जाट, मराठे, सतनामी, सिख, बुंदेले, सब फिर से आजाद होने लगे थे। इधर मेवात भी मराठों, जाटों तथा अलवर के नरूका शासकों की लालच का शिकार हुआ। अंग्रेज़ जो कि हिन्दुस्तान को लूटने के इरादे से आए थे, अब पूरी तरह इस मुल्क के मालिक बन बैठे थे। इन्होंने 1803 ई. तक सभी का काम तमाम कर दिया और मेवात को भी अपने कब्ज़े में ले लिया। मेवात को नवाब शम्सुद्दीन के हवाले कर दिया। शम्सुद्दीन ने मेवात को ठीक से व्यवस्थित किया। उसने दिल्ली रेजीडेट विलियम फ्रेजर की बदनीयती का नतीजा उसका कत्ल करके ही सांस ली और फांसी पर चढ़ गया। यहां यह बताना ज़रूरी है कि हिन्दुस्तान के मशहूर शायर मिर्ज़ा ग़ालिब की पेंशन इसी मेवात से जाती थी और मशहूर शायर दाग़ का ताल्लुक भी मेवात के शम्सुद्दीन से ही था।

पूरे मुल्क में अंग्रेज़ों की ज़्यादतियों से बग़ावत का माहौल बन रहा था। भला मेवाती पीछे कैसे रहते। जैसे ही 10 मई 1857 में मेरठ में बग़ावत की चिंगारी भड़की पूरा देश उसकी आग में लिपट गया। मेवात तो मुल्क की राजधानी के पास ही था, अतः यहां के आज़ादी पसंद रणबांकुरों ने भी विदेशी सत्ता को उखाड़ फैंकने का इरादा बना लिया। उधर रेवाड़ी, झज्जर, बल्लभगढ़, पलवल,, मथुरा और आस पास सभी ने इस जंग में हिस्सा लिया। दिल्ली में तो अंग्रेज़ों तथा उनकी बहु-बेटियों को मार डाला गया। इनमें शामिल थी गुड़गावां के सहायक कलक्टर की बहन भी। अफ़वाहों का बाज़ार गर्म था। जैसा कि इतिहासकार एस.एन. सेन ने अपनी पुस्तक *अठारह सौ सत्तावन* में लिखा है कि गुड़गावां के सहायक कलक्टर मि. कल्लिफर्ड ने सुना कि उसकी बहन और उसकी एक सहेली जेनिकस को महल में नंगाकर दिया गया और उसी अवस्था में उनको तोपों को ले जाने वाली गाड़ियों के पहियों में बाँधा गया था। उन्हें दिल्ली के चांदनी चौक में घसीट कर लाया गया था और वहां बादशाह के पुत्रों की मौजूदगी में उनहें टुकड़े-टुकड़े क़र काट डाला गया। कल्लिफर्ड के मन में यह बात भी थी कि उसकी बहन का वध करने से पहले उसके साथ बलात्कार भी किया गया था। इसलिए स्वभावतः वह बदले के अतिरिक्त और कुछ सोच नहीं सकता था और उसने एक अंग्रेज़ को लिखा भी था जो भी उसके सामने आया उसको उसने मरवाया और स्त्रियों और बच्चों को भी नहीं छोड़ा। बाद में खोजों से पता चला कि उनकी हत्या महल में की गई थी और उनसे कोई बुरा बर्ताव नहीं किया गया था। (पृ. 414-15)

मुगल बादशाह ने मिर्ज़ा ग़ालिब को उन दिनों रोज़नामचा लिखने के लिए हुक्म दिया था। कुंवर मोहम्मद अशरफ जो कि मेवाती तो थे ही लेकिन अपने समय के बहुत बड़े इतिहासकार हुए हैं उन्होंने एक पर्चा 'मिर्ज़ा ग़ालिब और 1857 का विद्रोह' लिखा था। इस पर्चे में वह बताते हैं कि मिर्ज़ा ग़ालिब ने अपने रोज़नामचे में लिखा था कि 7 अक्टूबर तक दिल्ली फिर से अंग्रेज़ों के हाथ आ चुकी थी फिर भी असंख्य विद्रोही बरेली, फरुखाबाद में दल बनाकर हर कदम पर लड़ने मरने को तैयार थे। दिल्ली के पड़ौस में सोहना व नूंह के मेवों ने इतना गदर और बवाल मचा रखा था जैसे कोई पागल ज़ंजीरों को तोड़ कर भागा हो। तुलाराम की सेना में देवी मेव ने कमान संभाल रखी थी जिसने अंग्रेज़ों के खिलाफ अलग रंग दिखाया (*1857 का विद्रोह,* पृ. 251–52)

बेशक, 1857 एक जंगे आज़ादी थी जिसका भारतीय इतिहास में अहम मकाम है। यह लड़ाई केवल दिल्ली की नहीं बल्कि मेरठ, कानपुर, लखनऊ, रूहेल खंड, बुंदेलखंड, पंजाब, मेवात और पूरे देश में लड़ी गई थी। रानी लक्ष्मी बाई, तात्यां टोपे, नाना फड़नवीस, राव तुला राम, नाहर सिंह, सभी ने मुग़ल बादशाह का साथ दिया था। भले ही सभी के अपने अपने स्वार्थ थे पर अंग्रेज़ों से सभी परेशान थे। मेवात में अंग्रेज़ों द्वारा लगाए टैक्स इतने ज़्यादा थे कि आम आदमी परेशान था। जैसा कि हम जानते हैं कि मेवात शुरू से ही कृषि में पिछड़ा प्रदेश है यहां पहाड़ों में झाड़ियां हैं या फिर मैदानों में रेत। ऐसे में करों का बोझ। सबसे बड़ी बात अन्दर ही अन्दर आज़ादी की तलब। बस फिर क्या था ऐसे में जब पूरा देश बग़ावत पर उतर आया हो तो वे पीछे क्यों रहें। मजबूरी यह थी कि उनके पास और कोई रास्ता नहीं था इसलिए मुग़लों को ही अपना स्वामी बनाया था।

हमें यहाँ एक बात नहीं भूलनी चाहिए कि मेवातियों ने दिल्ली के अलावा बल्लभगढ़, रेवाड़ी, फरूखनगर, ग्वालियर, इंदौर के राजाओं की सेनाओं में भर्ती होकर अपनी जगह बना ली थी। इसके अलावा मेवात में सोहना, नूंह, फिरोज़पुर झिरका के जागीरदारों की सेवा में भी बड़ी संख्या मेवातियों की ही थी। इसलिए जब बग़ावत की बात आती है तो मेवातियों का नाम सबसे पहले आता है। पर यह हमारे इतिहासकारों की कमी रही है कि मेवात के बारे में उनका ध्यान ही नहीं जाता। अकेले शहज़ादा फिरोज़शाह की सेना में 10,000 सैनिकों में 5,000 मेवाती थे जिसने अंग्रेजों के खिलाफ मंदसौर, इंदौर, ग्वालियर, बरेली, रामपुर में लड़ाई लड़ी और बाद में तात्या टोपे के साथ अपने जीवन का अंतिम युद्ध सीकर

(12 जनवरी, 1859) में लड़ा जहां उसे हार मिली। यह शहज़ादा देश विदेश में भेष बदल कर घूमता रहा। कभी काबुल तो कभी समरकंद और कभी बुखारा और या फिर कुस्तुनतुनिया में और आखिरकार मक्का शरीफ़ में 17 दिसम्बर 1877 में आखिरी सांस ली। और क्या आप जानते हैं कि उसकी विधवा बेगम को कितनी पेंशन मिलीं? महज़ 5 रुपये माहवार। ऐसे थे हमारे आज़ादी के दीवाने। यह तो एक मिसाल थी।

इसी प्रकार न जाने कितने मेवातियों ने अन्य राजाओं, जागीरदारों की सेना में रहकर अंग्रेज़ों के खिलाफ जंग लड़ी और अपनी जानें कुर्बान की। सबसे बड़ी बदकिस्मती यह है कि अंग्रेज़ इतिहासकारों और यहां तक हमारे खुद के भारतीय इतिहासकार मेवातियों को डाकू व लुटेरे का नाम देते हैं। जेलों में बंद मेवाती क्या डाकू-लुटेरे थे? नहीं! वे सभी तो ज़मीन से जुड़े हुए हमारे किसान भाई थे, आम नागरिक थे, नौकरीपेशा लोग थे।

सन सत्तावन की बग़ावत में जहां मेवाती मुल्क की आज़ादी के लिए शहीद हो रहे थे वहां कुछ जागीदार अपनी पुरानी रंजिश का बदला ले रहे थे। जैसा कि नूंह के खानज़ादों ने कितने ही मेवातियों को मौत के घाट उतार दिया था। इस दौरान हज़ारों मेवातियों ने अपनी जान दी। अंग्रेज़ों ने उन्हें तोपों से उड़ाया, पेड़ों पर लटका कर फांसी दी, कईयों के टुकड़े टुकड़े कर दिये गए। परंतु ये आज़ादी के दीवाने पीछे नहीं हटे। कई मेवातियों ने तो अंग्रेज़ों को इनकी तारीफ करने पर मज़बूर कर दिया। जैसे झज्जर के अब्दुस्समद को अंग्रेज़ों की बीसीओं गोलियों लगीं पर वह हार नहीं माना और आखिरकार शहीद हुआ। महाराजा अलवर की सेनाओं ने मेवों के कई गांवों को जलाकर खाक कर दिया लेकिन अंग्रेज़ों ने बदनाम किया मेवों को लुटेरे बताकर। मेवातियों पर झूठे इल्ज़ाम लगाए गए, उनकी सम्पति ज़ब्त कर ली गई, नौकरी से निकाल दिया गया, झूठे मुकद्दमे चलाए गए, कईयों की तनख्वाहें रोक दी गईं।

पिनगवां के सदुद्दीन ने अंग्रेज़ों को निशाना बनाया, नूंह के खानज़ादों ने बड़ी कोशिश की मेवातियों को दबाने की और अंग्रेज़ों का साथ दिया परंतु कामयाब न हो सके। नूंह के बाद होडल व हथीन में मेवातियों का बराबर दबदबा बना रहा। अली हसन खाँ ओर उसके ससुर अब्दुस समद खाँ, राव तुलाराम और उसके चचेरे भाई गोपाल कृष्ण, नाहर सिंह, नवाब अब्दुर्रहमान आदि अनेक देशभक्तों ने अंग्रेज़ों का डट कर मुकाबला किया। जून के मध्य में जयपुर से ईडन अपने 7,000 घुड़सवारों और 7 तोपों के साथ मेवात पंहुचा और बग़ावत को ठंडा

किया। लेकिन कुछ स्थानीय राजाओं में ढुलमुल की नीति अपनाई जिससे बग़ावत कामयाब न हो सकी। जैसा नूंह में खानज़ादों ने, बृज और पलवल में जाटों ने, फिरोजपुर झिरका में चांद खां और कबीर, रेवाड़ी में अहीरों ने अलवर में भी मेवों से पुरानी दुश्मनियां निकाली गई। मेवाती फिर भी पीछे नहीं हटे। रूपड़का में 3,500 मेवातियों ने अंग्रेज़ों के 400 फौजियों को मार गिराया। राव तुला राम को देश छोड़ना पड़ा। वह ईरान चले गये और वापसी में अफ़गानिस्तान में 38 वर्ष की आयु में मौत को प्राप्त हुए।

मेवात के दो गाँवों रायसीना व दोहा के मेवों ने कमाल कर दिया। अंग्रेज़ों के खिलाफ मरते दम तक जंग जारी रखी। कल्लिफर्ड को मौत के घाट उतार दिया। अंग्रेज़ों को खतरा पैदा हुआ कि कहीं हिन्दुस्तान छोड़ना न पड़े। महारानी विक्टोरिया ने घोषणा की कि सोहना, रिवाड़ी, पलवल, पुनहाना, फीरोजपुर झिरका आदि जहां भी अंग्रेज़ सेना में मेवाती हों उन्हें कोई सज़ा न दी जाए। अनेक मेवातियों ने इस घोषणा के कारण अपने आप को सरकारी अधिकारियों के हवाले कर दिया। लेकिन हुआ क्या? उन्हें बाद में सूली पर चढ़ा दिया गया। बग़ावत समाप्त हो चुकी थी। लेकिन इस जंगे आज़ादी ने यह साबित कर दिया कि अब अंग्रेज़ों को हिन्दुस्तान में रहना है तो यहां के बाशिन्दों को इंसान समझें, जानवर नहीं।

इस जंगे अजादी का इतिहास बहुत इतिहासकारों ने अपने अपने तरीके से लिखा है। इसके लिए सरकारी कागज़ों, कलैक्टरों के दफ्तरों से हासिल रिकार्ड आदि के बलबूते पर कई विचार धाराएं पनपी। कई तरह के आंकड़े भी सामने आए हैं। जैसे मेवात के बारे में पता चलता है कि ग्वालियर व पंजाब की फौजों में मेवात के 52 घुड़सवारों को फांसी दी गई थी। गुड़गावां के अहमबेग के साथ 98 मेवाती बिना कारण बताए फांसी पर चढाए गए। 25 लोगों पर मुकदमा चलाकर फांसी दी गई। 18 लोगों को 3 वर्ष से लेकर उम्र क़ैद की सजा दी गई। जिन बिस्वादारों ने अंग्रेज़ों का साथ नहीं दिया उनकी ज़मीनें ज़ब्त कर ली गई और कईयों पर जुर्माना लगा दिया। दोहा व रायसीना में मालिकाना हक छीन लिया गया। नूंह में मेवातियों की ज़मीनें खानज़ादों को दे दी गई। रिवाड़ी में तुलाराम और गोपाल कृष्ण की जागीरें ज़ब्त कर ली गईं, झज्जर के नवाब की जागीर छीन कर उसे गुड़गावां में मिला दिया गया। नसरूल्ला खां ने फिरोज़पुर झिरका में सरकारी खज़ाने को लूटने से बचाया था उसे 200 रुपये का इनाम दिया गया।

सन सत्तावन के गदर या जंगे आज़ादी को लेकर उस समय अनेक लोग गीत लिखे गए। मुझे कुछ साल पहले यहीं पास के कोलगांव (ज़िला मेवात) में सफेदा मिरासी से मिलने का मौका मिला जिसने यह गीत दोहराया:

सत्तावन का गदर की पड़ी, मुलक में रल्ल
गोरा मारा घेर के, दिल्ली गई दहल
अक्ल बड़ी और मन अडर, सही गरूरी रूआब
नंदन सू सब नरन पर ग़ालिब हुआ उक़ाब
आयो नंदन सू उक़ाब
बांधो कलकत्तो पर रूआब
तपके प्रताप ताप कौन झेले जंगी की
उत्तर दक्कन के सब भूप टोहे,
जदु बिन कौन टोहे ऐह कौन उपंगी की।
दूहल कुदावा चेतावा ऐसी चेटक रंगी की
कह मन सब कविराय, दीयो दूध पीवन लू गाय
दोहे में टोपी तो राख ली है फिरंगी की।

इसी प्रकार रायसीना के बारे में:

रायसीना के मेवों ने भला जगायो दीन,
खक्के मार तीन सौ, कुर्सी खाली कर दीन।
बंगला में मन न लगे, सूनी दीखे सेज,
रायसीना के गोरबे, देख बिना सीस अंग्रेज।

राजस्थान के महान क्रान्तिकारी स्वर्गीय विजयसिंह पथिक की कुछ पंक्तियां भी हमें इस जंगे आज़ादी की याद दिलाती है:

न भूल जाना खुशी के दिन,
तुम वतन परस्तों के वे फ़साने।
कि जिनके बदले हुए मुय्यसर हैं,
ये जश्न, महफिल और तराने।

लेटो पलंग पर तब याद करना,
उन नौजवानों की जान बाज़ी।
जिन्होंने फांसी के तख्त पर ही,
थे नींद लेने को पैर ताने।
और अंत में बिस्मिल के वो शब्द
शहीदों की चिताओं पर लगेंगे हर बरस मेले,
वतन पर मरने वालों की यही बाकी निशां होगा।

जयहिन्द!

Appendix VII

समकालीन ग्रंथों में मेवातः तेरहवीं से सोलवीं शती*

I

तेरहवीं शती के आरम्भ में उत्तरी भारत पर तुर्क शासन-व्यवस्था स्थापित होने के साथ ही दिल्ली सल्तनत की स्थापना हुई। इस काल का इतिहास-लेखन समकालीन फारसी के विद्वानों ने कलमबद्ध किया। इन फारसी इतिहासकारों का मुख्य उद्देश्य दिल्ली के सुल्तानों एवं शासक वर्ग का इतिहास, जिसमें उनकी विजयों, शासन प्रबन्ध, बाह्य आक्रमणों एवं स्थानीय विद्रोहों को दबाना एवं इस्लामी पताकाओं की प्रशंसा करना था। उस काल की मुख्य घटनाओं, प्रसिद्ध व्यक्तियों, सूफी व आलिमों के बारे में भी उनकी कलम ने कुछ काम किया। इसके अतिरिक्त मध्यकालीन व्यापार-उद्योग, कृषि, व्यापारिक मार्गों नगरों, कबीलों की गतिविधियों सम्बधी भी उक्त फारसी साहित्य में जानकारी मिलती है। दिल्ली सल्तनत के इतिहास के साथ-साथ हमें प्रांतीय इतिहास-लेखन का भी पता चलता है जिनमें मुख्यतः राजपूताना के विभिन्न राज्यों, बंगाल, गुजरात, कश्मीर, सिंध, मालवा, जौनपुर, विजयनगर बहमनी आदि थे परंतु मेवात सम्बन्धी किसी ग्रंथ का उल्लेख नहीं मिलता। इसके पीछे मुख्य कारण यह था कि मेवात पर किसी पर शक्तिशाली राजवंश का शासन नहीं रहा था। यद्यपि

*यह लेख 'मेवात बोर्ड राजस्थान' अलवर में राष्ट्रीय संगोष्ठी 'मेवातः इतिहास एवं संस्कृति' 30-31 अगस्त, 2008 में पढ़ा गया।

खानज़ादों द्वारा दो-तीन सौ वर्षों का शासन, जैसा कि बाबरनामा से पता चलता है, मेवात क्षेत्र पर रहा, उन्होंने शासन तो किया परंतु कोई शासन पद्धति नहीं चलाई। उनका समय दिल्ली के सुल्तानों के विरुद्ध संघर्ष करने में ही बीत गया। उन्होंने इतिहास-लेखन में कोई रूचि नहीं दिखाई। हाँ, उस काल में निर्मित कुछ इमारतों व किलों का पता अवश्य चलता है। मध्यकालीन मेवात का इतिहास वास्तव में दिल्ली सल्तनत के इतिहास का ही एक अंग है जिसकी जानकारी हमें समकालीन फारसी ग्रंथों या फिर *बाबरनामा* में मिलती है। इस शोध-पत्र का उद्देश्य मध्यकालीन मेवात को मध्य नज़र रखते हुए उक्त ग्रंथों की समीक्षा करना है।

सर्वप्रथम *तबकाते नासिरी* के लेखक मिनाहाजुद्दीन उसमान बिन सिराजुद्दीन मुहम्मद जूज़जानी का नाम आता है जिसे हम मिनहाज सिराज के नाम से अधिक जानते हैं। मिनहाज का जन्म 1193 ई. में गोर में हुआ। इसके पिता मुहम्मद गौरी की सेना में काजी थे। मिनहाज 1226 ई. में भारत के लिए रवाना हुआ और 14 मई, 1227 को उच्च पहुँचा जहाँ उसे मदरसये फीरोज़ी सौंपा गया। तत्पश्चात वह शम्सुद्दीन इल्तुतमिश की सेवा में अनेक पदों पर रहा। इल्तुतमिश की मृत्यु के बाद वह उसके उत्तराधिकारियों के काल में भी अनेक ऊंचे पदों पर आसीन रहा। मिनहाज अपने समय का बहुत बड़ा विद्वान था जिसने *तबकाते नासिरी* दिल्ली के सुल्तान नासिरूद्दीन महमूद शाह (शासनकाल 1246-66 ई.) को समर्पित की। इसमें 23 तबके अर्थात् अध्याय हैं जसमें आदम से लेकर नासिरूद्दीन महमूद के काल तक विस्तार से वर्णन किया गया है। इसमें संसार के प्रत्येक उन भागों के सुल्तानों का हाल है जिनके विषय में उस समय के विद्वानों को ज्ञान था। उसके द्वारा लिखा गया इहिास अनेक प्राचीन ग्रंथों के अध्ययन तथा स्वयं की जानकारी पर आधारित था। तबकाते नासिरी की विश्वसनीयता का पता इस बात से चलता है कि ज़ियाउद्दीन बरनी ने अपनी तारिखे फीरोजशाही में मिनहाज द्वारा लिखे गये इतिहास को पढने के बाद विश्व इतिहास लिखने का विचार त्याग दिया। उसने अपना ग्रंथ बल्बन के सिंहासनारोहण से आरम्भ किया।

तबकाते नासिरी मध्यकालीन भारत के इतिहास, विशेषकर तेरहवीं शताब्दी का महत्त्वापूर्ण मुख्य ग्रंथ है। जैसा कि विदित है इस ग्रंथ में मुख्य रूप से सुल्तानों की विजयों, मंगोल आक्रमाणों, प्रसिद्ध अमीरों का संक्षिप्त जीवन परिचय आदि का विस्तार से वर्णन है। मेवात सम्बंधी जानकारी हमें इस ऐतिहासिक स्त्रोत में

अधिक नहीं मिलती परंतु जो भी जानकारी मिली है वह मध्यकालीन मेवात के सदंर्भ में बहुत ही महत्त्वपूर्ण है। इस ग्रथं का भारत सम्बंधी वर्णन हिन्दी अनुवाद सैयिद अतहर अब्बास रिज़वी ने किया है जो बहुत ही महत्त्वपूर्ण है। मेजर आर. जी. रेवटी द्वारा पूरे ग्रंथ का अंग्रेज़ी में व्याख्या सहित अनुवाद उपलब्ध है।

सबसे पहली जानकारी मेवात के बारे में मिनहाज हमें उलुग खाँ की संक्षिप्त जीवनी लिखते समय देता है और बताता है सुल्तान बहरामशाह के काल में जब उलुग खा को रिवाड़ी की अक्ता प्रदान की गई थी तो उसने पहाड़ी मवासात के निवासियों को अपनी वीरता द्वारा कठोर दण्ड दिये और उस प्रदेश पर अधिकार कर लिया।[1] इसके बाद मेवात का उल्लेख हमें वर्ष 1248 ई. के अंत में मिलता है जब उलुग खाँ को एक बड़ी सेना देकर रणथम्भोर तथा मेवात के पर्वतीय प्रदेशों और नाहर देव के, जो हिन्दुस्तानी रायों में सबसे बड़ा समझा जाता था, के विरूद्ध भेजा गया। उसने वह प्रदेश तथा आस-पास के क्षेत्रों को विध्वंस कर दिए।[2]

ऐसा प्रतीत होता है कि मेवात पूरी तरह से नियंत्रण में नहीं लाया जा सका क्योंकि दस वर्ष के बाद पुनः उलुग खाँ को मेवात में सैनिक अभियान लेकर जाना पड़ा। इस बार मिनहाज लिखता है ''नये वर्ष में सफर 658 हि. (जनवरी-फरवरी, 1260 ई.) में उलुग खाँ मुआज्ज़म ने कोहपाया (पर्वतों के आँचल) की ओर प्रस्थान करने का दृढ़ संकल्प कर लिया। इस कोहपाया में आज्ञायों के उल्लंघन करने वाले दल सर्वदा लूटमार किया करते थे और मुसलमानों की धन सम्पत्ति लूट ले जाते थे तथा प्रजा को कष्ट पहुँचाते थे। वे हरियाना, सिवालिक तथा भियाना के ग्रामों में लूटमार किया करते थे।'' मिनहाज यहाँ लिखता है कि किस प्रकार ''इसके 3 वर्ष पूर्व उलुग खाँ के दास तथा ऊँटों का एक गल्ला हाँसी की विलायत के निकट से ले जा रहे थे। इन उपद्रवकारियां का नेता एक हिन्दू था, जिसका नाम मल्का था। उसने भूतों के समान झपट कर ऊँटों तथा दासों का गल्ला छीन लिया। उन लोगों ने उन्हें कोहपाया से लेकर रतनपुर (रणथम्भोर) तक के हिन्दुओं में बाँट दिया। उस समय एक युद्ध का आयोजन हो रहा था और उलुग खाने मुअज्ज़म को सामान ले जाने के लिए ऊँटों की विशेष आवशकता थी। इससे उलुग खाने मुअज्ज़म तथा समस्त मलिकों, अमीरों और सैनिकों को विशेष कष्ट पहुँचा किंतु वे उन पर किसी प्रकार चढ़ाई न कर सकते थे क्योंकि मुग़ल (मंगोल) सेना इस्लामी नगरों की अर्थात

सिन्ध, लाहौर तथा ब्याह नदी की सीमा पर धावे मार रही थी।''

''उलुग खाँ एवं अन्य मलिकों ने देहली की सेना के साथ 20 जनवरी, 1260 ई. को कोहपाया पर चढ़ाई कर दी। पहले ही धावे में वे 50 कोस तक पहुँच गये और अचानक उस ओर के विद्रोहियों पर टूट पड़े। उन पर्वतीय प्रदेशों तथा ऊबड़ खाबड़ और नदी नालों के निवासियों को मुसलमानों ने तलवार के घाट उतार दिया। बीस दिनों तक उलुग खाने मुअज़्ज़म कोहपाया के चारों ओर धावे मारता रहा। उन पहाड़ियों के निवास स्थान पहाड़ों की चोटियों तथा ऊँची-ऊँची चट्टानों पर स्थित थे और ऐसा ज्ञात होता था कि वे आकाश अथवा सितारों के निकट बने हैं।''

''उलुग खाने मुअज़्ज़म ने उन सब स्थानों को, जो कि सिकन्दर की दीवार के समान दृढ़ थे, विध्वंस कर दिया। वहाँ के निवासी हिन्दुओं, चारों तथा डाकुओं को तलवार के घाट उतार दिया। उलुग खाँ ने यह आदेश दे दिया था कि मुसलमान सैनिकों में से जो कोई एक कटा हुआ सिर लायेगा उसे एक चाँदी का तंका प्रदान किया जायेगा, और जो कोई एक पुरूष को जीवित पकड़ कर लाये उसे दो चाँदी के तंके खज़ानेदार प्रदान करा दे। सत्य का पालन करने वालों ने उलुग खाँ मुअज़्ज़म के आदेशानुसार ऊबड़-खाबड़ स्थानों तथा नदी-नालों को पार करके कटे हुए सिर तथा बन्दियों को लाना आरम्भ कर दिया; विशेषकर अफगानों में से प्रत्येक बड़ी वीरता से युद्ध करके सौ सौ हिन्दुओं को पर्वत तथा जंगलों से पकड़ कर लाया। · · · वह विरोधी हिन्दू, जिसने ऊँटों को छीन लिया था, अपने परिवार सहित गिरफ्तार हुआ और लगभग 250 प्रतिष्ठित विरोधी बंदी बना लिये गए। 142 घोड़े शाही अस्तबल में पहुँच गए। तंकों से भरे हुए 60 बोरे, जिनमें 30 हजार तंके थे, पहाड़ी प्रदेशों के राजाओं से प्राप्त हुए और खज़ाने में भेज दिए गए। 20 दिन में उलुग खाँ ने बड़ी वीरता तथा योग्यता से इतनी सफलता प्राप्त की। 24 रबी उल-अव्वल 658 हि. (9 मार्च, 1260 ई.) को उलुग खाने मुअज्जम दरबार वापस आया।''[3]

इसके आगे मिनहाज लिखता है ''सुल्तान के आदेश पर पहाड़ों तथा भूतों के समान हाथियों को, जो क्षण भर लोगों को मृत्यु के घाट उतार देते थे, काफ़िरों को दण्ड देने के लिए देहली में हौज़े रानी के मैदान में उपस्थित किया गया। कुछ विद्रोहियों को हाथी के पैरों के नीचे कुचलवा दिया गया। तुर्कों की रक्त बहा देने वाली तलवारों ने दो-दो हिन्दुओं के चार-चार हिन्दू कर दिये। कई सौ

विद्रोहियों की खाल चाकू से उतरवा ली गई। खालों में घास भूस भर कर शहर के द्वार पर लटका देने का आदेश दे दिया गया।'' लेखक का मानना था कि इस प्रकार का कठोर दण्ड हौज़े रानी के सामने देहली के द्वार के समक्ष किसी को कभी न दिया गया था और न इस प्रकार के दण्ड की किसी ने कोई कथा ही सुनी थी।[1]

एक अन्य स्थान पर मिनहाज इस घटना का उल्लेख इस प्रकार करता है ''नया वर्ष आरम्भ हुआ। 13 सफर (29 जनवरी, 1260 ई.) को खाने मुअज्ज़म देहली से पर्वतों की ओर मेवातियों का, जिनसे भूत भी भयभीत रहते थे, दमन करने के लिए रवाना हुआ। लगभग 10 हजार वीर रक्तपायी सवार उसके साथ में थे। दूसरे दिन उसे अत्यधिक धन सम्पत्ति तथा पशु प्राप्त हो गए। उसने पर्वतों के कठिन मार्गों को पार करके हिन्दुओं का वध किया। इस विजय के उपरांत इस इतिहास का अंत होता है।[5]

मिनहाज की *तबकाते नासिरी* से प्राप्त उक्त जानकारी से पता चलता है कि लेखक मेवात के सम्बंध में अधिक नहीं जानता था। वह हरियाना, शिवालिक, रणथम्भोर तथा अन्य स्थानों पर विद्रोहों व लूटमार का कार्य मेवातियों के सिर मढ़ देता है। वह कहीं मेवाती तो कहीं हिन्दू शब्द का प्रयोग करता है। दिल्ली सुल्तानों की शाही सेनाओं के सामने उक्त लूटमार किसी संगठित दल अथा टोलियों के बिना सम्भव न थी। ऐसा लगता है कि तुर्कों द्वारा पराजित राजपूत शासक अपने समर्थकों द्वारा दिल्ली के आसपास ही पुनः सत्ता प्राप्त करने के लिए संघर्षरत थे, अतः य लोग स्थानीय लोगों को संगठित करके तुर्की सेनाओं से भिड़ जाते थे। साथ ही साथ उन स्थानों पर, जहाँ सुल्तानों का अधिकार नहीं था या फिर ढीला ढाला प्रशासन था, ये दल वहाँ प्रभावशाली ढंग से घुस पैठ करके शाही सम्पत्ति को लूट लेते थे और सुल्तानों की प्रजा विशेषकर मुसलमानों को परेशान करते थे। मिनहाज का लेखन वास्तव में सुल्तान नादिरूद्दीन शाह की प्रशंसा एवं उसके महत्त्वपूर्ण वज़ीर उलुग खा की प्रशंसा से भरा हुआ है, जिसमें मेवातियों की बहादुरी कम करके उनको केवल लुटेरे प्रदर्शित किया है, जो कि उचित प्रतीत नहीं होता।

मध्यकालीन मेवात सम्बंधी जानकारी देने वाला दूसरा प्रमुख फारसी ग्रंथ है— *तारीखे फीरोज़शाही*। इस ग्रंथ के लेखक ज़ियाउद्दीन बरनी का जन्म सुल्तान बल्बन के राज्यकाल में 684 हि. (1285–86 ई.) में हुआ था। वह माता की

ओर से कैथल के सैयिदों के वंश का था। बरनी का पिता मुईदुल्मुल्क सैयिद जलालुद्दीन के वंश की एक पुत्री का नाती था।

तेरहवीं शताब्दी में मंगोलों के आक्रमणों के कारण इस्लामी जगत के अनेक प्रतिष्ठित मुसलमान एवं विद्वान भारत आए थे और देहली इस्लामी शिक्षा का केन्द्र बन गया था। बरनी का आरंभिक जीवन इसी वातावरण में बीता। बरनी का पिता एक वज़ीरजादा था और उसका चचा अलाउलमुल्क सुल्तान अलाउद्दीन खलजी का सलाहाकार था। उसके पिता और चचा को अनेक ऊँचे पद प्राप्त हुए थे जिससे उसे उस काल की राजनैतिक घटनाओं को जानने में मदद मिली। बरनी ने अलाउद्दीन खलजी और उसके उत्तराधिकारियों के काल में बड़े सुख व आराम का जीवन व्यतीत किया। उसका अधिकांश समय विद्या अध्ययन व विद्वानों के साथ व्यतीत होता था। अमीर खुसरो तथा अमीर हसन उसके बड़े अच्छे मित्र थे।

ज़ियाउद्दीन बरनी सुल्तान मुहम्मद बिन तुग़लक का बड़ा विश्वासपात्र था और 17 वर्ष से भी अधिक समय तक उसके दरबार में रहा। मुहम्मद तुग़लक ने उसको अत्यधिक धन सम्पति प्रदान की और उस पर विशेष कृपा दृष्टि रखता था। सुल्तान मुहम्मद तुग़लक की मृत्यु के पश्चात बरनी के दिन बड़ी कठिनाइयों से बीते, जिसका उल्लेख वह अपने ग्रंथ में जगह-जगह पर करता है। सुल्तान फीरोज़शाह तुग़लक के सिंहासनरोहण के पश्चात उसका सब कुछ छिन गया था। न तो वह सुल्तान का विश्वासपात्र रहा और न ही उसके दरबार में उसे कोई मान प्राप्त था। वह अपने पुराने दिनों को याद करके रोया करता था। बरनी ने अपने इतिहास *तारीखे फीरोज़शाही* में बल्बन के राज्यरोहण से लेकर सुल्तान फीरोज़शाह तुग़लक के छः वर्ष के राज्य के इतिहास का वर्णन किया है। यद्यपि बरनी ने अन्य ग्रंथों की रचना भी की थी परंतु सर्वाधिक महत्त्वपूर्ण ग्रंथ *तारीखे फीरोज़शाही* ही है।

ज़ियाउद्दीन बरनी ने अपने इतिहास में अधिकतर उन्हीं घटनाओं का उल्लेख किया है, जिनकी सच्चाई पर उसे पूरा विश्वास था। उसका विचार था कि तारीखे फीरोज़शाही के समान कोई भी इतिहास पिछले एक हजार वर्ष से नहीं लिखा जा सका था परंतु बरनी के इतिहास में सबसे बड़ा दोष यह था कि बड़ी बड़ी महत्त्वपूर्ण घटनाओं को बड़े ही संक्षिप्त रूप में लिख देता है और घटनाओं का क्रमानुसार उल्लेख नहीं करता है। बरनी के इतिहास में समकालीन राजनैतिक,

आर्थिक अवस्था का पता चलता है। मुख्य रूप से सुल्तानों की विजयों, मंगोलों के आक्रमणों और उस काल के प्रतिष्ठित व्यक्तियों, सूफियों, उलेमाओं तथा अमीरों का हाल लिखा है। मेवात के सम्बंध में यद्यपि हमें थोड़ी ही जानकारी मिलती है फिर भी वह बहुत ही महत्त्वपूर्ण है।

जैसा कि ऊपर लिखा जा चुका है कि *तबकाते नासिरी* का लेखक मिनहाज अपने इतिहास को शाही सेनाओं द्वारा मेवों के दमन के साथ समाप्त करता है। वहीं ज़ियाउद्दीन बरनी अपनी *तारीखे-फीरोज़शाही* के आरम्भ में ही ग्यासुद्दीन बलबन के सिंहासनारोहण के प्रथम वर्ष में मेवों के विनाश का वर्णन करता है। बरनी के वर्णन से पता चलता है कि मेवों के उपद्रव अल्तमश (इल्तुतमिश) के काल में समाप्त तो कर दिये गए थे परन्तु उसके बाद किसी शासक ने भी मेवात की ओर ध्यान नहीं दिया था। लगता है कि बरनी ने *तबकाते नासिरी* का बारीकी से अध्ययन नहीं किया अथवा इतिहास लेखन के समय 1357 ई में 75 वर्ष की आयु में उसकी स्मरण शक्ति साथ नहीं दे रही थी। वैसे भी उसने बल्बन के काल से पहले के समय का इतिहास नहीं लिखा था और इस विश्वास के साथ कि जो मिनहाज लिख गया था, वह विश्वसनीय था, अतः दोहराना ठीक न था।

मेवात सम्बंधी बरनी की जानकारी दोषपूर्ण है। वह लिखता है कि शम्सुद्दीन अल्तमश के ज्येष्ठ पुत्रों की युवावस्था, असावधानी, मदिरापान, और भोग विलासिता और नसिरूद्दीन की अयोग्यता व निर्बलता के कारण देहली के निकट मेव बड़े शक्तिशाली बन बैठे थे। नासिरूद्दीन के काल में ही उलुग खाँ द्वारा मेवों का दमन किया गया था। वास्तव में मेवों द्वारा अरावली की श्रृख्लाओं में छापामार युद्ध प्रणाली उनके लिए वरदान थी जिस कारण वे अवसर पाते ही पुनः संघर्षशील हो जाते थे।

बरनी के अनुसार अधिकतर तो यह होता था कि वे रात को नगर पर धावा बोल देते और घरों को तहस नहस कर डालते; वे सर्वसाधारण को बड़ा कष्ट पहुँचाते। लोगों को मेवों के उत्पातों के भय से रात में नींद न आती। शहर (देहली) के निकट के घर मेवों ने विध्वंस कर डाले थे। शहर के आसपास के मेवों की लूटमार के भय से किबला (पश्चिम) दिशा के द्वार संध्या के नमाज के पश्चात बन्द हो जाते और किसी को इस बात का साहस न था कि शाम की नमाज के पश्चात निकल सके; किसी बुजुर्ग के दर्शन हो सकें;

आमोद-प्रमोद के लिए कोई हौज़े सुल्तान (सुल्तान शम्सुद्दीन का बनवाया हुआ शम्सी हौज) तक जा सके। बहुत से मेव शाम की नमाज के समय ही हौज़ के निकट पहुँज जाते। भिश्तियों, पानी भरने वाली दासियों को परेशान करते और उन्हें नंगा कर देते। उनके वस्त्र छीन लेते। आसपास के मेवों के भय के कारण देहली में हलचल मच गई थी। बरनी आगे लिखता है कि सुल्तान बल्बन ने मेवों के उपद्रव का दमन अपने राज्याभिषेक के प्रथम वर्ष से ही सभी कार्यों के अपेक्षा अत्यावश्यक समझा।[6]

बल्बन पूरा वर्ष मेवों के विनाश और आसपास के जंगलों को कटवाने में संलग्न रहा। सभी जंगल पूर्णतया कटवा डाले गये। मेवों की बहुत बड़ी संख्या कत्ल करा दी गई। उसने गोपालगीर में एक किला बनवाया। शहर (देहली) के निकट के स्थानों पर थाने बनवाये। वहाँ अफगानों को नियुक्त किया गया। थाने की भूमि को मफरूज (वह भूमि जो कि किलों की सेना के खर्च के लिए अलग कर दी जाती थी) कर दिया। इस युद्ध में सुल्तान के एक लाख खास आदमी मारे गये। सुल्तान ने अपनी तलवार के बल से अनेक मनुष्यों को मेवों की लूट मार और कत्लोगारत से बचा लिया। उस तिथि से प्रजा मेवों के भय से मुक्त हो गई।[7]

इस घटना से प्रतीत होता है कि मेवों की स्थिति पर्याप्त शाक्ति शाली थी ओर एक लाख शाही सैनिकों का मेवों द्वारा मारा जाना साधारण कार्य न था। मेवों का नेतृत्व किसी के हाथ में था? यह प्रश्न अभी तक बना हुआ है। फारसी ग्रंथों के लेखक अपनी रूचि केवल सुल्तान सम्बंधी कार्यों में अधिक रखते हैं और अन्य शक्तियों का केवल उल्लेख मात्र, वह भी तब, जब शासक वर्ग इन शक्तियों के विरूद्ध युद्ध अभियान ले जाता था।

फारसी इतिहासकारों की इस शृंखला में हमारा अगला विद्वान है—एसामी, जिसने अपने ग्रंथ *फुतूहुस्सलातीन* में मेवात अथवा मेवों का उल्लेख किया है। इमामी के पूरे नाम का पता नहीं चल सका है। इतनी ही जानकारी मिलती है कि उसके पूर्वज शम्सुद्दीन अल्तमश के काल में भारत आए थे, जिनमें से एक फखरूल्मुल्क एसामी था, जिसे अल्तमश ने सम्मानित किया और मंत्री पद प्रदान किया। इसी वंश में एसामी का जन्म 711 हि. (1311-12 ई.) के लगभग हुआ। एमामी ने अपनी बाल्यवस्था के सोलह वर्ष अपने दादा इज्जुद्दीन की संरक्षता में बिताये जो सुल्तान बल्बन का बहुत बड़ा विश्वासपात्र था। जब मुहम्मद

बिन तुग़लक ने दौलताबाद को बसाना आरम्भ किया तो एसामी भी अपने दादा के साथ अन्य अमीरों की भाँति दौलताबाद गया। रास्ते में ही उसके दादा का 90 वर्ष की आयु में देहांत हो गया। ऐसा प्रतीत होता है कि एमामी 751 हि. (1350–51 ई.) तक दौलताबाद में ही रहा और उसी वर्ष उसके अपने ग्रंथ फुतूहुस्सलातीन की रचना समाप्त की।

एमामी ने अपने ग्रंथ फिरदौसी के *शाहनामा* की भाँति कविता में लिखा। *शाहनामा* में आदम से लेकर महमूद गज़नवी तक का हाल लिखा गया है। एमामी ने महमूद गजनवी से लेकर 751 हि. (1351–52 ई.) तक का इतिहास लिखा है। एसामी ने लगता है कि बहुत सी पुस्तकें, जो उसके पास थीं, पढ़कर अपना ग्रंथ लिखा और बाकी जानकारी उसने अपने दादा से प्राप्त की होगी। देहली से दौलताबाद की यात्रा में तो वह स्वयं मौजूद था। उसके द्वारा लिखा गया दिल्ली के सुल्तानों का इतिहास बहुत ही महत्त्वपूर्ण है क्योंकि इसमें कई ऐसी घटनाओं का पता चलता है जो अन्य समकालीन ऐतिहासिक ग्रंथों में नहीं मिलती। मेवात सम्बंधी जानकारी यद्यपि पूर्ववर्ती विद्वानों द्वारा दी गई जानकारी पर आधरित है, फिर भी इसमें कुछ अतिरिक्त अंश जोड़े गये हैं। *फुतहुस्सलातीन* के हिन्दी अनुवाद में रिज़वी महोदय ने संक्षिप्त रूप में इतना ही लिखा है कि बल्बन ने दिल्ली के आसपास के जंगल कटवा डाले और गोपालगिरी के किले का निर्माण कराया।[8]

फुतूहुस्सलातीन का अंग्रेज़ी अनुवाद डा. महदी हुसैन ने तीन भागों में किया है। छटे अध्याय का अनुवाद करने के पश्चात डा. महदी हुसैन ने पृ. 359 से पृ. 359 तक इसकी टीका लिखी है। इस टीका से पता चलता है कि अल्तमश ने 623 ही. (1226 ई.) में अक्से देहली अर्थात देहली के आसपास एक अभियान चलाया जिससे देहली की सीमा पर अधिकार हो सके। वास्वत में उसने मेवात को अपने नियंत्रण में किया जो अनुवादक के अनुसार मुइज्ज़ुद्दीन मुहम्मद गौरी की मृत्यु के बाद भट्टी राजपूतों के अधिकार में था।[19] इसी टीका में एक अन्य स्थान पर मेवात में हिन्दुओं के विद्रोह को नष्ट करने का मात्र उल्लेख ही है।[10] सुल्तान बल्बन के राज्यकाल की घटनाओं पर टीका करते समय अनुवादक इस घटना की पुनर्रावृति करते हुए लिखता है कि बल्बन ने सुल्तान बनने से पूर्व एक से अधिक बार मेवों का दमन किया था। अपने राज्यकाल के प्रथम वर्ष में ही बल्बन ने मेवों के उत्पात को समाप्त किया, जिन्होंने अपनी स्थिति फिर से

मजबूत बना ली थी, मार्गों को अवरूद्ध कर दिया था और राहगीरों को लूट लेते थे। अगले वर्ष बल्बन ने मेवों को देहली से बाहर किया और किले का निर्माण कराया। अनेक स्थानों पर थाने और चौकियाँ स्थापित कराई।[11] अनुवादित पदों (3133–3135) में बल्बन द्वारा गोपालगिरी किले बनवाने का उल्लेख भी है।[12]

मलफूजाते तिमूरी अथवा *तुज़ुके तिमूरी*, तैमूर की आत्मकथा है जो चग़तई तुर्की भाषा में लिखी गई थी। इसका फारसी अनुवाद करके अबू तालिब हुसैनी ने मुग़ल सम्राट शाहजहाँ को समर्पित की थी। तैमूर की इस आत्मकथा का उद्देश्य अपने पुत्रों व उत्तराधिकारियों को उन योजनाओं सैनिक अभियानों, शासन, विधि, प्रशासनिक विचारों व संस्थाओं से अवगत कराना था जिनको कि उसने स्वयं प्रयुक्त अथवा प्रचलित किया। ऐसा प्रतीत होता है कि अपने जीवन के संध्याकाल में तैमूर ने स्वयं से सम्बंधित घटनाओं का, लिखित सामग्री के आध ाार पर पुनरावलोकन किया व तिथि क्रम पर बल न देते हुए उन घटनाओं को लेख बद्ध किया। भारत से सम्बंधित इस रचना का अंग्रेज़ी में अनुवाद इल्यिट डाऊसन की *हिस्ट्री आफ इंडिया,* भाग तीन में उपलब्ध है।

मेवात सम्बंधी जानकारी बहादुर नाहिर की तैमूर से भेंट व उसके द्वारा दिये गये दो तोतों की प्रशंसा को लेकर है जो शरफुद्दीन अली यज़दी की पुस्तक *ज़फरनामा* में दिए गए विवरण से मिलती जुलती सी है। तैमूर लिखता है कि उसने कोटला में बहादुर नाहिर के पास सैयिद शम्सुद्दीन एवं अलाऊद्दीन नायबे करकरी का दूत मंडल भेजा जो उसके हाथ का लिखा एक पत्र लाए जो सम्मानपूर्वक लिखा गया था। इस खत में बहादुर नाहिर ने तैमूर के दरबार में उपस्थित होने की बात लिखी थी। तैमूर लिखता है कि बहादुर नाहिर ने दो सफेद तोते भेजे थे, जो मनभावन बातचीत करते थे। दूतों ने वे तोते उसे भेंट किए और बताया कि वे दो तोते सुल्तान तुग़लक शाह के थे ओर हमेशा सुल्तानों के दरबार में रहे थे। तोतों की शक्ल व आवाज तैमूर को बड़ी संतुष्टि प्रदान करती थी। इस कारण उसने ये निर्देश दिए कि वे प्रतिदिन पिजरों में उसके सामने प्रस्तुत किए जायें जिससे कि वह उनकी बातचीत सुन सके।[12]

शरफुद्दीन अली यज़दी द्वारा रचिता *ज़फरनामा* तैमूर के राज्यकाल का पूर्ण इतिहास है। लेखक तैमूर के पुत्र सुल्तान शाहरूख (1405 से 1447 ई.) का विश्वास पात्र था और बाद में दरबार से जुड़ा रहा। यज़दी अपन विद्वता तथा पांडित्य के लिए प्रसिद्ध था और अपनी काव्यमयी फारसी रचनाओं के लिए

उसने बड़ी ख्याति प्राप्त कर ली थी। उसकी सर्वाधिक प्रसिद्ध पुस्तक *ज़फरनामा* ही थी, जिसे उसने 1424-25 ई. में समाप्त किया। तैमूर के भारतवर्ष पर आक्रमण का लेखक ने अपनी काव्यमयी भाषा में बड़े उत्साह से विवरण किया है। मेवात सम्बंधी जानकारी लेखक की इस कृति के भाग दो में विशेष स्थान रखती है।

ज़फरनामा में पहली बार स्पष्ट होता है कि बहादुर नाहिर मेवात का शासक था न कि वली या हाकिम का। यज़दी लिखता है कि तैमूर ने 801 हि. (जनवरी 1399 ई.) में सैयिद शम्सुद्दीन तथा अलाउद्दीन नायब कोकरी को कोटला भेजा गया था आर उस स्थान के शासक बहादुर नाहिर ने आज्ञाकारिता प्रदर्शित की थी और तैमूर से भेंट करने का विश्वास दिलाया था। यज़दी आगे लिखता है कि बहादुर नाहिर के भेजे हुए दो तोते राजदूतों ने प्रस्तुत किये और निवेदन किया कि दोनों तोते तुग़लक शाह के राज्यकाल से जीवित थे और बहुत समय तक वे सुल्तानों की सभाओं में मीठी-मीठी बातें करते रहे थे। साहेब किरान (तैमूर) ने उन पक्षियों की प्राप्ति को अपने लिए शुभ समझा · · · निश्चित दिन बहादुर नाहिर तथा उसका पुत्र कुल्ताश उचित प्रकार के उपहार लेकर शाही दरबार में उपस्थित हुए और भूमि चूमने के सम्मान से सम्मानित हुए।[13]

यहया बिन अहमद बिन अब्दुल्लाह सहरिन्दी की *तारीखे मुबारकशाही* एक समकालीन ग्रंथ है जिसमें मुइज्जुद्दीन बिन साम से लेकर 1434 ई. तक का दिल्ली के सुल्तानों का है। लेखक को सैय्यद सुल्तानों का आश्रय प्राप्त था तथा समकालीन कुलीनों, दरबारियों, उच्चधिकारियों के सम्पर्क में रहा था और अनेक घटनाओं का वह प्रत्यक्षदर्शी रहा था। यहया ने अपने ग्रंथ की रचना सैय्यद सुल्तान मुबारक शाह की मृत्यु के बाद की थी। बरनी और अफीफ के इतिहास को आगे बढ़ाने में इस ग्रंथ का काफी महत्त्व है। इस ग्रंथ की विशेषता यह है कि यह फीरोजशाह तुगलक के अंतिम दिनों का विस्तार पूर्वक इतिहास है। लगता है कि यहया ने उस समय उपलब्ध ग्रंथों का भी अध्ययन किया होगा। बाद के इतिहासकारों ने यहया की *तारीखे मुबारकशाही* से काफी मदद ली है। यूँ तो ग्रंथ में मुख्यतः दिल्ली के सुल्तानों, उनकी विजयों आदि का कालक्रम से वर्णन ही है फिर भी बहादुर नाहिर व मेवात सम्बंधी जानकारी अति महत्त्वपूर्ण है जो सर्वप्रथम यहया ने उपलब्ध कराई है।

मेवात का उल्लेख इस ग्रंथ में सर्वप्रथम फीरोज़शाह तुग़लक के शास काल

के अंतिम दिनों में आता है जब सुल्तान के पुत्र शाहज़ादा मुहम्मद खाँ ने सुल्तान के वजीर खानेजहाँ का घर लूट लिया और उसे मेवात की ओर भागने पर विवश किया। खानेजहाँ ने महारी (अलवर के दक्षिण में माचेरी) में कोका चौहान के पास शरण ली परंतु बाद में जब शाही सेनाएँ महारी भेजी गईं तो कोका चौहान ने खानेज़हाँ का वध करा दिया।[44]

फीरोज़शाह तुग़लक की मृत्यु के बाद उसका पौत्र फतह खाँ सुल्तान के पद पर आसीन हुआ। शाहज़ादा मुहम्मद खाँ विद्रोह करके सिरमूर की पहाड़ियों की ओर भाग गया। उसके विरूद्ध मलिक फीरोज़ अली व बहादुर नाहिर को भेजा गया।[15] इस घटना से यह पता चलता है कि बहादुर नाहिर शाही सेवा में आ चुका था और दरबार में उसे कोई उच्च पद प्राप्त था।

यहया लिखता है कि किस प्रकार बहादुर नाहिर की सहायता से फीरोज़शाह तुग़लक के एक अन्य पौत्र अबू बक्र शाह ने दिल्ली का शासन प्राप्त किया था।[16] अगले वर्ष फीरोज़शाह के कुछ प्राचीन दासों ने अबू बक्र शाह के विरूद्ध विद्रोह कर दिया और मुहम्मद शाह से मिल गये। अबू बक्र शाह अनेक अमीरों और अनुयाइयों के साथ देहली से भाग कर बहादुर नाहिर के पास चला गया, जो कोटला में था। कुछ दिन पश्चात फीरोज़शाह के कुछ प्राचीन दास भी अपने परिवारों को लेकर कोटला पहुँच गये।[17] यहया के इस विवरण से पता चलता है कि बहादुर नाहिर कोटला को राजधानी बना कर मेवात पर शासन कर रहा था और इतना शक्तिशाली बन गया था कि शाही परिवारों को सुरक्षा प्रदान कर रहा था।

तारीखे मुबारकशाही से पता चलता है कि जब अबू बक्र शाह और फीरोज़ी दास बहादुर नाहिर के पास शरण लिए हुए थे तो सुल्तान मुहम्मद शाह ने उनके विनाश के लिए शाहज़ादा हुमायूँ खाँ, इस्लाम खाँ, गालिब खाँ, राय कमालुद्दीन एवं राय जुलजी को एक शक्तिशाली सेना देकर भेजा। उपरोक्त अमीर महेन्दवाली कस्बे में पहुँचे। मुहर्रम 793 हि. (दिसम्बर-जनवरी 1390-91 ई.) में अबू बक्र शाह, बहादुर नाहिर तथा फीरोज़ी दासों ने एक साथ एकत्र होकर प्रातः काल उपयुक्त सेना पर आक्रमण कर दिया और बहुत से आदमी मार डाले। इस्लाम खाँ अपनी सेना सुव्यवस्थित करके आक्रमणकारियों से युद्ध करने लगा। शाहज़ादा अपने अनुयाइयों सहित घोड़े पर सवार हुआ और उसने पहले ही आक्रमण में शत्रुओं का पराजित कर दिया। शाही सैनिकों ने पलायन करने वालों का पीछा

किया। उनमें से अधिकांश ने कोटला में शरण ली। कुछ मार डाले तथा कुछ बन्दी बना लिए गए। इस समाचार के पहुँचते ही सुल्तान ने भी दिल्ली से युद्ध-स्थल की ओर प्रस्थान किया और कोटला पहुँच कर धाँड (झील) के तट पर पड़ाव किया। अबू बक्र शाह तथा बहादुर नाहिर ने शरण की प्रार्थना की और वे सुल्तान से मिलने आये। बहादुर नाहिर को एक खिलअत प्राप्त की और वापस भेज दिया गया। अबू बक्र शाह को सुल्तान खण्डी ले गया, जहाँ से वह अमरोहा भेज दिया गया। वहीं उसके बन्दी बनाने का आदेश हुआ और बन्दीगृह में ही उसकी मृंत्यु हो गई।[18] इस घटना से यहाँ लगता है कि सुल्तान मुहम्मद शाह के लिए दिल्ली दरबार की राजनीति व षडयंत्रों के कारण मेवात पर अधिकार जमाना और उस पर शासन करना कठिन रहा होगा अन्यथा बहादुर नाहिर को खिलअत से सम्मानित करके वापस न भेजता।

दो—तीन वर्ष बाद जब मुहम्मद शाह की स्थिति थोड़ी मज़बूत हो गई तो उसने शव्वाल 795 हि. (अगस्त-सितम्बर 1393 ई.) में मेवात के विरूद्ध कूच किया और उसे विध्वंस किया और मुहम्मदाबाद से होकर जतेसर लौट गया, जहाँ वह बीमार हो गया। बहादुर नाहिर ने दिल्ली के समीपवर्ती स्थानों को लूट लिया। सुल्तान ने पुनः बहादुर नाहिर को पराजित किया। शाही सेनाओं ने कोटला में उसका पीछा किया और बहुत से आदमी बन्दी बना लिए गए तथा उनके घोड़ों, अस्त्र-शस्त्रों एवं सामानों को लूट लिया गया। बहादुर नाहिर कोटला से भाग खड़ा हुआ तथा जहर (झिर या झिरका?) नामक पर्वत में छिप गया। सुल्तान पुनः मुहम्मदाबाद लौट गया।[19]

यहया उल्लेख करता है क फीरोजशाह तुग़लक का एक पौत्र नुसरत खाँ पुत्र फतह खाँ मेवात में था जिसे रबी उल अव्वल 797 हि. (दिसम्बर-जनवरी 1394-95) में नासिरूद्दीन नुसरत शाह की उपाधि ग्रहण करा कर फीरोज़ाबाद में सिंहासनारूढ़ किया गया। नासिरूद्दीन के दरबार में शिहाब नाहिर मेवाती का ज़िक्र होता है जिसे सुल्तान ने शिहाब खाँ की उपाधि से सम्मानित किया।[20]

तारीखे मुबारकशाही के अनुसार उस समय दो बादशाह थे एक देहली में तथा दूसरा फीरोज़ाबाद में। मुकर्रब खाँ ने (वह सुल्तान महमूद नासिरूद्दीन शाह के पुत्र मुहम्मद का वजीर था) बहादुर नाहिर तथा उसके अनुयाइयों को अपने साथ मिला और उसे प्राचीन देहली के दुर्ग का रक्षक बना दिया।[21] देहली और फीरोज़ाबाद में प्रतिदिन युद्ध होता रहता था परंतु कोई भी दल किसी अन्य दल

पर विजय प्राप्त न कर सका। अन्त में शव्वाल 800 हि. (जून-जुलाई 1398 ई.) में मुकर्रब खाँ के ही साथी ने षडयंत्र करके नासिरूद्दीन नुसरत शाह से मिल गये और सुल्तान महमूद नासिरूद्दीन शाह, मुकर्रब खाँ और बहादुर नाहिर दिल्ली के किले में बन्द कर दिये गये।[22] इस घटना के बाद लेखक बहादुर नाहिर का उल्लेख तब करता है जब तैमूर के दिल्ली आक्रमण के समय उसके भय से मसनदे आला खिज्रखाँ (सैयद वंश का संस्थापक) ने मेवात के पर्वतों में शरण ली। बाद में खिज्र खाँ एवं अन्य अमीरों के साथ तैमूर की भेंट से बहादुर नाहिर भी सम्मानित हुआ।[23]

तैमूर के चले जाने के उपरांत नासिरूद्दीन नुसरत शाह फीरोज़ाबाद के सिंहासन पर वैठा। शिहाब खाँ मेवात से दस हाथियों तथा सैनिकों के साथ उससे दिल्ली आ मिला।[24] परंतु अगले ही वर्ष 803 हि. (दिसम्बर-जनवरी 1401 में) इकबाल खाँ ने बरन से दिल्ली पर चढ़ाई कर दी तो नुसरत शाह फीरोज़ाबाद छोड़ कर मेवात की ओर चल दिया और उसकी वहीं मृत्यु हो गई।[25]

इस घटना के बाद खिज्र खाँ द्वारा 814 हि. (1411-12 ई. में) मेवात पर आक्रमण करने का उल्लेख मिलता है। यहया लिख्ता है कि मेवात में तिजारा, सरहथ (सरहटा) तथा खरोल नामक कस्बों को नष्ट कर दिया गया और मेवात के अधिकांश स्थानों को विध्वंस करता हुआ वह दिल्ली पहुँचा।[26]

816 हि. (जुलाई-अगस्त 1413 ई.) में पुनः खिज्र खाँ द्वारा मेवात पर आक्रमण करने का उल्लेख है। इस बार खिज्र खाँ के अमीर जलाल खाँ की बहादुर नाहिर से भेंट का उल्लेख है।[27] लगता है मेवात को पूरी तरह अपने अधिकार में नहीं किया जा सका था क्योंकि पुनः 824 हि. (1421 ई.) में सुल्तान बनने के बाद खिज्र खाँ मेवात की ओर प्रस्थान करता है। कुछ मेवाती बहादुर नाहिर के कोटले (किले) में घिर गये और कुछ ने युद्ध किया। *रायते आला* (खिज्र खाँ) ने कोटले के निकट पड़ाव किया। मेव युद्ध करने लगे। प्रथम आक्रमण ही में कोटला (किले) पर विजय प्राप्त हो गई। मेव भाग कर पर्वत में प्रविष्ट हो गये। *रायते आला* ने कोटला को नष्ट भ्रष्ट कर दिया।[28] लगता है इसके बाद मेव शाही सेना में भर्ती हो गए। खिज्र खाँ की मृत्यु के पश्चात उसका पुत्र अबुल फतह मुबारकशाह 20 मई, 1421 ई. को दिल्ली की गद्दी पर सिंहासनारूढ़ हुआ। उसके राज्यकाल में मेवातियों का उल्लेख शाही सेना के अग्रिम भाग में मिलता है जिन्होंने ग्वालियर के अलप खाँ के शिविर को नष्ट

करने में अपनी भूमिका अदा की।[29]

रजब 828 हि. (मई–जून 1425 ई.) में सुल्तान मुबारकशाह द्वारा मेवों के विद्रोह का समाचार प्राप्त होते ही मेवात की विलायत में जाने और उसे विध्वंस करने का उल्लेख है। यहया लिखता है, "मेव समस्त विलायत को वीरान करके जहरा (?) नामक पर्वत में, जो अत्यंत दृढ़ स्थान है, घुस गये। उस पर्वत के अत्यंत दृढ होने के कारण उस पर विजय प्राप्त न हो सकती थी। अनाज की कमी हो गई, अतः संसार को शरण प्रदान करने वाला स्वामी (सुल्तान) सुरक्षित एवं लूट की धन-सम्पत्ति सहित शहर की ओर लौट आया और शुभ नक्षत्र में रजब 828 हि. (मई–जून 1425 ई.) में *कूशके दौलत* (राजमहल) में पहुँचा।[30]

अगले ही वर्ष 829 हि. (1425–26 ई.) में मुबारक शाह ने पुनः मेवात पर चढ़ाई कर दी। "बहादुर नाहिर के नाती जल्लू तथा कद्दू और कुछ अन्य मेव, जो उनसे मिल गये थे, अपने-अपने स्थानों को नष्ट करके इन्दौर के पर्वत में प्रविष्ट हो गए। वे कुछ दिन तक फिरते रहे। जब विजयी सेना (शाही सेना) ने शक्ति का प्रदर्शन किया तो वे इन्दौर के किले को खाली करके अलवर पर्वत में चले गए। दूसरे दिन संसार के स्वामी ने इन्दौर के किले को नष्ट-भ्रष्ट करके अलवर की ओर प्रस्थान किया। जब वह निकट पहुँचा तो जल्लू तथा कद्दू ने उस स्थान पर भी किलेबन्दी की। विजयी सेना निरंतर आक्रमण करती रही। फलतः विवश होकर उन्होंने क्षमा-याचना कर ली और शरण की प्रार्थना की। उनकी प्रार्थना स्वीकार कर ली गई। कद्दू सुल्तान के चरणों के चुम्बन द्वारा सम्मानित हुआ। वह पुनः भाग कर पर्वत में प्रविष्ट होना चाहता था, अतः उसे पकड़ कर बन्दी बना लिया गया। संसार के स्वामी ने मेवात की विलायत तथा अधिकांश ग्रामों को नष्ट भ्रष्ट कर दिया। कुछ समय तक उसने कोहपाया में विश्राम किया। तत्पश्चात उस प्रदेश में अनाज तथा चारे की कमी के कारण वह राजधानी (देहली) वापस चला गया और शाबान 829 हि. (जून-जुलाई 1426 ई.) में शुभ मुहूर्त तथा नक्षत्र में दौलतखाने के कूश्के में पहुँचा। दूसरे वर्ष मुहर्रम 830 हि. (नवम्बर-दिसम्बर 1426 ई.) को सुल्तान ने ब्याना की ओर प्रस्थान किया और मेवात की विलायत में होता हुआ तथा उनकी दुष्टता एवं विद्रोह के लिए दंड देता हुआ ब्याना पहुँचा।"[31]

अब तक की घटनाओं से यही लगता है कि मेवात क्षेत्र न केवल शाही परिवार के लोगों के लिए बल्कि क्षेत्रीय मुक्ताओं के लिए एक शरणास्थल बन चुका था।

26 रजब (11 मई 1428 ई.) को जब सुल्तान ने ब्याना की ओर प्रस्थान किया तो मुहम्मद खाँ (ब्याना का इक्तादार) अपने सहायकों सहित मेवात की ओर चल दिया।[32]

वास्तव में फ़ीरोज़शाह तुगलक की मृत्यु के साथ ही दिल्ली सल्तनत छिन्न-भिन्न होनी आरम्भ हो गई और उस पर तैमूर के आक्रमण के बाद स्थानीय शक्तियाँ सिर उठा रही थीं। जौनपुर, बंगाल, गुजरात, मेवाड़ आदि सभी विलायतें बढ़ चढ़ कर दिल्ली की राजनीति में रूचि दिखा रहीं थीं। जहाँ तक मेवातियों का प्रश्न है यहया के लेखन से यह प्रतीत होता है कि उन्होंने जौनपुर के शासकों से तालमेल बनाया हुआ था। यहया लिखता है कि मेवात का मलिक कद्दू जौनपुर के सुल्तान इब्राहीम से मिल गया था। इस अपराध के लिए शव्वाल 831 हि. (जुलाई-अगस्त 1428 ई.) में सुल्तान मुबारक शाह ने उसकी घर के भीतर ही हत्या करा दी। मलिक सरवरूलमुल्क को मेवात की ओर विद्रोह शांत करने तथा उस विलायत को सुव्यवस्थित करने के लिए भेजा गया। उनके कुछ कस्बे तथा ग्राम, जो जंगलों में बसे हुए थे, नष्ट करके पर्वत में चला गया। मलिक कद्दू का भाई जलाल खाँ तथा अन्य सरदार उदाहरणार्थ अहमद खाँ, मलिक फखरूद्दीन, मलिक अली तथा उनके सम्बंधी अश्वारोहियों तथा पदातियों सहित इन्दौर के किले में एकत्र हो गए। जब मलिक सरवरूलमुल्क उपर्युक्त किले के निकट उतरा तो वह मुकाबला न कर सके। उन्होंने संधि की वार्ता आरम्भ कर दी और यह निश्चय हुआ कि वह दासों के समान कर भेजा करेगा। तदनुसार धन, कर तथा दासों को लेकर मलिक सरवरूलमुल्क सेनाओं सहित शहर को लौट गया।[33]

तारीखे मुबारक शाही से ऐसा लगता है कि मेवात के अमीरों ने नाममात्र की ही अधीनता स्वीकार की थी और कर देना बन्द कर दिया था अन्यथा सुल्तान को फिर से मेवात पर आक्रमण करने की आवश्यकता न पड़ती। यहया लिखता है सुल्तान ने कोहपाया मेवात पर चढ़ाई करने का संकल्प किया और हौजे खास पर बारगाह (शिविर) लगवाई। राज्य के चारों ओर से अमीर तथा मलिक सुल्तान की सेवा में उपस्थित हुए। वहाँ से वह मंहदवारी (?) के कूश्क में उतरा। कुछ समय तक वहाँ ठहरा रहा। जलाल खाँ मेव, तथा अन्य मेवों ने विवश होकर धन, कर तथा उपहार प्रथानुसार अदा करना स्वीकार कर लिया।[34]

यह अधीनता अधिक समय तक नहीं रही और फिर से वह दिल्ली से सम्बंध विच्छेद करके स्वतंत्रता का बोलबाला शुरू हुआ। लेकिन दिल्ली के

समीप विद्रोही गतिविधियों का केसे पनपने दिया जा सकता था अतः रबी-उल-अव्वल 836 हि. (अक्तूबर-नवम्बर 1432 ई.) में पुनः सुल्तान को मेवात की ओर प्रस्थान करना पड़ा। पहाड़ियों में शिविर लगाये गये और निरंतर कूच करते हुए सुल्तान ताऊस (तावड़ू) कस्बे के निकट पहुँचा। जलाल खाँ मेव को जब यह समाचार प्राप्त हुए तो वह अत्याधिक सेना लेकर अन्दबर (इंदौर?) के किले में, जो मेवातियों के किलों में अत्यंत दृढ़ था, बन्द हो गया। यहया लिखता है, "दूसरे दिन बादशाह ने तैयार होकर उस किले पर अधिकार जमाने के लिए आक्रमण किया। अभी विजयी सेना का अग्रिम दल भी वहाँ न पहुँचा था क जलाल खाँ किले के भीतर आग लगाकर कोटला की ओर भाग गया। जो सामग्री, वस्त्र अनाज इत्यादि उसने किले में बन्द होकर युद्ध करने के लिए एकत्र किये थे उनमें से अधिकांश विजयी सेना के हाथ लग गये। *रायाते आला* ने वहाँ से कूच करके तजारा कस्बे में पड़ाव किया और अधिकांश मेवात प्रदेश नष्ट कर दिया। जब जलाल खाँ विवश तथा व्याकुल हो गया तो उसने आज्ञाकारिता स्वीकार कर ली और प्रथानुसार धन तथा कर प्रदान किया। तजारा कस्बे में मलिक एमादुलमुल्क ब्याना की अक्ता से अत्याधिक अश्वारोहियों तथा पदातियों को लेकर सुल्तान की सेवा में उपस्थित हुआ।"[35]

मुहम्मद बिहामद खानी की *तारीखे मुहम्मदी* यहया की *तारिखे मुबारकशाही* के समान विभिन्न घटनाओं के क्रम का पता लगाने के लिए बड़ा ही महत्त्वपूर्ण ग्रंथ है। विशेषकर फीरोज़शाह तुग़लक के उत्तराधिकारियों के काल के इतिहास की जानकारी के लिए इतिहासकार इसी ग्रंथ पर निर्भर हैं। मुहम्मद बिहामद खाँ ऐरिच (बुंदेलखंड में) के अक्तादार मलिक बिहामद खाँ का पुत्र था। लेखक एक सफल सैनिक था और अनेक युद्धों में भाग ले चुका था। बाद में ऐरिच के एक सूफी युसुफ बुद्ध का शिष्य हो गया और धार्मिक कार्यों में तल्लीन हो गया। अपनी कृति *तारीखे मुहम्मदी* में उसने मुहम्मद साहब से लेकर 842 हि. (1438-39 ई.) तक का हाल लिखा है। अपने समकालीन इतिहास में उसने कालपी के सुल्तानों का हाल तथा सुल्तान मुहम्मद बिन तुग़लक शाह के बाद के सुल्तानों का हाल कुछ अपनी जानकारी के आधार पर लिखा है। मेवात एवं मेवातियों सम्बंधी जानकारी काफी महत्तवपूर्ण है।

सर्वप्रथम, मेवात का उल्लेख अबू बक्र शाह द्वारा मेवात के. वाली (अधिकारी) बहादुर खाँ से जाकर मिलने का है।[36] तत्पश्चात फीरोज़शाह के प्राचीन दासों का

मेवात में अबू बक्र शाह के पास चले जाने का है।[37] यहाँ मुहम्मद बिहामद खाँ का विवरण यहया से भिन्न है और लिखता है कि मेवात के बहादुर खाँ ने अबू बक्र शाह को अपनी शरण में ले लिया और उसके सिर पर चत्र बहुत बड़ा विद्रोह उठ खड़ा हुआ। सुल्तान नासिरूद्दीन मुहम्मद शाह पुत्र फीरोजशाह मेवात की ओर अबू बक्र शाह को भागने तथा बहादुर खाँ के विनाश हेतु निकला और निरंतर प्रस्थान करते हुए कोटला किले के क्षेत्र में, जो मेवात का सबसे बड़ा किला था, उतर पड़ा और युद्ध की तैयारियाँ कराने लगा। बहादुर खाँ, जो अपने समय का बहुत बड़ा योद्धा था, अबू बक्र शाह को चत्र पहना कर सुल्तान के मुकाबले में युद्ध करके उन्हें पहले आक्रमण में ही पराजित कर दिया। अबू बक्र शाह अपने अत्याधिक पदातियों एवं अश्वारोहियों का विनाश कराके कोटला के किले में घुस गया। सुल्तान मुहम्मद शाह ने उसका पीछा किया और हाथी एवं सेना कोटला के किले के द्वार पर ले गया और इस दृढ़ किले को जिवय कर लिया एवं ध्वंस करा दिया। अबू बक्र शाह तथा बहादुर खाँ ने सुनाम पर्वत की कन्दराओं में शरण ले ली। सुल्तान ने उस पर्वत की कन्दराओं की ओर प्रस्थान किया और युद्ध तथा रक्तपात किया। बहादुर खाँ ने अपने आप को विनाश के निकट पाकर अबू बक्र शाह को बन्दी बना दिया। विजय एवं सफलता प्राप्त करने के उपरांत राजधानी की ओर लौट आया। अबू बक्र शाह की कुछ समय उपरांत मृत्यु हो गई।[38]

यहया की भाँति मुहम्मद बिहामद खानी भी महमूदशाह के काल के आरम्भ में ही अमीरों के मतभेद के कारण बहादुर खाँ, मुकर्रव खाँ तथा मल्लू खाँ द्वारा पुरानी देहली में हिसार, जहाँ पनाह तथा कूश्के सीरीं पर अधिकार प्राप्त करने का उल्लेख करता है। मुकर्रब द्वारा नुसरत शाह से जाकर मिल जाने से परिस्थितियाँ बदल गईं। बहादुर खाँ अपनी विलायत मेवात चला गया।[39]

इस काल का अंतिम ऐतिहासिक स्त्रोत बाबर द्वारा लिखित उसकी स्वयं की आत्मकथा *तुज़ुके बाबरी* है। मूल रूप में तुर्की भाषा में लिखी गई इस कृति का बाद में अकबर द्वारा फारसी में अनुवादित कराया गया। आज इस बहुमूल्य ग्रंथ का अनुवाद विश्व की अनेक भाषाओं में उपलब्ध है। *बाबरनामा* से प्रसिद्ध इस पुस्तक में सोलहवीं शताब्दी के राजनैतिक, सामाजिक एवं आर्थिक इतिहास का पता चलता है। इसमें मध्यएशिया एवं उतरी भारत का पर्याप्त वर्णन है। भारत की जलवायु, पर्वत, नदियाँ जंगल, फल, फूल, जानवर एवं यहाँ के लोगों के रहन

सहन सम्बंधी जानकारी इस ग्रंथ की मुख्य विशेषता है। इस लेख में *बाबरनामा* के ए. एस. बेवरिज द्वारा किया गया अंग्रेज़ी अनुवाद प्रयोग में लाया गया है।

मेवात सम्बंधी जापकारी तो बाबर के स्वयं के अनुभव एवं आँखों देखी घटनाओं पर आधारित है। इस काल के सभी इतिहासकारों में केवल बाबर ही ऐसा है जो हसन खाँ मेवाती के बारे में लिखता है जिसे वह स्वयं मिल चुका था। इसके अतिरिक्त बाबर द्वारा मेवात पर खानज़ादों के दो सौ वर्षों के शासन का उल्लेख बहुत ही महत्त्वपूर्ण है।

मेवात का सर्वप्रथम उल्लेख *बाबरनामा* में तब मिलता है जब बाबर आगरा के किले में बंद इब्राहीम लोदी के अमीरों का विवरण देता। इन अमीरों में एक फीरोज खाँ मेवाती भी था। इन लोगों ने आगरा में हुमायूँ का अधिक विरोध किया था। इसी कारण उन्हें आगरा में बंद कर दिया गया और बाद में मौत का आदेश दिया गया। कुछ लोगों के बीच में पड़ने से उन्हें माफ कर दिया गया और उनकी सम्पत्ति आदि लौटा दी गई।[41]

तत्पश्चात बाबर हिन्दुस्तान की पर्वत श्रेणियों का वर्णन करते हुए अरावली पर्वतमाला एवं मेवात का विवरण देता है। वह लिखता है कि अरावली पर्वत श्रेणी उत्तर से दक्षिण की तरफ चली जाती है। यह श्रृंखला दिल्ली में एक छोटी से चट्टान से शुरू होती जहाँ फीरोजशाह (तुग़लुक) ने अपना महल जहाँनुमा बनवाया था। यहाँ से यह छोटी-छोटी पहाड़ी चट्टानों के रूप में प्रतीत होती है। मेवात को पार करके ये पर्वतमाला बयाना प्रदेश में प्रवेश करती है। सीकरी, बारी और दूलपुर (धौलपुर) के पहाड़ भी इसी का भाग हैं।[42]

पानीपत में इब्राहीम लोदी के साथ युद्ध में बाबर हसन खाँ मेवाती के बेटे नाहर खाँ मेवाती का हाथों में पड़ जाने का उल्लेख करता है जिसे बंधक बनकर रखा गया था। इसके फलस्वरूप हसन खाँ बाबर के पास आता-जाता रहता था। वह अपने बेटे के छोड़ने का अनुरोध करता रहता था। कुछ लोगों को लगा कि यदि उसके बेटे को छोड़ दिया जाए तो सम्भव था हसन खाँ मेवाती बाद में बाबर का समर्थन करे। उक्त परामर्श से बाबर ने नाहर खाँ को खिलअत प्रदान की और पिता के लिए वादा कराकर छोड़ दिया गया। परंतु हसन खाँ मेवाती जैसा कि हम जानते हैं राणा साँगा से मिला हुआ था, नहीं लौटा[43] और बाद में खनुआ के युद्ध में बाबर की सेनाओं का सामना करता है।

बाबरनामा में इस घटना के पश्चात मेवात को लूटने का विवरण मिलता है।

24 फरवरी 1527 ई. को बाबर ने शेख जमाल फर्मूली को दोआब से जितने भी तीरंदाज़ मिलें, उन्हें लेकर मेवात में लूट मार का आदेश दिया और इतनी अशांति हो जाए कि कुछ भी न बचे जिससे शत्रु को उधर की चिंता हो। मुल्ला तर्क अली को, जो काबुल से आया था, आदेश दिया कि वह शेख जमाल के साथ जाकर उसकी सहायता करे और मेवात को हर तरीके से नष्ट भ्रष्ट कर दे। मगफ़ूर दीवान को भी इसी आशय का आदेश दिया गया। इन लोगों ने मेवात के कोनों में जाकर कुछ ग्रामों को विध्वंस किया और कुछ लोगों को कैदी बनाया परंतु इससे शत्रुओं को जरा भी खटका न हुआ।[44]

खनुआ के युद्ध में हसन खाँ राणा साँगा का साथ देता है। बाबर लिखता है कि उसके पास 12000 घुड़सवार थे।[45] हसन खाँ इस युद्ध में मारा जाता है। बाबर के अनुसार किसी बन्दूक चलाने वाले ने उसे अपना निशाना बनाया था[46] खनुआ के युद्ध के बाद बाबर मेवात पर आक्रमण के कारण बताता है और लिखता है कि किस प्रकार हसन खाँ मेवाती की मक्कारी से वह उत्तेजित हुआ और राणा साँगा से युद्ध करने का विचार त्याग कर मेवात को विजयी किया।

बाबर के अनुसार मेवात दिल्ली के निकट था जिसकी वार्षिक मालगुज़ारी 3 या 4 करोड़ थी। हसन खाँ मेवाती और उसके पूर्वजों ने एक के बाद एक पूरी स्वतंत्रता से एक या दो सौ वर्षों तक शासन किया था। उन्होंने दिल्ली के सुल्तानों को अधूरा समपर्ण किया था।

दिल्ली के सुल्तानों ने अभी तक मेवात को अपने अधिकार में लेने को लिए कभी चेष्टा नहीं की थी। इसका कारण क्या था? बाबर यह नहीं समझ पाया था। शायद इसलिए कि उनके पास स्वयं एक विशाल क्षेत्र था अथवा इसलिए कि उन्हें मेवात के बारे में कुछ करने का अवसर नहीं मिला क्योंकि यह पहाड़ी प्रदेश था। बाबर एक विलीक्षण निरीक्षक था और लिखता है कि सुल्तान केवल नाम मात्र की अधीनता स्वीकार करा कर ही संतुष्ट हो जाते थे। बाबर भी अपनी हालत सुल्तानों की भाँति बताता है और इसी कारण हसन खाँ मेवाती के साथ मेलजोल का व्यवहार बनाए रखा।[47]

हसन खाँ चालाकी से बाबर बहुत दुखी था। इसी कारण राणा साँगा के राज्य पर आक्रमण करने का इरादा टालना पड़ा था। बाबर का ध्यान मेवात की ओर गया क्योंकि उसके शासक के व्यवहार से काफी क्षुब्ध था इसलिए सोच विचार के साथ बाबर अपनी सेना के साथ मेवात पर आक्रमण करने के लिए रवाना

हुआ। मार्ग में चार रातें बिताने के बाद बाबर ने अलवर से 6 कोस की दूरी पर मानसनी नदी के किनारे शिविर लगाया। इन दिनों मेवात के शासक अलवर को अपनी राजधानी बनाए हुए थे। बाबर का मानना था कि हसन खाँ और उसके पूर्वजों की राजधानी तिजारा में थी। उसका विचार था कि जब वह पंजाब में था तो हसन खाँ ने बड़ी बुद्धिमता से अपने रहने के लिए अलवर के किले में महल बनवा लिया था। तत्पश्चात बाबर लिखता है कि जब हसन खाँ मेवाती का पुत्र नाहर उसके पास बंधक था तो हसन खाँ ने अपने एक विश्वास पात्र कर्मचंद को आगरा भेजा था जो उस लड़के की उपस्थिति में उसके पास पहुँचा था तथा शाँति की प्रार्थना की थी। अब्दुर्रहीम शकावल उसके साथ अलवर गया और शाही सम्मान पत्र प्रदान किए गए। वापसी में नाहर खाँ के साथ लौटा और नाहर को पुनः सम्मनित करके उसे कई लाखों के परगने दिए गए।[48]

खनुआ के युद्ध में कौशल दिखाए जाने के बदले अलवर खुसरो को दे दिया गया और साथ में 50 लाख उसके खर्च के लिए मेवात की व्यवस्था कर दी गई। परंतु खुसरो ने यह प्रस्ताव ठुकरा दिया। उसके स्थान पर चीन तिमूर को मेवात की राजधानी तिजारा के साथ-साथ 15 लाख भत्ते के रूप में दिए गए। अलवर और 15 लाख का भत्ता तरदी यक्का को दिया गया और अलवर के खजाने से जो भी मिला वह हुमायूँ को दिया गया।[48]

13 अप्रैल 1527 ई. बुधवार के दिन बाबर शिविर से चलकर अलवर से 2 कोस की दूरी पर पड़ाव डाला। वहाँ से वह अलवर का किला देखने गया और रात वहीं बिताई और अगले दिन शिविर में पहुँचा और और वहाँ पुनः मानसनी नदी पर शिविर लगाया। बाबर ने फिरोज़पुर के झरने और कोटला की झील के बारे में काफी प्रशंसा सुन रखी थी। इसी को ध्यान में रख कर उसने दोनों स्थानों की यात्रा की। फिरोज़पुर और इसके झरने की यात्रा के बाद लिखता है कि घाटी कनेर के फूलों से भरी हुई थी। वह स्थान आकर्षक तो था पर उतना नहीं जितनी प्रशंसा की गई थी। बाबर ने वहाँ पत्थर का 10 × 10 का एक हौज बनाने का आदेश दिया और रात वहीं बिताई और अगले दिन कोटला झील के लिए निकल पड़ा। झील पर्वतों से घिरी हुई थी। उसने सुना था कि मानसनी नदी इस झील में आकर गिरती थी। झील इतनी बड़ी थी कि एक किनारे से दूसरा नहीं दिखता था।इसके बीच में एक टीला था जिसके चारों ओर छोटी छोटी नौकाएँ थीं जो वहाँ के लोग किसी संकट अथवा अव्यवस्था के समय अपने बचाव के लिए

प्रयोग में लाते थे। बाबर के पहुँचने पर भी कुछ लोग नौकाओं में बैठकर झील के बीच भाग गये थे।[50]

बाबर के वर्णन से लगता है जैसे हम आँखों देखा हाल सुन रहे हैं। बाबर की लेखनी सरल और आकर्षक है और मेवात सम्बंधी विस्तृत उल्लेख बाबर से पूर्व अथवा बाबर के बाद इस काल में किसी ने भी नहीं किया।

निकट समकालीन इतिहासकारों में मुहम्मद कासिम हिन्दू शाह उपनाम फरिश्ता की *तारीख़े फ़रिश्ता* मध्यकालीन भारत के इतिहास को जानने के लिए एक महत्त्वपूण ग्रंथ है। इसे लेखक ने 1606 ई. से 1611 ई. के बीच पाँच वर्ष की कड़ी मेहनत से पूरा किया, जिसमें तीन अध्याय हैं। प्रथम अध्याय में अठारह खंड हैं, जिनमें गजनी शासकों का इतिहास है। द्वितीय अध्याय में चवालीस खंड हैं, जिनमें दिल्ली के सुल्तानों से लेकर मुग़ल सम्राट अकबर के शासन काल का इतिहास है। इसी अध्याय में सूर शासकों का भी वर्णन है। तृतीय अध्याय में अठारह खंड हैं, जिनमें दक्षिणी भारत एवं बहमनी शासकों का हाल है। *तारीखे फरिश्ता* का यूँ तो अंग्रेजी में अनुवाद जॉन ब्रिग्स द्वारा चार भागों, प्रथम बार लन्दन से 1829 में और दूसरी बार वर्ष 1908 एवं 1966 में कलकत्ता से छप चुका है। हाल ही में उत्तर प्रदेश हिन्दी संस्थान, लखनऊ से इस ग्रंथ का हिन्दी अनुवाद डा. नरेन्द्र बहादुर द्वारा 2003 ई. में प्रकाशित हुआ है।

फरिश्ता का जन्म 1570 ई. में केस्पियन सागर के तट पर अस्त्राबाद में हुआ और बचपन ही में यह अहमदाबाद आ गया था। वहाँ उसने शाही परिवार के सदस्यों के साथ शिक्षा ग्रहण की और युवा अवस्था में निज़ामशाह और इब्राहीम आदिल शाह द्वितीय की सेवा में रहा, जिसने फरिश्ता को 'हिन्दुस्तान में इस्लामी शासन काल' का इतिहास लिखने की आज्ञा दी जो *तारीखे फरिश्ता* ने नाम से प्रसिद्ध हुई। लेखक ने इस ग्रंथ के लिए 32 सम्बंधित ऐतिहासिक ग्रंथों का अध्ययन किया था। इसके अतिरिक्त उस काल के विभिन्न लोगों से जानकारी भी प्राप्त की। सुल्तानों के काल का इतिहास क्योंकि पहले से उपलब्ध ऐतिहासिक ग्रंथों पर आधारित था, अत कई घटनाएँ ज्यों की त्यों लिखी मिलती है। मेवात सम्बंधी घटनाओं की जानकारी में भी ज्यादा परिवर्तन नहीं है।

नासिरूद्दीन महमूद के काल में उलुग खाँ द्वारा 1259 ई. में सुल्तान की आज्ञा से कोहपाया, रणथम्भोर और शिवालिक पर आक्रमण का उल्लेख फरिश्ता भी करता है। वह लिखता है कि मेवात और शिवालिक के राजा ने विशाल सेना

संगठित की और दुर्गम रास्तों पर शाही सेना से मुकाबला करने आये। उलुग खाँ ने इन विद्रोहियों को आड़े हाथों लिया · · · उलुग खाँ ने लगभ तीन–चार महीने तक उन गैर मुसलमानों से लड़ाई जारी रखी लेकिन शत्रुओं के अनेक शरण स्थालों को जीता न जा सका। लेखक यहाँ शत्रुओं के बन्दी बनाकर जीवित लाने पर दो तंके और सिर काट लाने पर एक तंके की बात भी लिखता है। शत्रुओं के ढाई सौ अमीर और सरदारों को ज़िन्दा गिरफ्तार किया गया। नासिरूद्दीन ने इस गिरोह के कत्ल का हुक्म दिया। उन सबको देहली के बाज़ार में विभिन्न प्रकार से मारकर समाप्त कर दिया।[51]

अगली घटना बल्बन के प्रथम वर्ष में 'मेवाती लुटेरों की समाप्ति' शीर्षक से वर्णन की गई, जिसमें बल्बन एक लाख मेवातियों को मौत के घाट उतार देता है। इस घटना से लगता है कि फरिश्ता ने बरनी की *तारिखे फ़ीरोज़शाही* की नकल की लगती है परंतु मेवातियों की संख्या एक लाख बताने के पीछे लगता है कि फरिश्ता ने कुछ ग्रंथों में पढ़ा होगा, जो आज उपलब्ध नहीं है। एक अतिरिक्त जानकारी जो अब तक किसी भी इतिहासकार ने नहीं दी, वह यह कि मेवातियों को मरवाने के बाद बल्बन ने जंगलों को जिसमें ये लुटेरे रहा करते थे, बिल्कुल साफ करवा दिया और उस ज़मीन को खेती करने योग्य बनवाकर कृषकों में बाँट दिया। बल्बन ने इन स्थानों पर पुलिस चौकियाँ भी स्थापित कराईं। इन चौकियों की सुरक्षा के लिए अपने कुछ विश्वसनीय अधिकारियों को वहाँ रख दिया और दिल्ली वापस आया।[52]

तारीखे फरिश्ता के अंग्रेज़ी अनुवाद से पता चलता है कि रणथम्भोर और शिवालिक के पर्वतीय क्षेत्रो में राजाओं और मेवात के राजपूतों ने उत्पात मचा रखा था। उलुग़ खाँ के कई अधिकारी मारे गए थे। 10,000 हिन्दू और 200 हिन्दू मुखिया कैदी बनाकर दिल्ली लाये गए थे। मुखिया लोगों को मरवा दिया गया और शेष को दास बना दिया गया।[53]

इसी प्रकार बल्बन द्वारा सुल्तान बनने के बाद मेवात के अभियान का अंग्रेजी अनुवाद में कुछ इस प्रकार मिलता है'

मेवातियों ने राजधानी के दक्षिणी–पूर्व में 80 मील तक के क्षेत्र पर अपनी अधिकार जमा रखा था और दिल्ली के द्वार तक आक्रमण किया करते थे। यह कहा जाता है कि इस अभियान में एक लाख मेवातियों को मौत के घाट उतारा गया था। 100 मील घेरे तक जंगल साफ कराये गये और भूमि कृषि योग्य बन

गई।[54]

निष्कर्ष में हम यह कह सकते हैं कि मेव क्योंकि कबीले के रूप में थे, अतः स्वतंत्र जीवनयापन के आदि थे। जब जब भी किसी शक्ति ने उनकी स्वतंत्रता में बाधा डालने का प्रयत्न किया, वे उनके विरूद्ध सिर उठाते रहे। बल्बन द्वारा एक लाख से भी अधिक मेवों को मौत दे घाट उतारने के बाद उनकी शक्ति घट गई। दपुनः जब फीरोज़शाह तुगलक के काल में जब मेवों ने इस्लाम ग्रहण करके खानजादा पद प्राप्त किया तो वे एक राजनैतिक शक्ति के रूप में उभर कर मेवात के शासक बने। इनमें बहादुर नाहिर व हसन खाँ मेवाती ने नाम कमाया। खानज़ादों ने केवल अपनी स्वतंत्रता बनाये रखने के लिए दिल्ली की शाही सेनाओं में बार-बार टक्कर ली और समयानुसार कभी कभी अधीनता भी स्वीकार की। शासन व्यवस्था के नाम पर उन्होंने कुछ स्थायी प्रबंध नहीं किया आर न ही अपने शासक होने का कोई चिन्ह जैसे सिक्के चलाना अथवा अपना इतिहास लेखन बध कराना जैसा कोई काम नहीं किया। हाँ इतना अवश्य किया कि अनेक भवनों, इमारतों आदि का निर्माण बखूबी कराया, जो आज भी उनकी याद दिलाते हैं।

टिप्पणियाँ

1. सैयिद अतहर अब्बास रिज़वी, *आदि तुर्क कालीन भारत,* अलीगढ़, 1956 पृ. 82
2. वही, पृ. 85
3. वही, पृ. 94-95
4. वही, पृ. 96
5. वही, पृ. 55
6. वही, पृ. 163
7. वही, पृ. 163-74
8. वही, पृ. 304
9. एसामी, *फुतुहुस्सलालीन,* अंग्रेज़ी अनुवाद आगा मेंहदी हुसैन, भाग 2, अलीगढ़, 1976, पृ. 340
10. वही, पृ 354
11. वही, पृ. 353
12. वही, पृ. 291

13. इलियट एण्ड डाऊसन, *हिस्ट्र आफ इंडिया ऐज़ टोल्ड बाई इटस ओन हिस्टोरियनज़,* खण्ड 3, पृ. 449
14. सैयिद अतहर अब्बास रिज़वी, *तुग़लक कालीन भारत,* भाग 2, पृ 260
15. वही, पृ. 205
16. वही, पृ. 207
17. वही, पृ. 210
18. वही, पृ. 211
19. वही, पृ. 212
20. वही, पृ. 214 कन्निंघम के अनुसार बहादुर नाहिर कोटिला छोड़कर फिरोज़पुर झिरका भाग गया था। देखें एलेक्जेंडर कन्निंघम *रिर्पोट आफ ए टूर इन ईस्ट्रन राजपूताना इन 1882-83* खण्ड, xx, वाराणासी, 1969, पृ. 127
21. *तुग़लक कालीन भारत,* भाग 2, पृ. 217
22. वही, पृ. 217
23. वही, पृ. 217-18 तथा इलियट एंड डाऊसन, खण्ड 4, पृ. 33
24. वही, पृ. 220
25. सैयिद अतहर अब्बास रिज़वी, *उत्तर तैमूर कालीन भारत,* भाग 1, पृ. 3
26. वही, पृ. 4
27. वही, पृ. 11-12
28. वही, पृ. 12
29. वही, पृ. 21
30. वही, पृ. 28
31. वही, पृ. 29
32. वही, पृ. 29-30
33. वही, पृ. 33 के.एस. लाल, *टवीलाइट ऑफ द सल्तनत,* नई दिल्ली 1980), पृ. 102-4
34. वही, पृ. 34
35. वही, पृ. 35
36. वही, पृ. 44
37. *तुग़लक कालीन भारत,* भाग 2, पृ. 231-31
38. वही, पृ. 233
39. वही, पृ. 233
40. वही, पृ. 237-38
41. *बाबरनामा,* अंग्रेज़ी अनुवाद ए. एस. बेवरिज, नई दिल्ली, 1970 पृ. 477-78
42. वही, पृ. 485-86
43. वही, पृ. 45
44. वही, पृ. 551
45. वही, पृ. 562

46. वही, पृ. 573
47. वही, पृ. 578
48. वही, पृ. 577–78
49. वही, पृ. 578–79
60. वही, पृ. 580
51. *तारीखे फ़रिश्ता* हिन्दी अनुवद नरेन्द्र बहादुर, लखनऊ, 2003, पृ. 164–65
52. वही, पृ. 173
53. हिन्दू कासिम शाह फ़रिश्ता, *तारीखे फरिश्ता* अंग्रेज़ी अनुवाद जॉन ब्रिग्स शीर्षक *हिस्ट्री आफ मोहमडन पावर इन इंडिया*, पृ. 244–45
54. वही, पृ. 255–56

۵-شمس الدین شمس: میوز آف انڈیا، دیرَ کسٹمس اینڈلا، نئی دہلی ۱۹۸۳
۶- نور محمد (ایڈ) انڈین مسلمس، نئی دہلی ۱۹۹۹ء
۷- پرتاپ اگروال: کاسٹ ریلیجین اینڈ پاور- این انڈین کیس سٹڈی، نئی دہلی ۱۹۷۱ء
۸- ہاشم امیر علی: دی میوز آف میوات، نئی دہلی ۱۹۷۰
۹-شیل مایارام: اگینسٹ ہسٹری اگینسٹ اسٹیٹ، کولمبیا یونیورسٹی پریس ۲۰۰۳ء
۱۰- کے۔ایس۔سنگھ: انڈیاز کمیونٹیز، آکسفورڈ یونیورسٹی پریس ۱۹۹۸ء
۱۱- ڈینزل ایبٹسن: پنجاب کاسٹس، انڈین ری پرنٹ، پٹیالہ ۱۹۸۱
۱۲- امپیریل گزیٹر آف انڈیا، ج (XVII) ۱۹۰۸ء
۱۳- ندیم حسین اور شیخ ابرار حسین: شیعاز اینڈ شیعہ اسلام ان انڈیا، نئی دہلی ۱۹۸۹ء
۱۴-مسز میر حسن علی: آبزرویشنس آف مسلمانس آف انڈیا ۱۸۸۲ کی طبع ثانی، نئی دہلی ۱۹۷۳ء
۱۵- انسائیکلو پیڈیا آف اسلام، نیا ایڈیشن، ج VII، ای، جے، برل ۱۹۹۳ء
۱۶- انٹرویو (گفتگو)
۱/- مفتی جمال الدین، الور
۲- محمد پلٹو خاں ایڈوکیٹ، الور
۳- صالح خان ایڈوکیٹ، فیروز پور جھرکا، ضلع گوڑگاؤں
۴- ڈاکٹر جگ مندر نایل، راج رشی کالج، الور
۵- بھوپ سنگھ پوسوال، ایڈوکیٹ، الور

لیے پلاؤ نہیں کھایا کہ اسے مسلمانوں نے پکایا تھا اور اسے بھینس کے گوشت میں بنایا گیا تھا۔

پہلی جولائی ۱۹۶۴ء کو پورے میوات میں حسینؓ کے 'چالیہے' (حسینؓ کے انتقال کی برسی کے چالیسویں دن) پر میلے لگے۔ چاونڈی کلاں کا کوئی شخص کسی میلے میں شریک نہیں ہوا لیکن زیادہ تر گھروں میں اس دن کچھ میٹھا ضرور پکایا گیا۔

جیسا پہلے بھی ذکر کیا جا چکا ہے ہریانہ میں محرم کچھ ہی گاؤوں میں منایا جاتا ہے جب کہ راجستھان میں یہ روایت اب بھی بہت سے گاؤوں اور شہروں میں باقی ہے۔ مثال کے طور پر الور میں اب بھی تعزیے کا جلوس میو بورڈنگ ہاؤس سے نکلتا ہے اور ایک جگہ جسے ابھی تک کربلا کہا جاتا ہے، وہاں لے جاکر دفن کیا جاتا ہے۔اس سے پہلے یہ جگہ قبرستان (ڈمپنگ گراؤنڈ) ہی تھی مگر اب یہاں عمارتیں کھڑی ہوگئی ہیں۔ پھر بھی حکومت نے اس کے ایک حصے کو تعزیے دفن کرنے کے لیے مختص کردیا ہے اور اسے ابھی کربلا ہی کہا جاتا ہے۔

یہ بات بھی یاد رکھنے کی ہے کہ جلوس کے دوران میونیاں حسینؓ کی یاد میں جو کچھ گاتی ہیں وہ ان کی مادری زبان 'میواتی' میں ہوتا ہے جو برج بھاشا اور راجستھانی سے ملی جلی زبان ہے۔ ہندو تہوار منانے کا رواج میووں میں اب لگ بھگ ختم ہوتا جارہا ہے پھر بھی ایسے موقعوں پر یہ دوستوں کو مبارکباد دے کر اور مٹھائی کھاکر خوشی منالیتے ہیں۔ بھیروں جی کا چبوترہ، اب بھی تمام فرقوں میں عام طور پر مقبول ہے، جس میں میو بھی شامل ہیں۔ اس طرح ہم ملک کے اس حصے میں ایک مخلوط کلچر کی جھلک دیکھ سکتے ہیں اور اس پر فخر کرسکتے ہیں۔

کتابیات:

۱- جی۔ڈی گلاٹی: میوات ڈیورنگ تھرٹینتھ سنچری، پنجاب ہسٹری کانگریس کی کارروائی، پروسیڈنگس میں شائع ہوئی، پٹیالہ ۱۹۸۱

۲- یوگندر اسکند: دی اوریجن اینڈ ڈیولپمنٹ آف دی تبلیغی جماعت (۲۰۰۰-۱۹۲۰)' نئی دہلی ۲۰۰۲ء

۳- ابوالفضل: آئین اکبری، ترجمہ: ایچ بلوشمین، ج ا، تیسرا ایڈیشن، طباعت ثانی، نئی دہلی

۴- میجر پاؤلیٹ: گزیٹر آف الور، لندن ۱۸۱۷ء

۵- شمس الدین شمس: میوز آف انڈیا، دیئر کسٹمس اینڈلا، نئی دہلی ۱۹۸۳

۶- نورمحمد (ایڈ) انڈین مسلمس، نئی دہلی ۱۹۹۹ء

۷- پرتاپ اگروال: کاسٹ ریلیجین اینڈ پاور- این انڈین کیس سٹڈی، نئی دہلی ۱۹۷۱ء

۸- ہاشم امیر علی: دی میوز آف میوات، نئی دہلی ۱۹۷۰

۲۲ مئی، محرم کے نویں دن پیکوں نے پھر ناچنا شروع کیا۔ انہوں نے پورے گاؤں میں گھوم کر ہر گھر سے پیسہ جمع کیا۔ اس میں سے نصف روپیہ تعزیے کے اخراجات کے لیے تھا، اس کے علاوہ کچھ پیسہ دوسری رسموں کے لیے لیا گیا۔

دس محرم (۲۳ مئی) دوتانا میں ایک میلا لگایا گیا۔ بانسوں اور رنگین کاغذوں کا بنا ایک تعزیہ لایا گیا۔ تعزیے کے اخراجات کے لیے سات گاؤں نے چندہ دیا تھا۔ تعزیہ کا ڈھانچہ، جسے حسینؓ کے مزار کی نقل مانا جاتا ہے، لگ بھگ چھ میٹر اونچا تھا اور اس پر ایسی علامتیں بھی تھیں جن سے ان کے بھائی حسنؓ کے مزار کا اشارہ ہوتا ہے (تعزیے کے نیچے) دونوں طرف بانسوں کو کافی آگے بڑھا کر لگایا جاتا ہے تاکہ لوگ اسے کندھوں پر اٹھا سکیں۔ تعزیے کے آگے ایک نقارہ رکھا جاتا ہے جسے ہندو مسلمان دونوں دن بھر بجاتے رہتے ہیں۔ تعزیے کے آگے سقّے پانی پلاتے ہیں۔ کچھ لوگ تعزیوں کے آگے اپنی طرف سے پانی چھڑکنے کے لیے پیسے بھی دیتے ہیں۔ اس عمل کو نیک کام سمجھا جاتا ہے، اور اسے کربلا میں حسینؓ اور ان کے ساتھیوں پر پانی بند کردیے جانے کی نشانی کے طور پر انجام دیا جاتا ہے۔ کچھ لوگ پکے ہوئے کھانے بھی چڑھاتے ہیں جو تعزیے کے کسی خدمتگار کو دے دیا جاتا ہے، جو عام طور پر ملاّ ہوتا ہے۔ چاونڈی کلاں کے ایک بوڑھے بنیے نے بتایا کہ: ''پرانے وقتوں میں ہم بھی محرم میں شامل ہوتے تھے۔ ہم تعزیے کے خدمتگار کو میٹھے چاول دیا کرتے تھے جیسا میو کرتے ہیں، مگر اب جب کہ میو لوگ کٹر مسلمان ہوگئے ہیں اور انہوں نے ہمارے تہواروں میں شریک ہونا بند کردیا ہے تو ہم نے بھی تعزے پر چڑھاوے بند کردیے ہیں''۔

سیکڑوں لوگ، جن میں زیادہ تر میو ہوتے ہیں میلے میں آتے ہیں۔ مرد، عورتیں، بچے اپنے بہترین لباس پہنے خوش خوش میلے میں آتے ہیں۔ اس دن میو اپنے گھروں میں کوئی میٹھی چیز بھی پکاتے ہیں۔ میلے میں بہت سی دکانیں لگ جاتی ہیں جن میں کھانے پینے کا سامان، ہلکے پھلکے زیور اور کھلونے بکتے ہیں۔ کوئی چار بجے تعزیے کو بڑھایا جاتا ہے، ایک وقت میں کچھ میٹر۔ اسے عیدگاہ کے پاس تالاب تک سورج غروب ہونے تک پہنچنا ہوتا ہے۔ یہاں اسے توڑ کر پانی میں ڈبودیا جاتا ہے۔ جب تعزیہ میلہ میدان سے آگے بڑھایا جاتا ہے تو یہاں کھیل تماشے شروع ہوتے ہیں۔ جیسے کشتی کے دنگل وغیرہ ہوتے ہیں۔

محرم کے تیرھویں دن (۲۵ مئی ۱۹۶۴ء) چاونڈی کلاں میں ایک تعزیہ کھانا ہوا۔ پیکوں، نے

رات نہ لوٹنے، اپنے دورے کے درمیان بیل گاڑی پر سواری کرنے اور حسینؑ کی نافرمانی پر سرزنش کرنی شروع کردی۔ اس نے ایک فقیر کو بھی ڈانٹا جس نے ان پیکوں کے ساتھ رہنے کے فرض کو پورا نہیں کیا تھا۔ چند منٹ بعد وہ اٹھا اور حاجی پیر کے مزار کی طرف دوڑا اور وہاں سجدے کی حالت میں کچھ دیر پڑا رہا۔ پھر وہ سیدھا لیٹا تو لگتا تھا اس کا جسم اکڑ گیا ہے۔ ایک چھوٹے سے مٹی کے برتن میں اپلا سلگا کر اس پر کسی قسم کے گوند (غالبًا لوبان) کا سفوف ڈال کر اس کے پاس رکھ دیا گیا۔ اس کی دھونی نے اسے آہستہ آہستہ کچھ سکون پہنچا، اور کچھ دیر بعد وہ ہوش میں آ گیا۔ گاؤں کے ایک بزرگ سے پوچھنے پر مجھے بتایا گیا کہ اس نوجوان کو کئی سال سے اس قسم کے دورے پڑ رہے ہیں، اور یہ اس وقت سے پڑنے شروع ہوئے ہیں جب سے وہ پاکستان سے واپس آیا ہے، جہاں وہ تقسیم ملک کے بعد ہجرت کر گیا تھا۔ وہاں سے واپسی پر اسے معلوم ہوا کہ اس کی زمین کسی پنجابی رفیوجی کو الاٹ کی جا چکی تھی۔ اسی وقت سے اس کی یہ پریشانی شروع ہوئی ہے''۔

تقریباً دوپہر کے وقت پیک پھر کچھ آس پاس کے گاؤں کا دورہ کرنے چلے گئے اور رات کو نو بجے کے آس پاس واپس ہوئے۔ پیکوں کی کمر میں لپٹی پٹیوں میں لگی گھنٹیوں کی آواز پر گاؤں کے میدان میں مہندی کی تھالیاں پہنچنی شروع ہوئیں۔ پانچ خاندان بلاناغہ مہندی لاتے ہیں، ویسے جو چاہے وہ لاسکتا ہے۔ اس وقت یہاں صرف چار مہندیاں تھیں۔ ایک پچھلی رات یعنی مہندی کی رات کو ہی مسجد لے جائی گئی تھی۔

پیک گاؤں کے مختلف حصوں میں ناچتے ہوئے رفتہ رفتہ پکی مسجد کی طرف بڑھتے رہے مہندی کی تھالیاں اٹھانے والے ان کے ساتھ ساتھ چلتے رہے۔ کافی بڑی تعداد میں لوگ اس جلوس میں شامل تھے جو لگ بھگ دو بجے رات کو مسجد پہنچا۔ یہاں بھی پیک کچھ دیر ناچتے رہے پھر آرام کرنے رک گئے۔ انہیں مہندی کی تھالیوں سے شربت اور کھانا دیا گیا۔ چھوٹے چھوٹے چراغوں کو مسجد کے طاقوں میں رکھ دیا گیا۔ اس کے بعد ہر شخص خالی تھالیوں کے ساتھ اپنے گھر کو چلا گیا۔ تھالیوں میں مہندی اب بھی لگی ہوئی تھی جسے بعد میں دھو دیا جاتا ہے۔

۲۲ مئی، محرم کے نویں دن پیکوں نے پھر ناچنا شروع کیا۔ انہوں نے پورے گاؤں میں گھوم کر ہر گھر سے پیسہ جمع کیا۔ اس میں سے نصف روپیہ تعزیے کے اخراجات کے لیے تھا، اس کے علاوہ کچھ پیسہ دوسری رسموں کے لیے لیا گیا۔

پر سوار ہونے کی بھی ممانعت ہوتی ہے''۔[1]

اس دن دوپہر کے وقت یہ پیک، گاؤں کے میدان میں جمع ہوتے ہیں۔ ایک نوجوان ڈکوٹ برہمن جوان کا سربراہ (انچارج) ہوتا ہے، ایک لال ڈوری (لال دھاگہ جو ہندو لوگ مذہبی رسوم ادا کرتے وقت استعمال کرتے ہیں) ان کی کلائیوں پر باندھتا ہے اور مرثیہ خوانی کرکے ان کی سربراہی کرتا ہے۔ گاؤں کے میدان میں ایک نقارہ رکھ دیا جاتا ہے جسے دو آدمی ایک ساتھ مار مار کر بجاتے ہیں۔ پیک اس کی تال پر ایک گھنٹے تک ناچتے کودتے ہیں۔ اس کے بعد وہ کچھ دیر آرام کرتے ہیں اور پھر گاؤں کے دورے پر نکل جاتے ہیں۔

یہ لگ بھگ ہر گاؤں میں جاتے ہیں، پہلے اس گاؤں کے میدان میں ناچتے ہیں پھر گھر گھر جاتے ہیں، ناچتے ہیں اور پیسے جمع کرتے ہیں، اس طرح جو پیسہ جمع ہوتا ہے اسے کسی مذہبی عام منصوبے پر خرچ کیا جاتا ہے۔ جیسے نگاڑے کی مرمّت وغیرہ۔ رات کو یہ لوگ کسی گاؤں میں آرام کرتے ہیں مگر صرف زمین پر فرش بچھا کر۔ اگلی صبح یہ اپنا دورہ پھر شروع کردیتے ہیں اور روزانہ پانچ، چھ گاؤں پورے کرلیتے ہیں۔ یہ محرم کے ساتویں دن اپنے گاؤں واپس آجاتے ہیں۔

گاؤں کے زیادہ تر مرد کم سے کم ایک بار یا اس سے زیادہ مرتبہ جوانی میں پیک بنتے ہیں، مگر چاونڈی کلاں میں ہمیں ہندو اور سکھ لڑکے بھی پیک کا روپ بھرنے والے نظر آئے۔ پچھلے کچھ سالوں میں گاؤں کا ایک سکھ اور ایک ہندو نائی لڑکا حسینؑ کے سپاہی بنے تھے۔ جن ماں باپ کی اولاد مرجاتی ہے وہ اس امید میں کہ ان کا لڑکا زندہ رہے گا اپنے بچوں کو پیک بنانے کی منّت مان لیتے ہیں۔[2]

سات محرم کی شام کو بہت سے خاندان مہندی کی رسم مناتے پیکوں کی واپسی پر، ان کا استقبال کرنے، گاؤں کے میدان میں جمع ہوتے ہیں۔ اس موقع پر یہ لوگ دس بارہ روشن دیے، شربت کا ایک گلاس، ایک پیالی کھیر اور پسی ہوئی مہندی رکھ کر ایک پیتل کی تھالی سجاتے ہیں۔ اگر آدھی رات تک پیک واپس نہیں آتے، ایسا کبھی کبھار ہی ہوتا ہے، تو 'مہندی' کی یہ روایت اگلی رات میں پوری کی جاتی ہے۔

چاونڈی کلاں گاؤں کے پیک محرم کے آٹھویں دن صبح کو لوٹتے ہیں۔ تھوڑی دیر آرام کرکے وہ

۱- پرتاپ سی۔ اگروال، کاسٹ ریلیجین اینڈ پاور- این انڈین کیس سٹڈی، نئی دہلی ۱۹۷۱ء، ص ۶۵-۱۶۱

۲- ایضاً، ص ۶۲-۱۶۱

میرے بچپن کے زمانے میں ہم لوگوں نے ہر سال اس مہینے کو دھوم دھام سے نہ صرف مناتے ہوئے دیکھا ہے بلکہ اسے ایک مبارک مہینہ سمجھتے ہوئے ہم میووں کے جلوس میں شریک بھی ہوئے ہیں، ان کے ساتھ گاؤں، گاؤں گھوم کر ٹھنڈا شربت پلایا ہے اور حسینؑ اور حسنؑ سے برکتوں کی دعا بھی کی ہے۔ مقامی لوگ تعزیے کے جلوس میں کسی تعزیے کے نیچے سے نکلنا ایک محترم اور مقدس عمل سمجھتے تھے اور اسے اپنے مستقبل کی بہتری کا ضامن مانتے تھے۔ اس پورے علاقے میں محرم کی رسوم کے لیے بہت سے مقررہ مرکز تھے۔ ان رسومات کی ادائیگی کی تفصیلات بیان کرتے ہوئے ایک ماہر علم البشر (اینتھر وپولوجسٹ) نے، جس نے میوات کے چاونڈی کلاں نام کے ایک گاؤں میں مہینوں تک قیام کیا تھا اور ان کے ساتھ رہا تھا، لکھا ہے کہ یہ گاؤں اپنی وسعت، محلِ وقوع، ذات پات کے ڈھانچے اور معاشی اور سماجی تنظیم وغیرہ ہر لحاظ سے میوات کا اچھا نمونہ پیش کرتا ہے۔ یہ گاؤں راجستھان کے ضلع الور کی تحصیل میں قومی راجدھانی دہلی سے ۱۴۰ کلومیٹر دور 'تجّارہ' تحصیل میں واقع ہے۔

کئی لیڈروں اور میوات کے بہت سے بزرگوں سے گفتگو کر کے میں اس نتیجے پر پہنچا کہ اس علاقے میں ہریانہ کے ضلعوں کے لوگ ماہِ محرم کے پہلے ہفتے کو کوئی خاص اہمیت نہیں دیتے۔ لیکن ہمارے ماہر علم البشر دوست نے راجستھان کا کچھ مختلف منظر پیش کیا ہے جیسا کہ اوپر بیان کیا گیا۔ انہوں نے لکھا ہے:

''چاونڈی کلاں میں محرم کی رسومات کے سلسلے میں سب سے پہلے، گھروں میں، ایک میٹھی چیز پکائی جاتی ہے۔ نوجوان لوگ پیک کا سا لباس پہنتے ہیں اور آس پاس کے گاؤں میں جاتے ہیں۔ ۱۹۶۴ء میں اس ٹولی میں چار میو اور ایک سقّہ شامل تھے۔ اس وقت ان کا مخصوص لباس، جسے وہ اپنے عام کپڑوں پر ہی پہن لیتے ہیں، ایک سرخ لنگی ایک سبز الغی (مستطیل کپڑا، جس میں بیچ میں ایک سوراخ یا شگاف سا ہوتا ہے، اور اسے سر پر ڈال لیا جاتا ہے)، ایک لال اور سفید 'گنڈا' (رنگین دھجیوں سے بٹی ہوئی ایک لمبی ڈوری جسے پگڑی، سینے، پیٹھ اور کمر کے چاروں طرف لپیٹا جاتا ہے)، چمڑے کی یا دھاگوں کی ایک پٹی جس میں چھوٹی چھوٹی گھنٹیاں لگی ہوتی ہیں اور ہاتھ میں ایک تلوار یا لکڑی، پر مشتمل ہوتا ہے۔ پیکوں کو جوتا پہننا منع ہوتا ہے۔ انہیں چارپائی پر سونے اور پہیّے والی گاڑی پر سوار ہونے کی بھی ممانعت ہوتی ہے''۔[1]

اس دن دوپہر کے وقت یہ پیک، گاؤں کے میدان میں جمع ہوتے ہیں۔ ایک نوجوان ڈکوٹ

اسلامی کلینڈر کا پہلا مہینہ محرم اسلامی معاشرے میں بہت اہم مانا جاتا ہے۔ پوری دنیا میں، جس میں ہندوستان بھی شامل ہے اسے پورے جوش وخروش، شان وشوکت، اور گہرے جذبے کے ساتھ ایک مذہبی فریضے کے طور پر منایا جاتا ہے۔

مسلمانوں میں شیعہ فرقے کا عقیدہ ہے کہ پیغمبر محمدؐ کے نواسے حسینؑ خلافت کے حقدار و جانشین تھے۔ یہ لوگ ان کی شہادت کا سوگ مناتے ہیں جو دس محرم ۶۱ھ/۶۸۰ء میں کربلا کی جنگ میں واقع ہوئی تھی۔ حسینؑ کے بھائی حسنؑ (جنہیں شیعوں کے یقین کے مطابق زہر دیا گیا) انہیں بھی اس موقعے پر یاد کیا جاتا ہے۔ ملک میں سنی فرقہ عام طور پر محرم کے اس سوگ میں شریک نہیں ہوتا مگر میو اس سے مستثنیٰ ہیں کیونکہ یہ سنی ہوتے ہوئے بھی محرم میں شریک ہوتے ہیں، ہاں کسی طرح کا سوگ نہیں مناتے۔ حقیقت میں اس سانحے کی یاد میں عام شیعہ انداز کے برعکس ان لوگوں میں کربلا کے غمناک واقعات سے کسی قسم کے ذاتی لگاؤ یا جذبے کا فقدان نظر آتا ہے۔ جیسا کہ پہلے ذکر کیا گیا نسلی اعتبار سے ان کا راجپوت سلسلے اور ہندوؤں سے ایک دیرینہ تعلق اور ان کے میلوں اور تہواروں میں شریک ہوتے رہنے کی وجہ سے محرم بھی ن کے لیے اور بہت سے تہواروں کی طرح ایک تہوار ہی ہے۔

جہاں تک میوات میں محرم کی رسومات کی ابتدا کا سوال ہے ہم مشکل ہی سے کوئی تحریری شہادت حاصل کرسکتے ہیں، بہرحال یہ بات بالکل صاف ہے کہ یہ صوفی اثرات کا نتیجہ ہوسکتا ہے یا ان کے راجپوت نسل سے تعلق کا۔ اس کے علاوہ صدیوں سے ان کے ہندو میلوں ٹھیلوں اور تہواروں میں حصہ لیتے رہنے کے نتیجے میں وہ اس علاقے میں ثقہ قسم کے مسلمان کا روپ اختیار بھی نہیں کرسکتے تھے۔ ہم ان کے تبدیلی مذہب اور مغلوں کی خدمات انجام دینے کا ذکر کرچکے ہیں۔ مغل خود ہی ایک مخلوط کلچر کی ابتدا کرنے والوں میں سے تھے۔ یہ بھی یاد رکھنا چاہئے کہ ہمایوں اور بیرم خان دونوں نے میو لڑکیوں سے شادی کی تھی جس سے ہندوستان میں اپنی رعیت کی طرف ان کے نرم رویّے کا اظہار ہوتا ہے۔ اکبر کے دربار میں کئی شیعہ عالم بھی موجود تھے۔ عبدالرحیم خانخاناں جسے عام طور پر رحیم کہا جاتا ہے، ایک میونی کا ہی بیٹا تھا۔ اب اس بات کو باور کرلینے میں کوئی دقت نہیں ہونی چاہئے کہ اس دور کے میو وہی مذہبی روایات پوری کررہے تھے جو اس وقت کے مذہبی ماحول اور ان کے دوسرے بھائیوں، یعنی ہندوؤں کے ساتھ رہنے سے مطابقت رکھتی تھیں۔ ایسی صورت حال میں سنی مذہب کی راسخ الاعتقادی ان پر کوئی بہت گہرا اثر نہیں ڈال سکتی تھی۔ چنانچہ انہوں نے آزاد روش اور اسلام کا وہ

نگاہ سے دیکھتے تھے، ان کے ہاتھ کا پکا کھانا کھانے سے انکار کردیتے تھے اور انہیں اپنی رسوم میں گندگی پیدا کرنے والا ذریعہ سمجھتے تھے۔ اسی دوران تبلیغی جماعت تحریک بھی علاقے میں داخل ہوچکی تھی، جنھوں نے میووں کو ایک سچے مسلمان کی حیثیت سے اپنی شناخت بنائے رکھنے کی تلقین کی۔ اس طرح سے میووں کو ایک طرف تبلیغی جماعت کے پرچار اور دوسری طرف جدید تعلیم کے اثر سے اپنے مسلمان ہونے کا احساس ہوا۔ مدرسوں کا قیام اور مسجدوں کی تعمیر، ان کے توسط سے ہوئی۔ اسلامی تعلیمات نے انہیں ایک علاحدہ مذہبی گروہ کی شکل دے دی اور انہیں پہلے سے زیادہ متحد کردیا۔

۱۹۴۷ء کی تقسیم ملک نے میووں کے لیے حقارت اور پریشانی کے نئے دروازے کھول دیئے تھے۔ تقسیم کے بعد جو فسادات ہوئے اس میں میووں کی بہت سی زمینوں پر نچلی ذاتوں کے ہندو قابض ہوگئے، پھر جو میو پاکستان چلے گئے ان کی زمینوں کو حکومت نے پنجابیوں کو الاٹ کردیا جو مغربی پنجاب سے آئے ہوئے ہندو اور سکھ تھے۔ ایک وقت چونکہ تبلیغی جماعت نے ان میں سے بہت سے لوگوں کو اسلام کو کم سے کم ظاہری طور پر اپنا لینے کی طرف راغب کردیا تھا تو ان نئے بیرونی عوامل نے ان میں اسلامیت کے نفوذ کو اور تیز کردیا۔ آمد و رفت کی بہتر سہولتوں نے میوات میں تبلیغی دوروں میں بہت تیزی سے اضافہ کیا جن میں باہر کی تبلیغی جماعتیں اور خود میووں کی اپنی جماعتیں شامل تھیں جو اس پورے خطے میں اور باہر آتی جاتی تھیں۔ اسلامی ادب اور اسلامی تعلیم دونوں سے میووں نے اور زیادہ واقفیت حاصل کی جس سے رفتہ رفتہ ان میں ایک اسلامی شناخت اور پورے ملک کے مسلمان فرقے سے ان کی ایکتا اور یکسانیت کا احساس اور بڑھا۔ بابری مسجد کے بحران سے مذہبی شناخت کے احساس میں خاص طور پر اور اضافہ ہوا۔ چنانچہ آج میو ہندو روایت کو چھوڑ رہے ہیں مگر یہ لوگ دونوں مذہبوں کی ہلکی پھلکی اور دلچسپی کی حامل رسوم میں ضرور شریک ہوتے ہیں۔ یہ صورت حال ہریانہ میں زیادہ واضح ہے جہاں میو زیادہ تعلیم یافتہ اور معاشی اعتبار سے بہتر حالت میں ہیں لیکن راجستھان میں اپنی غربت کی وجہ سے وہ اب بھی پرانی روایات کو اپنائے ہوئے ہیں۔[۱]

اسلامی کلینڈر کا پہلا مہینہ محرم اسلامی معاشرے میں بہت اہم مانا جاتا ہے۔ پوری دنیا میں، جس میں ہندوستان بھی شامل ہے اسے پورے جوش و خروش، شان و شوکت، اور گہرے جذبے کے ساتھ

۱- مزید مطالعہ کے لیے یوگیندر اسکند، سابقہ حوالہ ملاحظہ ہو، ص ۱۴۸ تا ۱۷۴، نیز ملاحظہ ہو نور محمد (ایڈ) انڈین مسلمس، نئی دہلی ۱۹۹۹ء، ص ۱۸۳

رسم و رواج اور اداروں کو جیسے گوتر، اور پال کا نظام اور نچلی ذاتوں سے چھوا چھوت کے عمل کو برقرار رکھنے کی وجہ سے ایک حد تک اسلامیت قبول کر لینے کے باوجود میووں نے اس علاقے کے سماجی درجات میں ایک اونچے درجے کی دعوے داری قائم رکھی۔ غیر مسلم دستکار، خدمتگار، یہاں تک کہ برہمن تک زرعی پیداوار میں ایک حصے کے بدلے میں اپنے میو مربّیوں کی خدمت کرتے رہے۔ جب تک ان گاہک یا خدمت گزار قسم کی ذاتوں کی معاشی اور سماجی زندگی میں کوئی اختلال پیدا نہیں ہوا، ان ذاتوں کے لوگوں نے میووں کی مخلوط سی مذہبی شناخت کو نظر انداز کرنا مناسب سمجھا۔ اس لیے میووں نے بھی ان دونوں فرقوں (ہندو اور مسلمان) میں سے کسی طرف بھی زیادہ جھکنے کی کوئی ناگزیر مجبوری محسوس نہیں کی کیونکہ ان کی حیثیت میوات میں محفوظ تھی۔ میوات کی دوسری ذاتوں کے گروہوں نے بھی اس علاقے پر میووں کے غلبے پر کوئی سوال نہیں اٹھایا۔[1]

دوسری طرف، چونکہ میو عام طور پر دہلی کے مسلم حکمرانوں سے مخالفانہ رویہ رکھتے تھے اس لیے ان کی عام مذہبی روایات انہیں ایک علاحدہ شناخت کا احساس دلاتی رہتی تھیں، جو ان کے شاہی مخالفوں سے بالکل متضاد تھی۔ دلچسپ بات یہ ہے کہ میوات کا مقامی جاگیردار اعلیٰ طبقہ 'خان زادے'، میووں کے مقابلے میں اسلامیت کا زیادہ حامل تھا، اپنی عورتوں کو سخت پردے میں رکھتا تھا اور دوسری اسلامی روایات کا زیادہ پابند تھا۔[2]

اگلے چند برسوں میں مختلف سماجی، معاشی دباؤ اور مجبوریوں کے سبب میووں کی حالت امید افزا نہیں رہی، میووں کو لگ بھگ معینہ وقفوں کے ساتھ بہت سخت قحط جھیلنے پڑے جن کے نتیجے میں یہ جین اور ہندو بنیوں، ساہوکاروں وغیرہ سے لیے ہوئے قرضوں کے بوجھ میں بری طرح دب گئے۔ بیسویں صدی کے ابتدائی حصے میں ان کی معاشی ابتری میں نہ صرف بہتری نہیں ہوئی بلکہ اس میں بہت تیز گراوٹ آئی، جس کا اظہار پنجاب گورنمنٹ کی انتظامی رپورٹ ۱۹۱۶ء سے ہوتا ہے۔ جیسے جیسے میو غربت و افلاس میں نیچے اترتے رہے انہیں شدت سے یہ بھی احساس ہوتا رہا کہ بنیے نہ صرف ان کی مصیبتوں سے فائدہ اٹھا رہے ہیں بلکہ حقیقت میں وہ اس صورت حال کی جڑ بھی ہیں۔ اور چونکہ بنیے اعلیٰ ذات کے ہندوؤں کی زندگی کا ایک مقامی منبع سمجھے جاتے تھے اس لیے ان کے خلاف بڑھتے ہوئے جذبات رفتہ رفتہ بحیثیت مجموعی ہندو مذہبی روایات سے دوری کی صورت میں ظاہر ہوئے اور

۱۔ شمس الدین شمس، میوز آف انڈیا، ص ۳۵ ۲۔ یوگیندر اسکند، سابقہ حوالہ، ص ۱۱۴

اپنے لباس کے سلسلے میں بھی یہ لوگ میوات میں آباد دوسری کسان ذاتوں کے لوگوں سے کسی طرح ممتاز نہیں کیے جاسکتے تھے۔ میونیاں (میوعورتیں) راجستھانی لہنگا اور بلاؤز پہنتی تھیں اور چاندی کے بھاری بھاری زیور۔ زیادہ تر میو سر پر چوٹی یا بودھی بھی بڑھاتے تھے جو ہندوؤں میں عام رواج تھا۔[2] جہاں تک اسلامی ظاہری امور کا سوال ہے ان میں مردوں میں ختنہ، نکاح اور دفن کے سلسلے کے امور پورے کیے جاتے تھے گو کہ ان امور کو بھی کسی حد تک ہندو سانچے میں ڈھال لیا گیا تھا۔ انہوں نے کبھی ماضی بعید میں اسلام ایک مذہب کے طور پر قبول کرلیا تھا اور انہیں خود کو مسلمان کہے جانے پر فخر بھی تھا۔ لیکن وہ ملک کے باقی حصے کے مسلمانوں کے مقابلے میں میوات کے ہندوؤں سے قریب تر تھے۔ اس طرح میو تمدن کا مطالعہ کرنے والا یہ سوچنے پر مجبور ہے کہ میوؤں میں ایک ایسی شعوری کوشش یا فکر موجود تھی کہ وہ ہندو اور مسلمان دونوں کلچروں کے عناصر کو اپنائے رہیں اور ایک ایسا انداز پیدا کریں جو بنیادی طور پر میواتی ہو۔ دونوں فرقوں کے صوفی سنتوں کا احترام و عقیدت، اور دونوں فرقوں کی مقدس کتابوں اور روایات سے لگاؤ ان کے یہاں بالکل واضح نظر آتا ہے۔ میوؤں کے ثقافتی ورثے میں دونوں جزو لازم کی طرح سموئے ہوئے ہیں۔[3] انہیں ہندوستان کے مخلوط کلچر کی بہترین مثال کہا جاتا ہے۔ ایک بہت عام کہاوت، جس میں ہندو جاٹوں اور مسلمان میوؤں کے انداز میں مماثلت کا اندازہ ہوتا ہے اس طرح ہے: 'جاٹ کیا ہندو! اور میو کیا مسلمان!'۔[4]

میوؤں کی بارہ 'پالوں' اور لگ بھگ باون 'گوتروں' میں تقسیم سے بھی ان کے راجپوت سلسلے سے تعلق رکھنے کی نشاندہی ہوتی ہے۔ یعنی یادو، تومر، اور کچھواہا شاخیں۔ ہر پال اور گوتر اپنی ایک الگ شناخت رکھتا تھا اور میوات میں کئی کئی گاؤں پر مشتمل ہوتا تھا۔ بہرحال، اب میو ایک وسیع علاقے میں آباد ہیں جو ملک کی چار ریاستوں ہریانہ، راجستھان، اترپردیش اور مدھیہ پردیش میں پھیلا ہوا ہے۔

جیسا کہ جدید محققین کا خیال ہے میوؤں کی مذہبی روایت ان کے لیے خاصی فائدہ مند ہی ثابت ہوئی ہے۔ میوات کی زراعتی زمینوں میں سے زیادہ تر زمینوں پر میو کاشتکار ہونے کی وجہ سے متصرف رہے۔ اس علاقے میں عددی اعتبار سے میو یہاں کی غالب ذات تھے۔ اپنے علاقے کے غیر اسلامی رسم و رواج اور اداروں کو جیسے گوتر، اور پال کا نظام اور نچلی ذاتوں سے چھوا چھوت کے عمل کو برقرار

۱- میجر پاؤلیٹ، گزیٹر آف الور، لندن ۱۸۷۸ء، ص ۳۸ ۲- یوگیندر اسکند، سابقہ حوالہ، ص ۱۱۳

۳- شمس الدین شمس، میوز آف انڈیا، ویئر کسٹمس اینڈ لاز، نئی دہلی ۱۹۸۳، ص ۳۶ ۴- ایضاً، ص ۳۶

بہترین جاسوس ہیں اور بڑی اچھی ہوئی خدمات بجالا سکتے ہیں۔ ایسے ہزاروں لوگ موجود ہیں جو احکام بجالانے کے لیے ہر وقت حاضر ہیں''۔[1]

ان کے اسلام قبول کرنے کے سلسلے میں کئی نظریے سامنے آتے ہیں۔ کچھ لوگوں کا خیال ہے کہ سالار مسعود غازی (جو محمود غزنوی کے ساتھ آئے تھے) کے میووں پر گہرے اثر کی وجہ سے ان میں تبدیلیِ مذہب کی ابتدا ہوئی۔ کچھ دوسرے لوگوں کا خیال ہے کہ قرون وسطیٰ میں اس خطے میں بہت سے صوفی داخل ہوئے، جس کے نتیجے میں کئی صدیوں کے دوران میووں میں تبدیلیِ مذہب کا سلسلہ شروع ہوا مگر ان کی 'اسلامیت' بہت جزوی سی ہی تھی۔ اس سلسلے میں انہوں نے اسلام کے کچھ عمل اپنا لیے لیکن ساتھ ہی اپنے مقامی کلچر اور مذہب کی روایات کو بھی باقی رکھا۔ وقتاً فوقتاً صوفیائے کرام اور علمائے عظام اس بات کی کوشش بھی کرتے رہے کہ ہندو کلچر کے جو بہت واضح عمل ان میں باقی نظر آرہے تھے انہیں ختم کردیں۔ بہرحال یہ تبدیلیِ مذہب جزوی اور برائے نام ہی رہی۔[2] انیسویں صدی کے آخری ربع میں ریاست الور کے سیٹلمنٹ آفیسر میجر راولینٹ کے الفاظ میں:

''اب تمام میو مسلمان ضرور ہیں لیکن ان کے گاؤں کے دیوی دیوتا وہی ہیں جو وہاں کے ہندوؤں کے ہیں اور یہ لوگ کچھ تہوار بھی وہی مناتے ہیں۔ چنانچہ میووں میں ہولی کھردرے قسم کے کھیلوں کا تہوار ہے اور اسے اتنا ہی اہم تہوار سمجھا جاتا ہے جتنا محرم، عیداور شب برأت، اور یہ اسی طرح جنم اشٹمی، دسہرا اور دیوالی بھی مناتے ہیں۔ یہ لوگ شادی کی تاریخ مقرر کرنے کی غرض سے نوٹ (پیلی چٹھی) لکھنے کے لیے ایک برہمن پجاری کو بھی متعین کرتے ہیں، خود کو ہندو ناموں سے پکارتے ہیں مگر ان میں رام شام نہیں ہوتا۔ بہرحال سنگھ عام طور پر ناموں میں شامل کیا جاتا ہے۔ اماوس کے دن جو ہر مہینے سورج اور چاند کے ملاپ کا دن ہوتا ہے، میو ہندو اہیروں اور گوجروں وغیرہ کے ساتھ محنت مزدوری چھوڑ دیتے ہیں، یا جب وہ کوئی کنواں بناتے ہیں تو اس سلسلے کا سب سے پہلا عمل 'بیرو جی' یا ہنومان کے لیے ایک پلیٹ فارم بنانا ہوتا ہے۔ اپنے رسم و رواج کے اعتبار سے آدھے ہندو ہوتے ہیں۔ ان کے گاؤں میں مشکل سے ہی کوئی مسجد نظر آتی ہے۔ میووں کی عبادت گاہیں ان کے پڑوسی ہندوؤں جیسی ہی ہوتی ہیں۔ مثال کے طور پر 'پنچ پیر' 'بھاٹیا' اور 'چاہنڈ' وغیرہ۔ چاہُنڈ اور کھیرا دیو،

۱- ابوالفضل، آئین اکبری، ترجمہ: ایچ بلوشمین، ج ۱، تیسرا ایڈیشن، طباعت ثانی، نئی دہلی، ص ۲۶۲

۲- یوگیندر اسکند، سابقہ حوالہ، ص ۱۱۲

Appendix VIII

Observation of *Muharram* in Mewat (Urdu)

میوات کے میووں میں محرم کی رسمیں

ڈاکٹر جی ڈی گلاٹی ☆

میووں کا علاقہ 'میوات' راجستھان کے الور اور بھرت پور ضلعوں کے بڑے حصوں اور ہریانہ میں گوڑگاؤں اور فریدآباد اور اترپردیش میں متھرا اور آگرہ کے کچھ حصوں پر مشتمل ہے۔ اب حکومت ہریانہ نے اس خطے میں ایک الگ ضلع بھی بنادیا ہے جس کا صدر مقام نوح ہے۔

روایات کے اعتبار سے میو لوگ راجپوت نسل سے تعلق رکھنے کا دعویٰ کرتے ہیں۔[1] اب میو مذہباً مسلمان ضرور ہیں لیکن اپنی تمام ثقافتی اور مذہبی قدیم روایات کو اپنائے ہوئے ہیں۔ تبلیغی جماعت ایک کے مبلّغ اور ترجمان نے لکھا کہ: ''میو لوگ نماز کے نام تک سے ناواقف تھے''۔[2] اگر اتفاقاً کوئی مسلمان ان کے علاقے میں چلا جاتا تھا اور نماز پڑھنے لگتا تھا تو اس کے چاروں طرف لوگ جمع ہوکر حیرت سے دیکھتے تھے کہ یہ کیا کرنا چاہتا ہے۔ ان کے خیال میں اس کے پیٹ میں درد ہورہا ہوتا یا وہ بالکل مخبوط الحواس ہوچکا ہوتا، جس کی وجہ سے وہ بار بار اٹھک بیٹھک لگاتا نظر آتا تھا۔

یہ بات واضح نہیں ہے کہ کب اور کیسے اسلام کی جڑیں میوات میں جمیں۔ قرون وسطیٰ کے ہندوستان میں دو دارالسلطنتوں دہلی اور آگرہ کے درمیان رہتے ہوئے[3] بھی یہ ترکوں اور مغلوں دونوں سے الجھتے رہے۔ پھر بھی مغلوں کے تحت انہوں نے شاہی خدمات بھی انجام دیں اور اکبر کے دور میں انہیں دوڑنے والے (ہرکارے) کی حیثیت میں ملازم رکھا گیا۔ ابوالفضل نے ''آئین اکبری'' میں اکبر کی فوج کی تقسیم کی تفصیلات دیتے ہوئے میووں کا ذیلی سرخی ''میوڑے'' کے تحت تذکرہ کیا ہے۔ اس نے لکھا ہے: ''یہ میوات کے باشندے ہیں اور دوڑنے والوں کی حیثیت سے شہرت رکھتے ہیں۔ یہ بڑے دور دراز علاقوں سے بڑے جوش و خروش کے ساتھ ہر مطلوبہ چیز لے آتے ہیں۔

☆ دہلی یونیورسٹی

۱- تفصیلات کے لیے ملاحظہ ہو: ''میوات ڈیورنگ تھرٹینتھ سنچری'' از جی۔ڈی گلاٹی، پنجاب ہسٹری کانفرنس کے پندرھویں اجلاس کی روداد، پٹیالہ ۱۹۸۱ء، ص ٦۱

۲- منظور نعمانی کی ''تبلیغی جماعت، جماعت اسلامی اور بریلوی حضرات''، لکھنؤ ۱۹۸۹ء کا اقتباس یوگندر اسکند کی ''دی اوریجن اینڈ ڈیولپمنٹ آف تبلیغی جماعت'' (۱۹۲۰-۲۰۰۰)' نئی دہلی ۲۰۰۲ء، ص ۱۱۰

۳- جی۔ڈی گلاٹی، سابقہ حوالہ، ص ٦۴-٦۱

Bibliography

Abul Fazl, Allami, *Ain-i-Akbari,* Vol. II, English Translation by H.S. Jarret, reprint, New Delhi, 1978.

—, *Akbarnama,* English Translation by Henry Beveridge, Calcutta, 1948.

Afif, Shams Siraj, *Tarikh-i-Firuzshahi,* English Translation (extract) by Elliot and Dowson, Hindi translation by S.A.A. Razvi in *Tughluq Kalin Bharat,* Part II, Aligarh, 1957 and English translation by R.C. Janhari, Delhi, 2002.

Aftab-i-Mewat, An Urdu Magazine published in Lahore.

Aggarwal, P.C., *Castes Religion and Power: An Indian Case Study,* New Delhi, 1971.

Ahmad, Nizamuddin, *Tabakat-i-Akbari,* English translation by B.De., Vol. I, reprint, Calcutta, 1973.

Ahmad, Sharf Alauddin, *Murraqa-i-Mewat,* (Urdu), Hindi translation by Anil Joshi, Alwar.

Ali, Hashim Amir, *The Meos of Mewat: Old Neighbours of Delhi,* Oxford, 1970.

Ashraf K.M., *Life and Conditions of the People of Hindustan,* New Delhi, 1970.

—, 'Ghalib and the Revolt of 1857' published in the Proceedings of a Symposium entitled *Rebellion 1857: A Symposium* Ed. by P.C. Joshi, People's Publishing House, New Delhi, 1957.

Babur, Zahiruddin Muhammad, *Tuzuk-i-Baburi,* English translation by A.S. Bereridge under the title *Baburnama: Memoirs of Babur,* reprint, New Delhi, 1979 and by Wheelar

M. Thackston under the title *The Babumama: Memories of Babur, Prince and Emperor,* O.U.P., 1996.

Badaoni, Abdul Qadir bin Mulukshah, *Muntakhab-ut-Tawarikh,* English translation by S.A. Ranking, Vol. I, reprint, Patna, 1973.

Ball, Charles, *The History of Indian Mutiny,* Vol. II, Indian reprint, New Delhi, 1981.

Bansal, Tara Chand, *Firozepurjhirka: Itihas ke Jharokhe se* (Hindi) Firozepur Jhirka, 2002.

Barani, Ziauddin, *Tarikh-i-Ferozeshahi,* Ed. by Sayyid Ahmad Khan, Calcutta, 1862. English translation (extract) by Elliot and Dowson. Hindi translation by S.A.A. Rizvi.

Bhardwaj, Suraj Bhan, *Socio-Economic Conditions in the Mewat Region,* An unpublished Ph.D. thesis, J.N.U. 1990.

Bhargava, M.L., *Freedom Struggle in Uttar Pradesh,* 6 vols., Lucknow, 1957-61.

Bharucha, Rustam, *Rajasthan An Oral History-Conversation with Komal Kothari,* Penguin Books, New Delhi, 2003.

Bhatnagar, V.S., *Life and Times of Sawai Jai Singh (1688-1743),* Delhi, 1974.

Chand, Tara, *Influence of Islam on Indian Culture,* Allahabad, 1946.

Chand, Subhash, *Territorial Expansion and Organization of Dahangal Pal* (Hindi) M. Phil dissertation Jamia Millia Islamia, New Delhi, 2000.

Chirgh-i-Mewat, A progressive magazine of Mewati Culture, Alwar (Rajasthan).

Chopra, P.N., *Who is Who of Indian Martyrs,* 3 vols., Delhi, 1992.

Crooke, William, *Tribes and Castes of North Western Provinces and Oudh,* Calcutta, 1896.

Cunningham, Alexander, *Reports of Archaeological Survey of India,* vol. XX, reprint, Varanasi, 1969.

Dalrymple, William, *The Last Maghal: The fall of Dynasty,* Penguin Books, 2006.

Darling, M., *Punjab Peasant in Prosperity and Debt,* reprint, New Delhi, 1978.

Dogra, Bharat, *Rashtriya Ekta Ke Poster* (Hindi), New Delhi, 1991.

Doron, Richard M. (Ed.), *Handbook of American Folklore*, U.S.A., 1983.

Duff, J.G., *A History of the Maharattas*, 2 vols., Calcutta, 1918.

Elliot and Dowson, *History of India as told by its own Historians*, reprint, Delhi, 1996.

Ferishta, Hindu Shah Muhammad Qasim, *Tarikh-i-Ferishta*, English translation by John Briggs under the title, *History of the Rise of the Mahommedan Power in India*, vol. I, reprint, Calcutta, 1966. Hindi translation by Narender Bahadur, Lucknow, 2003.

Gazetters

District Gazetter of Agra, 1965.

District Gazetter of Aligarh, 1987.

District Gazetter of Allahabad, 1968.

District Gazetter of Alwar, 1968.

District Gazetter of Bharatpur, 1971.

District Gazetter of Bulandshahar, 1971.

District Gazetter of Gurgaon, 1884.

District Gazetter of Gwalior, 1965.

District Gazetter of Hissar, 1884.

District Gazetter of Itawa, 1965.

District Gazetter of Pilibhit, 1988.

Ghalib, Mirza, *Dastambuy: A Diary of the Indian Revolt of 1857* being the English translation of *Dastambuy* by Khwaja Ahmad Faruqi, Asia Publishing House, 1970.

Government of India, *Proceedings of the Trial of Bahadur Shah II*, Calcutta, 1985.

Guha, Ranjeet (Ed.), *Subaltern Studies* Oxford University Press, Delhi, 1989.

Gulati, G.D., 'Mewat during thirteen century,' *Proceedings of Punjab History Conference*, 1981, pp. 61-64.

—,'Folktore and History Writing: A case study of Mewat' presented at Nehru Memorial Library and Museum, New Delhi, 1989.

—, 'Village Bania as reflected in the folktales of Mewat'

presented at an International Conference on Folklare, University of Delhi in its South Campus, 1990. Revised version presented at the *Punjab History Conference* and Published it its Proceedings, 1966.

—, 'Folklore as Source of Regional History: A case study of Mewat' Presented at Symposium sponsored by the University Grants Commission held at Kurukshetra University, Kurukshetra, 1991.

—, 'Lal Das as the Symbol of Hindu-Muslim Unity' (Hindi), published in a National Daily *Nav Bharat Times,* New Delhi, November, 1991.

—, 'Jat-Meos Alliance Against Jaipur State: Evidence of *Murraqa-i-Mewat*' presented at a National Seminar on *Jats in History* held in January, 2001 under the auspicious of the Centre for Research and Publication of Surajmal Memorial Education Society, New Delhi.

—, '*Yasin Khan Ki Baat,*' presented at a National Seminar on the *Peasant Movements* held in March, 1999 at Kurukshetra University, Kurukshetra under the title 'Peasants' unrest in Mewat as reflected in a Folksong,' later presented under the same title at *Punjab History Conference* held at Patiala in March, 2004.

—, 'Babur's Observation of Mewat and the Mewatis' presented at *Punjab History Conference* held at Patiala in March, 2005 and was published in its proceedings (pp. 147-50).

—, '1857: Mewat and its Neighbouring Regions' was first presented under the title 'Martyrs of 1857: Gurgaon District' at a National Seminar on *Revolt of 1857 and the Pubjab: Historiographical Pespectives* held a Pubjab University, Patiala on 28 November, 2007. The Proceedings of the Seminar were published under the title *Rethinking 1857 and the Punjab* edited by Navtej Singh, Patiala, 2008, pp. 28-38.

—, *Central Asia Under the Mongols,* New Delhi, 2010.

—, 'Khanzadas and their buildings in Mewat' was prepared to bepresented at a Seminar to be held at Sitamau (M.P.)

26-28 December, 2010. Due to the Gurjar agitation, it could not be posible to reach Sitamau.

Habib, Irfan, *Atlas of the Mughal Empire: Political and Economic maps,* O.U.P., 1982.

Habib, Muhammad and K.A. Nizami, *Comprehensive Hisotry of India,* vol. V, Delhi, 1970.

Habibullah, A.B.M., *The Foundation of Muslim Rule in India,* revised edition, Allahabad, 1961.

Hasan, Mohibul, *Babur: Founder of the Mughal Empire in India,* New Delhi, 1985.

Haye, Chowdhary Abdul, 'The Freedom Movement in Mewat and Dr. K.M. Ashraf" in Horst Kruger (Ed.), *Kunwar Mohammad Ashraf: An Indian Scholar and Revolutionary* 1903-62, P.P.H. New Delhi, 1969, pp. 291-336.

Husain, Altaf, *Tarikh-i-Zila Gurgaon* (Urdu), Lahore, 1885.

Husain, Mahdi, *Tughlaq Dynasty,* Calcutta, 1963.

Ibettson, Denzil, *Panjab Castes,* 1986.

Imperial Gazetter of India, vol. XVII, Oxford, 1908.

Isami, *Futuh-su-Salatin,* English translation by Agha Mahdi Husain in 3 vols., 1978. Extracts in English by Elliot and Dowson and in Hindi by S.A.A. Rizvi.

Joshi, Anil, *Alwar At A Glance,* Alwar, 1988.

—, *Alwar Darshan* (Hindi), Alwar, 2004.

—, *Arjang-i-Tijara,* being the Hindi translation of the Urdu text written by Shaikh Muhammad Makhdum in 1878, Alwar, 1987.

—, *Muraqqa-i-Mewat* in Urdu, Hindi translation under the title *Tarikh-i-Mewat,* Alwar, 1989.

Khan, A.R., *Chieftains of the Mughals,* Shimla, 1970.

Khan, Maulana Wahiduddin, *Mewat Ka Safar,* New Delhi, 1988.

Kinger, Hors, *Kunwar Muhammad Ashraf: An Indian Scholar and Revolutionary,* P.P.H., Delhi, 1969.

Lal Das Ki Bani, a manuscript, Oriental Institute, Alwar.

Lal, K.S., *Twilight of the Sultanate,* second edition, New Delhi, 1980.

—, *History of the Khaljis,* third edition, New Delhi, 1980.

—, *Growth of Muslim Population in Medieval India,* New Delhi, 1973.

—, *Indian Muslims: Who Are They?*, New Delhi, 1990.

—, *Muslim Slave System in Medievel India,* New Delhi, 1984.

—, *Growth of Sheduled Tribes and Castes in Medieval India,* New Delhi, 1995.

Land Settlement Report of Gurgaon District, 1882.

Leach, Maria, *Standard Distionary of Folklore,* New Delhi, 1945.

Majumdar, R.C., *The Sepoy Mutiny and the Revolt of 1857,* Calcutta, second edition, 1963.

Mallson, (Ed.), Kaye's and Mallson's *History of the Indian Mutiny of 1857-58,* 6 vols., London, 1889.

Maulana, A.S., *Tarikh-i-Meo Chhatri* (Urdu), Nuh, 1974.

Malwa Akhbar 9-16 June 1857, Natnagar Shodh Samsthan, Sitamau (M.P.).

Mayaram, Shail, *Resisting Regemes Myth, Memory, and the Shaping of a Muslim Identity,* Delhi, 1997.

Meo Darpan, Annually published from Malwa region in Hindi, Chief editor Mohd. Iqbal Khan Meo, Indore, Madhya Pradesh.

Metcalfe, Charles Theophilus, *Two Native Narratives of the Mutiny of Delhi,* Translated from the originals, 1898.

Mewati, Lord Sannu Khan, *Mewati Dohe* (Hindi) Alwar.

Minhaj Siraj Jurjani, *Tabakat-i-Nasiri,* Ed., by W. Nassau, Lees, Khadim Husain and Abdul Hai, Calcutta, 1863-64. English translation by Major H.G. Raverty with annotation in 2 vols. reprint, Delhi, 1970.

Moore, Erin, *Conflict and Compromise: Justice in an Indian Village,* University of California, Berkeley, 1985..

Morwal, Bhagwan Das, *Kala Pahad (Hindi),* New Delhi, 1999.

—, *Kala Pahad,* a novel in Hindi, New Delhi, 1999.

Navin, Allen, *The Gateway to History,* Indian reprint, Bombay, 1968.

Nigam S.B.P., *Nobility under the Sultans of Delhi,* Delhi, 1968.

*Panjab Past and Presen*t, Patiala.

Pattanayak D.P. and Peter J. Clans (Ed.), *Indian Falklore,* I, Mysore, 1981.

Powlett, Major P.W., *Gazetteer of Ulwar,* Govt. Press, Lahore, 1878.

Proceedings of the Pubjab History Conference.

Propp. Vladimir, *Theory and History of Folklore,* translated by Ariand Y. Martin and Richard P. Mortin and others, Manchester University Press, 1984.

Qanungo, Kalika Ranjan, *Shershah and His Times,* Bombay, 1965.

—, *History of the Jats,* Delhi, 1987.

Qureshi, S.Y., *Haryana Rediscovered A Bibliographal Area Study,* Gurgaon, 1985.

Raiken, Charles, *Notes on the Revolt in the North-Western Province of India,* London, 1858.

Ranawat, M.S., *Bharatpur Maharaja Jawahar Singh Jat (Hindi),* Hindi Sahitya Mandir Jodhpur, 1974.

Rathee, C.R. 'Meos of Mewat: A Muslim Tribe of North India' in *Mainstream,* vol. 9, No. 35, 1971, pp. 19-28

Report dated 9th June, 1934 on the dispute over the shrine of Lal Das.

Rizvi, S.A.A., *Aadi Turk Kalin Bharat,* Aligarh, 1956.

—, *Khalji Kalin Bharat,* Aligarh, 1955.

—, *Tughlaq Kalin Bharat,* Part I, 1956; Part II, 1957.

—, *Timur Kalin Bharat,* Part I, 1958; Part II, 1958.

—, *Baburnama,* Aligarh, 1959.

—, *A History of Sufism in India* in 2 vols., 1983.

Rose, H.A., *Glossary of the Tribes and Castes of the Punjab and the North-west Province,* Patiala, 1970.

Sen, S.N., *Eighteen Fifty Seven,* Government of India Publication, 1957.

Shams, Shamsuddin, *The Meos of India: Their Customs and Laws,* Delhi, 1983.

Shangari, T.R., *Sant Charandas,* Hindi translation by R.P. Premi, Radha Swami Satsang Beas, fourth edition, Amritsar, 1996.

Sharma, G.N., *A Bibliography of Medieval Rajasthan,* Agra, 1965.

—, *Social Life in Medieval Rajasthan,* Agra, 1968.

Shodh Sadhna (Hindi, English), Natnagar Shodh Samsthan, Sitamau (M.P.).

Siddiqui, I.H., *Some Aspects of Afghan Despotism in India,* Aligarh, 1969,

—, English translation of *Waqiat-i-Mushtaqui* of Razqullah Murhatiqui, New Delhi, 1993.

Siddiqui, Majid Hayat, 'History and Society in a popular rebellion: Mewat 1920-33' in *Comparative Studies in Society and History,* July issue, 1986, pp. 463-74.

Singh J.P. and Mumtaz Khan, 'The Cultural Landscape of Mewat' in *Social Structure and Regional Development: A Social Geography* by Ahmad A. (Ed.), Jaipur, 1993, pp. 151-77.

Singh, Nagendra K. (Ed.), *Encyclopaedia of Muslim Biography,* vol. V, New Delhi, 2001.

Singh, Navtej, *Rethinking 1857 and the Punjab,* Patiala, 2008.

Sirhindi, Yahya bin Ahmad, *Tarikh-i-Mubarakshahi,* English translation by K.K. Basu, Baroda, 1932. Extracts in Elliot and Dowson and Hindi translation by S.A.A. Rizvi.

Spear, Perceival, *Twilight of the Mughals,* Oxford University Press, 1951.

Srivastava, M.P., *The Indian Mutiny, 1857,* Allahabad, 1979.

Steel, Flora, Annie, *Tales of the Punjab,* London, 1894.

Tayal, Jugmandir, 'Mewat ke Sant Laldas' presented at a seminar on *Historical Sources of Medieval Rajasthan,* sponsored by Indian Council of Historical Research, New Delhi and held at Dungargarh (Bikaner) in 2011

Thackston, W.M., *The Baburnama: Memoirs of Babur: Prince and Emperor,* being the English translation of *Baburnama,* New Delhi, 1996..

Thomsan, E.P., *The Voice of the Past: Oral History,* Oxford, 1978.

Timur, Amir, *Institutes,* English translation by Major Davy, Oxford, 1783.

—, *Malfuzat-i-Timuri,* English translation in Elliot and Dowson, Hindi translation in S.A.A. Rizvi. Also in English by Major Charles Steward, London, 1830.

Tod, *Annals and Antiquities of Rajasthan,* 2 vols., New Delhi, 1971.

Tripathi, R.P., *Some Aspects of Muslim Administration,* Allahabad, 1936.

Vansina, Jan, *Oral Tradition: A case Study: Historical Methodology,* Chicago, 1965.

Vinay Patrika, *Alwar Ank,* Raj Rishi College, Alwar, 1969.

Yadav, K.C., *Revolt of 1857 in Haryana,* Delhi, 1977.

—, *Haryana Ka Itihas* (Hindi), New Delhi, 1982.

Yazdi, Maulan Sharfuddin Ali, *Zafarnama,* English translation by Elliot and Dowson and Hindi translation by S.A.A. Rizvi.

Watson, J. Forbes and John William Kaye, *The People of Hindustan,* vol. 7, reprint, Delhi, 1987.

Wink, Andre, *Al-Hind: The Making of the Indo-Islamic World,* vol. I, New Delhi, 1990 and vol. II, Brill, Leiden, 2004.